# BARRETT WENDELL
# AND HIS LETTERS

# BARRETT WENDELL
# AND HIS LETTERS

BY

M. A. DeWolfe HOWE

WITH ILLUSTRATIONS

THE ATLANTIC MONTHLY PRESS

BOSTON

# NOTE

THERE will be few more such collections of letters as Barrett Wendell's — so voluminous, and all in manuscript. Now that the world has taken to time-saving through dictation, nobody appears to have the leisure for extensive correspondence. This was one of the constant expressions of Wendell's devotion to his friends, and in his letters not only that characteristic but many others stand clearly forth.

Before the material of this book was placed in my hands more than a year ago, Mrs. Wendell had sought and secured many letters from their recipients. To this collection substantial additions have since been made. Yet there are many friends — such as W. B. Shubrick Clymer, T. Russell Sullivan, and Arlo Bates, to name but three — quite unrepresented in the correspondence. In the processes of elimination required for making a book of reasonable proportions, the mere mention of many other friends has disappeared. The richness and scope of the human background of Wendell's life are none the less manifest. Against this background his intellectual and spiritual concerns, his highly distinctive personal traits, are revealed as fully as possible in his own words.

The book has been prepared for publication chiefly in the Boston Athenæum, a library with which Wendell himself was intimately identified. To its librarian, Mr. C. K. Bolton, and to the members of its staff, I am much indebted for specific and general help in the work. For the coöperation of Mrs. Wendell, notably generous in its freedom from even the suggestion of restrictions of any kind, I would record a peculiar gratitude.

M. A. DeW. H.

Boston, 26 *May*, 1924

# CONTENTS

# ILLUSTRATIONS

BARRETT WENDELL
AND HIS LETTERS

# BARRETT WENDELL AND HIS LETTERS

## I

### INTRODUCTORY

NEARLY thirty years after Barrett Wendell published his biography of Cotton Mather, he had occasion to write to a friend who had recently read the book with pleasure. Touching, in the course of the letter, upon what this early piece of work had taught him, he stated a theory of biography in general which his own biographer — if one who intends rather to act as an editor of letters may so be called — seizes upon as a statement not only sound in itself but also peculiarly applicable to the undertaking now invitingly, if somewhat bewilderingly, at hand. Thus he wrote: —

What I learned first, and most lastingly, is that whoever would tell the truth about any man must be, in the literal sense, his apologist. I do not mean that one should make apologies, or indeed write history as Mather did, to emphasize his own opinion. I mean that the first and perhaps the only duty of an honest biographer is, so far as may be, to set forth the man of whom he writes as that man saw himself, and to explain him on his own terms. Then judgment may best be left to those who read.

"To set forth the man of whom he writes as that man saw himself," to explain Barrett Wendell "on his own terms" — there lies the challenge. In the memoir of Wendell which his college classmate and lifelong friend, President Lowell, of Harvard University, prepared for the Massachusetts Historical Society, these significant words are found: "James Russell Lowell said of Wordsworth that he was two men, and this is, perhaps, peculiarly the case with men of letters. It was true of Barrett Wendell. There was the real man, and what he thought himself to be; and the former was the larger of the two." There will be many occasions in the pages that follow to bear these words in mind. With them the other true words, written soon after his death, may well be joined: "A certain playful exaggeration of speech, born of his innate detestation of pedantry, often tended to obscure the sound common-sense which underlay his most decided opinions; but those who knew him best did not take long to recognize the simplicity, unselfishness, and high sense of honor, which formed the basis of his character."

Accepting the task of presenting Barrett Wendell as he saw himself, his biographer, then, would have the reader constantly aware that what the subject of this book really was, and what he thought himself and wished others to think him, were frequently at variance. Throughout his life, which covered the time when dual, and even multiple, personalities were becoming objects of special scrutiny, he was appearing in the guises — sometimes disguises — which made him the "character" he was; yet, with all his propensity to the astonishing utterances which seemed to delight him in proportion to their capacity to make his hearers "sit up," he never succeeded in blinding those who really knew him to the essential "simplicity, unselfishness, and high sense of honor" which were his salient personal traits.

It is no wonder that confusion sometimes arose. A letter written to Barrett Wendell in 1906 by a graduate of Harvard then teaching history at Trinity College, Hartford, Connecticut, relates a significant incident: —

"The recent discovery here of a man who thought George Eliot was President of Harvard, found an added interest in the answer made by a man of the same class on my American History exam paper, which may be of interest to you. The man has been well drilled in English, in which your name is frequently mentioned, and writes:—

" 'The Abolition movement increased . . . by the orations and agitations of such men as Wm. Lloyd Garrison,

Barrett

Henry Ward Beecher, and ~~Barrett~~ Wendell ~~Phillips~~.'

"You will note he hesitated, but that you finally received the credit."

Nothing could have given Wendell himself more amusement than to find himself bracketed with the abolitionists. If he had lived in Boston — at least as an older man — at the time when Garrison was making himself peculiarly obnoxious to the more conservative elements of society, he would probably have joined the "mob of gentlemen" who tried to hang the reformer. If he had lived in Boston before the Revolution, it would have been entirely in keeping with the rôle of his maturer years to ally himself with the Tories, as a defender of the established order. But in whatever century or circumstances his incarnation might have fallen, he would still have been the same faithful, penetrating student and interpreter of letters and life, as he saw their interrelations, the same warm-hearted human being, often misunderstood, — partly, it may be, because he did not by any means always understand himself or greatly care that others should see beneath the contradictory surface, — the same constant exponent of all the loyalties which most nearly concern a man's life.

## II

## BACKGROUND, BOYHOOD, AND YOUTH

### 1855-1874

BARRETT WENDELL was born at 41 West Cedar Street, Boston, August 23, 1855, the eldest of the four sons of Jacob Wendell and Mary Bertodi (Barrett) Wendell. To "explain him on his own terms" it is as necessary to record his ancestry as to relate the experiences of his own existence, for he was intensely aware of the background which he shared with New Englanders of his own kind. In his books — notably the *Literary History of America* — he constantly spoke of Americans of "the better sort," meaning those upon whom the advantages of breeding and education had bestowed a position of social superiority less obvious to-day than it was in the three American centuries that have gone before. Conspicuously possessed of the historic sense, and therefore much given to identifying a living past with a living present, he brought to the past, as it concerned his own inheritances, a frankly personal interest. It would have been an affectation of a sort quite foreign to him to make any pretense to the contrary. Democracy, in the latest meanings of the word, made but a scant appeal to him. He was fond of using the word "gentleman," and prepared to accept equally the privileges and the responsibilities implied in the term.

Nearing the end of his life, Barrett Wendell wrote, in 1918, for his children, a memoir of his father, Jacob Wendell, the opening pages of which present the family history with a detail significant of its meaning to him. Those to whom it will mean much less may read the passage with a cursory eye. It runs as follows: —

My family was of Dutch origin. The first of them in this country, Evert Jansen Wendel, came from Emden, in East Friesland, to New York, about 1640, when some twenty-five years of age; his widowed mother was then living in a village called Upleward, where she died in the year 1657. In New York, Evert Jansen married Susanna du Trieux, who was probably descended from a Gascon Protestant, recorded as having taken refuge in Holland after condemnation by the Parliament of Bordeaux in the reign of Charles IX. Evert Jansen soon moved to Albany, where he passed the rest of his long life. There, in 1656, he was made ruling elder of the church, in honor of which dignity he had painted in one of the windows a probably assumed coat-of-arms, complacently borne by his descendants ever since. His eldest son, John, married Elizabeth, daughter of Abraham Staats, of Albany; flourished as a trader with Indians; was once mayor of Albany, — I think in Leisler's time, — and died rather prematurely, in 1691, leaving considerable landed property and ten or eleven children. His widow subsequently married John Schuyler, by whom she became the mother of the "American lady" recorded by Mrs. Grant of Laggan, and grandmother of the Revolutionary general, Philip Schuyler. Abraham Wendell was sent in boyhood to New York, where he lived for more than forty years, a merchant and a magistrate, of genially convivial habit and frequent carelessness of obligation. His wife was Catherine, daughter of Teinis and Catherine (Van Brugh) Dekey, through whom the family became kinsfolk of certain Bayards, Livingstons, and other remembered names. Meanwhile, Jacob Wendell, the youngest brother of Abraham, and in every sense a substantial man, had moved to Boston, where he flourished until after 1760, marrying an Oliver and becoming ancestor of Mr. Wendell Phillips and Dr. Holmes.

As early as 1714, he persuaded his brother Abraham to entrust his eldest son, John, to his care, convinced that educational opportunity in Boston was better than in New York. Though this John never entered Harvard College, after all, he lived comfortably in Boston from the age of eleven until his death, in 1762, at fifty-nine. He was convivial, like his father, he became a partner in his uncle's business, he was once in command of the Ancient and Honorable Artillery, and he married Elizabeth, daughter of the third Edmund Quincy, of Braintree. Her elder brother, the fourth Edmund Quincy, was father of Mrs. John Hancock; her younger brother, Josiah, was the ancestor of that line which preserved the distinction of the name throughout the nineteenth century; her younger sister, Dorothy, married Edward Jackson, and their descendants, under the names of Jackson, Lee, Higginson, Holmes, and more, continue to this day the most sturdy traditions of ancestral Massachusetts.

The eldest surviving son of John and Elizabeth (Quincy) Wendell, who bore his father's name, was born in Boston, in 1731. He took his degree at Harvard in 1750, and soon went to Portsmouth, where he married a Wentworth, cousin of Benning Wentworth, Governor of New Hampshire. There he lived all his life, a lawyer of speculative disposition, much concerned with the development of the unsettled regions of New Hampshire and Vermont, and patriarchally prolific. His second wife, who was akin to his first, was Dorothy, daughter of Henry Sherburne of Portsmouth. By the two he had some twenty children. My grandfather, Jacob Wendell, born in 1788, was his youngest surviving son. By that time, the family fortunes were pretty well ruined.

This record of family origin therefore becomes significant. My grandfather was akin to many notable families not only in New Hampshire but in both Massachusetts and New York as well. His circumstances, however, were those of the conventional poor boy, with his own way to make. He did his best to do so, meanwhile cherishing ancestral traditions with a fervor which he transmitted to his children. The War of 1812 seems to have brought him his first prosperity. He was successful in privateering ventures; and by 1816, when twenty-eight years old, he found himself in condition to marry. His wife was Mehitable, only child of Mark Rogers of Portsmouth; her father was first cousin, on the mother's side, of Sir John Wentworth, last royal governor of New Hampshire, and traced his descent, through the Reverend Nathanial Rogers of Portsmouth, John Rogers, President of Harvard, whose wife, born Denison, was grand-daughter of Thomas Dudley, and the Reverend Nathaniel Rogers of Ipswich, to the redoubtable Puritan divine, the Reverend John Rogers of Dedham in Essex, who died there the year when Harvard College was founded. Mark Rogers, however, had died young and poor. At the time of her marriage, the fortunes of my grandmother's family were as far from prosperous as those of the Wendells.

The next twelve years had a different story. My grandfather was engaged not only in shipping but in an attempt to establish on the Piscataqua such manufactures as were then founding the fortunes of the Merrimac. By the time of my father's birth, he was more than well-to-do and his affairs promised a fortune ample enough to restore the family to its traditional dignity. Two years later, he was completely ruined. The manufacturing venture proved beyond his resources. Of all his property he retained only the house where he lived; and that, for years, was heavily encumbered. He survived until 1865; but, though he never lost the personal respect won in his prosperous days, he was a broken man. I can clearly remember him — a small man, slight of figure, baldish but with a shock of strong, dark hair, with a tinge of chestnut which queerly contrasted with the white beard on his cheeks and under his chin. He was very quiet in manner, yet alert; he had a contagiously hearty laugh, never loud; and all his children loved him dearly.

My father, Jacob, was born on July 24, 1826. My father's earliest memories were of actual poverty. For a while the family could not afford a servant. In consequence, he sometimes had to get up before daylight, split wood, light fires from a tinderbox, and drive the cow to its pasture, a mile or more away, before breakfast and school. His school was good, however.

Accordingly, in the late summer of 1843, when a little past his seventeenth birthday, he secured some small employment in Boston where he literally knew no human being, and started out in search of fortune. His reward came; after some years in the employ of J. C. Howe & Co., selling agents for some of the principal cotton and woollen mills in New England, he was admitted to the firm as a junior partner, in 1853 or 1854. The business relations thus began lasted through all the rest of his life. He had taken about ten years to make good; and he was about twenty-eight years old.

Once secure of something like a reasonable income, my father, on October 24, 1854, married Mary Bertodi Barrett, under conditions which may fairly be called surprisingly happy. What is more, though neither he nor my mother was blessed with tranquil placidity of temper, nor ever quite ignored the inevitable annoyances of daily existence, they loved each other as dearly and as simply at the end of their forty-four years together as they had at the beginning.

They had met at Mr. Coolidge's church, when my mother was still a young girl. When Mr. Ripley's exodus to Brook Farm had threatened to break the church to pieces, one of the few men who stuck staunchly by the wreck and most helped to bring her safe to port was my grandfather, Nathaniel Augustus Barrett, then about forty years old. His grandfather, who had been a considerable man of business in Boston a century before, had been ruined by the Revolution. His father, the youngest of a large family whose few remaining letters show engaging traces of eighteenth-century pleasantry, had not married until well past the age of forty-five; his wife, a Newport Brown, was twenty-two years his junior. She had died with her fifth child, in 1802, when my grandfather was only two years old; and in 1810, when he was only ten, his father had died in turn, leaving four children, a very modest property, and some admirable family portraits, four of which are now in my possession. So, though related to many well-to-do people in both Massachusetts and Rhode Island, the little family was remarkably lonely; for their own cousins in Massachusetts were mostly old enough to be their parents, and as they lived in that part of Braintree now called Quincy, they had never seen much of their Boston relations.

My grandmother was Sally, fourth daughter and sixth of the nineteen children of John and Esther (Goldthwaite) Dorr, of Boston. The Dorrs came from Roxbury, where they had been respectable citizens for some generations; their fortune was based on trade in furs with China, after 1790, in more or less intimate relations with Mr. John Jacob Astor. As a family they were not intellectually powerful, nor unusually strong in character; but they were remarkably handsome, and all of them whom I remember had an extraordinary air of personal distinction. In the matter of character, too, my grandmother's father, John Dorr, seems to have been exceptional; he was extremely self-willed and dominant; yet his children not only respected and rather timidly feared him, but were genuinely fond of him. He died a month or so before I was born.

The memoir of Jacob Wendell from which this passage is taken does not record the fact that when Barrett Wendell was only eight years old, in 1863, his father's business, which had caused frequent visits to New York, led to the removal of his family from Boston to that city, where he became the representative of his firm. His characteristics have been summarized by President Lowell: "A quiet retiring man without the brilliance of his son, he had business capacity, sterling integrity, and commanded the confidence and respect of those who met him. Not himself a scholar, he believed in the value of scholarship, and of his own motion established a foundation for the highest scholar in the freshman class at Harvard College." Much of the value of his son's memoir of him lies in the self-revelations of its author. The following passage, for example, shows forth the Barrett Wendell of childhood as he saw himself in advancing years: —

As for me, for nearly four years an only child, and on my mother's side an only grandchild, and so perhaps fairly well spoilt before my memory begins, I must have been a rather disturbing puzzle to them both — as well as to my not naturally amiable self. So far as I can now discern, I was in one sense a good child — neither mischievous nor vicious, fairly conscientious and perhaps unusually pure of impulse. On the other hand, my nervous system was always a bit erratic — I can trace the trouble now through my father and his mother to hers, who had a startling experience of interrupted personality about 1800; I was morbidly self-conscious and pettily ill-tempered; I

disliked physical exercise; my most nearly favorite pastime —
I seldom got absorbingly interested in anything — was the
writing of far from poetic or imaginative plays. The first which
I remember completing was composed when I was eight years
old. It was clearly founded on the libretto of *Lucia di Lammer-
moor*, which I had once been taken to hear; it got along all
right to the very end — when I discovered with dismay that
one character, named Sally, had somehow survived; so with
what then seemed to me inspiration, I added some such words as:
"Enter Sally, who looks about her, and says, 'I die,' and dies."
Harmless as this literary propensity may have been, it was not
quite intelligible to parents whose own preoccupations, apart
from domesticity, were mostly concerned with matters of business or religion, and who assumed — quite sensibly — that
normal children ought to like playing out of doors. And I never
consoled them by delight in religious exercises. To this day I
detest hymns — except the *Dies Iræ;* and I was never graced
with the engaging vice of pretending to like, for the gratification
of others, anything which has excited my displeasure.

A letter which Barrett Wendell, not quite six years old,
wrote (June 27, 1861) to his uncle, George Wendell, came
to light when its writer was nearing sixty. It was a child's
request for the building of a toy "sailing vessel, steamer,
or schooner." His desires were definite: "I wish it to be
about middle size and very perfect. If I have to *pay* you,
in your answer to this you can tell me how much you
want, but as you are my uncle and say that you do not
need any pay, it will be most convenient for me. What
do you think about the times?" His own thoughts appear
in statements about troops he had seen in Boston, before
they went South. Commenting upon the letter, in 1912,
when he acknowledged its receipt from his cousin,
Arthur R. Wendell, he recalled the pleasant summers of
his childhood passed with his family at West Needham —
now Wellesley — Massachusetts, and remarked of himself, "I must have been a funny little prig at five years old.

BARRETT WENDELL AT ABOUT EIGHT (1863)

That I was dreadfully self-conscious, and therefore far from happy in personal feeling, I am sure. It took me thirty years at least to get an objective view of anything."

The autobiographic pages of the memoir already drawn upon contain another illuminating passage. It relates to a visit which Barrett Wendell, not quite eight years old, paid to New York with his father and mother, apparently shortly before their final removal from Boston in 1863. He had then never been further from Boston than Portsmouth, and never anywhere in a steamboat. "I was vastly impressed," he writes, "by the importance of the journey, which revealed to me my lifelong taste for travel"; and he proceeds: —

New York I found interesting but disconcerting. I have always been over-sensitive to the solitude of strangers in a great city; and even then New York was comparatively metropolitan. It still kept, to be sure, what now seem unimaginable traces of its Dutch origin; the little hand-carts of the ash-men and scavengers, for example, were drawn by dogs harnessed to the axle, and there was distinctly specialized street-cries — that of strawberries, with its shrill prolongation of the final syllable still echoes in my ears. The older houses, too, traces of which even now linger about Washington Square, had such spacious stolidity that to call their "stoops" steps would have been barbarous. At that time, besides, business still lurked downtown. Union Square, with its bronze equestrian Washington in one corner, was a shady, fenced, oval park surrounded by substantial brick dwellings of the better sort. Madison Square, where the Worth monument already kept an otherwise extinct memory safe behind an iron fence of sheathed swords, was at once more or less impressive; it was enclosed in shabby wooden palings painted a dingy brown, but the houses about it had risen in what I then supposed the supreme glory of brownstone, and on the corner of 23d Street reposed in all its white marble dignity the solid Fifth Avenue Hotel, unaltered to the eye until more than a generation later they pulled it down. In a small two-story structure, I think, wooden, where the Flat-iron building has long replaced it, was a bookshop, subsequently fascinating to me from the fact that its bibulous proprietor a few years later got into newspaper notoriety by shooting a now forgotten man of letters for undue sympathy with his wife. Fifth Avenue itself started, as I think it starts to this day, in the guise of Washington Square; but almost from 14th Street, blooming into brownstone fronts — as like one another as eggs. It seemed utterly secure from the intrusion of trade.

It was all very splendid; there was something depressingly monotonous, though, in the unbroken vistas of the rectangular streets, and something inhuman in the fact that they were not named but numbered. Compared with Boston, I can now see, it was surging with growth, which means incessant change; and change I have never found instantly sympathetic. At any rate, the nervous effect of it on small me must have filled my parents with dismay; for I vividly remember sitting down on a curbstone in 30th Street one evening and loudly bawling, because very sensibly they would not take me with them to Wallack's, at that time the most fashionable of American theatres. To do them justice, they delayed their start until they had condemned me to punitive bed, and made sure that I was miserably there. I soon went to sleep. I was given to understand the next morning that they had greatly enjoyed the play, which had been "too old" for me.

As Barrett Wendell's first memories of New York, which he never came to like, were closely knit with those of his father, so were his first memories of Europe, which he came to love. The following paragraph from the memoir should therefore be read at this point: —

The summer of 1868, now just fifty years ago, long remained the most delightful I could remember. Exactly why my father decided to take his first vacation from business I do not know. Very likely, our shaven, serene, jocose Doctor Crane had advised a long rest; and very possibly he had thought my mother, too, in need of relief from domestic monotony. At any rate, so far as I knew, they rather suddenly decided to go to Europe, and take me with them. Then my wonder-year of three months began. I can describe it no better than by saying that, although I knew little of Longfellow, I saw Longfellow's Europe — which still seems to me the most purely beautiful of all. My readiness for it, I rather think, had been preparing all my short life, for I cannot remember a time when my Aunt Sarah Barrett was not eagerly willing to tell me inexhaustible stories and legends of the Old World we all came from. The charm of Europe — its beauty, its variety, its fathomless humanity, its immemorial habit of life, its boundless wealth of historic and fantastic tradition, glorious fine art — is really there; and no one ever felt this charm more genuinely than I, even at the age of twelve. The evil of Europe, its sins, its crimes, its baseness, is really there too; but somehow they left me untouched. At worst, they were the fleeting shadows which made clearer the beautiful outlines of what seemed to me — as they seemed to Longfellow and his time — the true features. It was a dream world, suddenly real for a little while.

An old bit of memory rises. At home I thought theatregoing the height of earthly delight; in Paris, one evening, I heard someone say that he was going to the theatre, and found myself indignantly surprised that anybody should so waste time when Europe was there to enjoy.

Learning thus early that "Europe was there to enjoy," and profiting greatly from his own early enjoyment of it, Barrett Wendell was meanwhile undergoing more formal instruction in New York. There is an amusing memento of one of the private schools he attended in the form of a letter, written before he was nine years old, and addressed to "Mr. Sanford, 204 5th Ave., N. Y." In the painstaking script of early boyhood it reads: —

MR. SANFORD                    NEW YORK, *Feb.* 26th, 1869

DEAR SIR, — You wanted us to give you our different opinions about gentlemen, and how to distinguish them from other persons.

I think that any one can be a gentleman if he tries to be.

Gentlemen are not always to be judged by their manners. Lord Byron once said that he once had his pocket picked by the most gentlemanly person he ever met with.

Once in the country while we were taking tea, a man with a sword in his hand walked into our yard. We were surprised because we did not know him. Father and Uncle Frank went out to meet him, and Uncle Frank asked him what kind of a sword he had, and he handed it to him. He proved to be a man named Lynch. He was not a gentleman. Gentlemen are judged by their actions and not by their manners, always, as I said before. Gentlemanly actions and manners arise from a good heart. That man who picked Lord Byron's pocket had only much civility.

This is my opinion of Gentlemen.

Your pupil,

BARRETT WENDELL

The "man named Lynch," intruding upon the domestic scene, armed with a sword, and the *insouciance* of "Uncle Frank" in asking what kind of sword it was, suggest a pleasing element of imagination in a child whose heart, with respect to gentlemen, was evidently in the right place. A suggestive bit of evidence that it remained there is found in a maturer reference to gentlemen in Wendell's discussion of the variable meaning of words, in his *English Composition:* —

What does a man mean, for example, who asserts that another is or is not a gentleman? To one the question turns on clothes; to another on social position gauged by the subtle standards of fashion; to another on birth; to another on manners; to another on those still more subtle things, the feelings which go to make up character; to another still on a combination of some or all of these things. Last winter a superannuated fisherman died in a little Yankee village. He was rough enough in aspect to delight a painter; if he could read and write it was all he could do. But there was about the man a certain dignity and self-respect which made him at ease with whoever spoke to him, which made whoever spoke to him at ease with him. I have heard few more fitting epitaphs than a phrase used by a college friend of mine who knew the old fellow as well as I: "What a gentleman he was!" But one who heard this alone would never have guessed that it applied to an uncouth old figure, not over-clean, that until a few months ago was visibly trudging about the paths of our New England coast.

Of the schooling which immediately preceded Barrett Wendell's admission to Harvard College, he has himself written in the memoir of his father. After mentioning his "nervous over-sensitiveness," he says: —

It was thought best that I should no longer be exposed to the vexatious discipline of a large school. So, after a short period of private tuition by my mother's cousin John Adams, I joined a small class which he was preparing for college. He had taken what used to be the parlors of a pleasant old brick house on the Fourth Avenue side of Union Square, near 17th Street; and there I resorted daily, with Sam and Arthur Sherwood, and John du Fais — all three editors of the Harvard *Lampoon* when I was — and a few more. Yet he was not only a first-rate coach for examinations; he actually could manage to teach more than I ever quite believed that he knew. Under him, for one thing instead of copying the *Æneid*, as a punitive task, I read every line of it and of the *Bucolics* and the *Georgics* too. Though he may not much have cared for his classics, he recognized that they were literature.

In considering the boyhood which preceded Barrett Wendell's maturity, the notably significant point is that he appears clearly to have derived more from his informal than from his formal instruction. That he was far from robust in his physical and nervous equipment, that his father was able and ready to deal with this condition by supplementing his schooling with much travel, and that the boy had the wit and the character to make the most of the opportunities thus afforded — these facts provide the true link between his boyhood and his maturity.

The remarkably careful and competent diaries which he set himself to keeping, even in his most youthful journeyings, bear witness to this process of self-improvement. Journals of sightseeing, particularly of the young, are the most tiresome things in the world to quote, and young Wendell's shall not be quoted here. But his European diaries of the summer of 1868, when he was thirteen, and of 1871, when he was sixteen, are none the less extraordinary documents. They reveal to an uncommon degree, not only a capacity for close observation but also an appreciation of the significance of historical, artistic, and literary associations. Here was a notable foundation for future building. Here, too, is a clear suggestion that in his own early practice of daily writing he discovered the value of the "daily theme" as the exercise in English composition with which his work as a teacher was peculiarly associated. It is pleasant to think of what he might himself have done in later life by extending to the length of a daily theme the brief record of his visit to the Blarney Stone: — "I contented myself with touching it with Mr. Hitchcock's umbrella and then kissing that." His pupils might then have accounted for his chariness of meaningless praise.

In addition to the journals of travel there are documents of self-improvement in the shape of lurid manuscript plays, under such titles as "Raymond of Caen," "Redwing the Pirate," and "The Moor's Revenge." The most ambitious of them, "The Oubliette, a Story of the Black Forest," written in the year following the summer travels of 1868, bears an obvious relation to the diary-page recording a visit to the Alte Schloss near Baden-Baden. It should be mentioned merely in token of the fact that what the boy was seeing was both extending his knowledge and feeding his imagination, an endowment with which these crude *juvenilia* show at least that he was liberally equipped.

Of the summer travels of 1871 there is a characteristic

BARRETT WENDELL AT ABOUT SEVENTEEN (1872)

reminiscence in a letter written by Barrett Wendell in 1917, apropos of the Reverend Dr. Edward A. Washburn, rector of Calvary Church, New York: —

In '71 he took me abroad with him for three or four months. By that time he was a "rueful Christian," but the best of fellows and the wisest of old friends. He taught me on principle that one should never open a bottle that won't keep, without finishing it; and, dear old boy, never ordered more than a pint between us. On one thirsty occasion I insisted on a quart; he stuck to his half pint, made me drink the rest, and put me to bed. There was never better lesson for a youngster.

To the success of the summer as a whole the final page of the diary bears enthusiastic witness. It has, besides, in its self-appraisal, an autobiographic value which warrants its quotation:

So ended the pleasantest journey I have ever taken, and I very much doubt if I shall ever enjoy one so much again. I was just at the right age to be enthusiastic over what I saw, without being too critical — to see all the beauties and hardly any of the impurities of the lands I visited. And I can feel too how much older and more mature I have grown in many ways since I left home. I really think that mentally — and physically too for that matter, for I have not felt so strong for several years — I was a different Barrett Wendell who sailed away in June.

Well, those three months have wrought a change in me that will never be undone; and besides their *effect*, every memory of them is perfectly delightful. I am inclined to think that, live as long as I may, I shall never look back to any other period of my life with half the pleasure with which I shall remember this perfect summer of 1871.

In the following year young Wendell was admitted to Harvard College, a freshman in the Class of 1876. This, however, proved an untimely start, and after about six months his fragile health brought his first connection with the University to a premature end. The result of this break in his studies was in reality an important contribution to his equipment for the continuous pursuit of his college course which began in the autumn of 1874 with the Class of 1877. In the memoir of his father, already so freely drawn upon, his enriching experiences of 1873 and 1874 are summarized in his own words: —

A recurrence, in April if I remember, of my probably hysterical paralysis had sent me invalid home, where medical advice had forbidden study and recommended open air for some time to come. We passed the summer in a cottage at that part of Swampscott called Beach Bluff, the name of the pleasant and hospitable house of my grandmother Barrett's cousins, the Addison Childs, who then owned the whole neighborhood.

The following year was therefore probably the most important in my life. My New York friend, George Allen, the nephew of Doctor Bellows, had also been out of condition, and had been made purser on the Pacific Mail liner Colima, bound without passengers for San Francisco by way of the Straits of Magellan. He managed to arrange that I should be taken along, and thus have a voyage of six or eight weeks. This was to be supplemented by a voyage across the Pacific, and so around the world. We left New York about the first of October. The Colima broke her propeller somewhere off the coast of Brazil. We put into Rio de Janeiro for repairs; and there, having found conditions at sea other than had been expected, — the captain, for one thing, had tried to bully me into signing over to him a letter of credit for five hundred pounds, — I took myself into my own hands, and went to my beloved Europe.

There I travelled alone for nine or ten months; I visited southern Spain, — with an excursion to Tangiers and Tetuan, I went on to Malta, — in which voyage I accidentally met my dearest of English friends, Sir Robert White-Thomson, who died at eighty-seven, only a few months ago.[1] By February I

[1] The name of this friend, first as Colonel Thomson, then as Sir Robert White-Thomson, will frequently recur in the ensuing pages. For about forty years, from the late seventies till the end of 1917, shortly before Sir Robert's death, Wendell maintained a steadfast correspondence with him. Sir Robert preserved the letters from Wendell, bound in two volumes, from 1879 to 1912, and carefully arranged thereafter. When

had got to Rome, where I stayed for weeks, absorbing the delights I later tried to set forth in my first book, *The Duchess Emilia.* I passed most of May in Paris. Thence I started on an indefinite summer journey northward, in the course of which I went up the whole length of the Gulf of Bothnia, and saw the midnight sun from the top of Ava Saxa, on the Arctic Circle, and subsequently drove across Scandinavia, and made an excursion to St. Petersburg and Moscow, coming back by way of Warsaw and Berlin. I reached England in time to make my first visit to Sir Robert White-Thomson — then still Colonel Thomson — at Broomford in Devon, and another with his wife's parents, Sir Henry and Lady Ferguson-Davie, at their greater Devonshire house of Creedy. And finally I returned home, in mid-September, by the last side-wheel steamship — the Scotia — which ever carried passengers across the Atlantic, and reëntered Harvard with the Class of 1877.

The young traveller's journal of this *wanderjahr* is no more to be quoted than its predecessors, but its many pages abound in convincing evidence that an American youth, rapidly maturing, and inalienably American at heart, was educating himself to become, in a measure quite uncommon then or since, a genuine citizen of the larger world. This he did become, and in so doing grew to occupy a place that was quite his own among American teachers, thinkers, and writers.

If the temptation to quote must be resisted, there are a few pages in the journal of this period which may at least be paraphrased. They are sharply, even physically, separated from all the other pages by having been cut out of the book in which they were written and enclosed in an envelope marked "Not to be opened except by Barrett

Wendell went to England, as youth and man, a visit to Sir Robert at Broomford Manor, Exbourne, Devon, served periodically to cement the friendship, which grew to include the families of both friends. Sir Robert's eldest son was the late Remington Walter White-Thomson, master and head of a house at Eton. Younger sons were Leonard Jauncey White-Thomson, now Bishop of Ely, and Brigadier-General Sir Hugh Davie White-Thomson. His only daughter, Ada, is the Hon. Mrs. Edward St. Aubyn.

Wendell." In a somewhat maturer handwriting their author inscribed the words, "otherwise to be burned," and "over." On the back of the envelope he wrote: "By way of avoiding melodramatic legends, in case this packet should fall into the hands of an imaginative person, I shall state that the contents are certain leaves cut out of my journal, written while in Malta in January, 1874. They are of rather a religious nature, and so ridiculous that I did not dare leave them where anybody could get at them; and I keep them only with the hope of having a good laugh over them some time or other."

A biographer, finding the envelope already opened, owes it both to his subject and to his readers to touch upon these pages. They relate, with transparent honesty and admirably straightforward and thoughtful expression, the revolt of a sensitive youth of eighteen against the traditional Deity of New England theology, seen even through the tempered austerities of the Anglican forms in which the youth was reared; his acknowledgment of a God of his childhood, "a dear, kind, gentle, loving God, to whom I could always go for aid and consolation"; the impossibility of reconciling the public and the private Deity; his scorn of the hypocrisy he would have to show in any pretense to this end, and of his contemporaries ruled by no such scruples; his abhorrence of forcing his disbelief or belief, in which he was not happy, on others; his realization that his mind was "still in its teens," and that the pages represented no settled opinions.

Fifty years after they were written they do represent an intellectual and spiritual candor, in which the later workings of Barrett Wendell's mind and spirit had their roots.

# III

## COLLEGE AND LAW STUDY

### 1874–1880

If the two preceding chapters have accomplished their purpose, the reader will have seen that Barrett Wendell came to his college and law studies with a preparation for them quite unlike that of most American youths of his own or later days. The impression he made upon his undergraduate contemporaries at Harvard is clearly preserved in President Lowell's memoir of him[1]: —

"At college he stood high in his studies, though not among those at the top of his class, for his interest was rather literary than learned, and he had no ambition for rank as such. He was strongly individual, striking out for himself instead of following the conventional track. Partly perhaps from delicate health, partly from his experience in travel, he was more mature than his fellows. At this time also he appeared to them somewhat radical, or rather iconoclastic, in temperament. That was a period when American taste was very crude, uncongenial to people who, like himself, were familiar with the more mellow traditions of an older world; and a revolt was beginning against the tone of thought which they termed 'Philistine' and 'Chromo-civilized.' One outlet for his energy he found in the group of men who founded the *Lampoon*, said at the time to be the best product of student life in the University, and certainly the most original. To that publication he contributed freely while in college and the Law School."

[1] *Proceedings, Massachusetts Historical Society,* Dec. 1921

The early volumes of the *Lampoon*, begun in February 1876 by a small group of students which included several of Barrett Wendell's closest friends, may be scrutinized both as social documents and for what they reveal in Wendell himself. The paper owed its origin to the refusal of the *Advocate*, another undergraduate journal, to print an ironic picture and communication on the Art Club by R. W. Curtis, an *Advocate* editor, and J. T. Wheelwright, each of the Class of 1876. They joined to themselves Wheelwright's brother, E. M. Wheelwright, later a distinguished architect, Samuel and A. M. Sherwood, who had been schoolmates of Wendell's in New York, E. S. Martin, of Wendell's college class, 1877, now the wise and witty editor of *Life*, and, as business editor, W. S. Otis, then of the sophomore class.

The first issue of the *Lampoon* was dated February 10, 1876. The Art Club skit seems mild enough, after nearly half a century, yet fairly prophetic in its tone of much that the *Lampoon* was to print in later years. It might have happened last week, for example, that an imaginary archæologist should write in a letter from Crete: "I have a rare piece of frieze from an ancient ice-chest." But in general the pages of the early *Lampoons*, both in text and in picture, speak for a past remote enough to be taking on an historic aspect. The current crudities of American life, especially as revealed at Harvard College, became fruitful objects of humorous scorn, offset by admiration of Eastlake furniture, London clothing, and all the contemporary symbols of "the correct." Young men wearing incredibly long belted ulsters, with incredibly large plaids and incredibly wingèd wing-collars, stalk through the pages of the journal. With its second volume, beginning October, 1876, that admirable illustrator, F. G. Attwood, afterwards identified with *Life*, became a contributor of drawings and an editor. At the same time Barrett

THE LAMPOON BOARD, 1877

Standing, left to right: Barrett Wendell, F. J. Stimson, Robert Grant, W. S. Otis.  Sitting, left to right: C. A. Coolidge, J. T. Bowen, J. T. Wheelwright, J. T. Coolidge, Jr., F. G. Attwood, Francis McLennan

Wendell, who had contributed to the second and ninth numbers of the first volume, joined the staff. From that time forth, through his senior year, his year in the Law School, and the two following years of his law studies in New York and Boston, he remained a contributor and intermittently an editor.

The tone of his contributions is illuminating. They reveal a somewhat world-weary young man, both consciously and unconsciously clever, evidently fond of saying smart, "snobbish," and — to the more conventionally minded — irritating things, indulging himself freely in the venerable cynicism of youth, and obviously enjoying it all to the full. While still a junior in college, he imagines a young graduate spending his summer vacation with his family, and exclaiming, "I felt as if I had on a tight coat — I never dared to let myself out, for fear of making a split." Out of college himself he produces, in "A Want Supplied," an amusing outline of a "Boston peerage," prophetic of his own interest in genealogical matters. A paragraph from "Some Considerations concerning Shop and the Talk Thereof," which appeared during his year in the Harvard Law School, is characteristic enough to be quoted:—

Shop, in short, is the thing we devote our lives to. We come into the world in the shape of eight or nine pounds of red, squirming, squalling, ugly flesh, with no apparent object beyond squirming and squalling. We squirm and squall with infantile frankness for some years in pretty much the same fashion, whether we be high or low, rich or poor, European, Asiatic, African, or American. By and by we grow old enough to be circumspect. We exercise our powerful will. We make ourselves squirm more or less obstreperously, in the fashion most suited to our taste or our condition. We teach ourselves to squall as a habit on a single note. In short, unless we are happy enough to have our minds made up for us, we make up our minds as to what we shall be. We settle down into our shops; we talk about them with delicious unconsciousness that everybody has not as much interest in them as ourselves. We laugh at the shop-talk of more enterprising shopmen; and because we do not happen to do a very thriving business, we amuse ourselves with the idea that we are not in trade.

By no means a negligible bit of youthful social philosophy! Many others might be cited to exhibit a genuine though sometimes a rather desperate interest in life. The *Lampoon* served Wendell an excellent purpose as a medium for characteristic self-expression. It also bore a close relation to his lifelong friendships, for among its editors were his academic seniors, Robert Grant, of the Class of 1873, and Frederic Jesup Stimson, of the Class of 1876, each destined to distinction in letters and affairs, each close to Wendell through all his years. Of his many contributions to the *Lampoon*, none other has endured so long at Harvard as his invention of the generic student-name of "Hollis Holworthy."

Since Harvard College became Barrett Wendell's "shop," it is worth while to pause a moment more and look at him as an undergraduate. Not at all given to athletics, — which then as now afforded a passport to general prominence, — marked by peculiarities of manner and temperament which at a time of life when human beings are most ruled by conventions set him apart from his fellows, he made the social and intellectual affiliations pertaining to the larger clubs, a place on the editorial staff of the *Crimson* before his association with the *Lampoon*, and membership in the now defunct "O. K.," a society of "literary" proclivities; but attained the distinction neither of undergraduate election to Phi Beta Kappa nor of membership in one of the more rigorously selective social clubs. Near the end of his sophomore year, in May 1875, prompted whether by the lure of congenial companionship or by military ardor, he joined the First Corps of Cadets in Boston. In this relation Wendell must have come nearer than in any other to participation in vigorous physical exercise. During his young manhood an injury to his back brought on a lameness, observable only to the most watchful, yet sufficient to cause his habitual use of a cane in walking. Throughout his life he was seldom far from the limits of his physical and nervous strength.

Of all his teachers at Harvard there was none whose influence appears to have counted more permanently with him than James Russell Lowell, the discursive scholar, also a man of the world, who cared much more for the spirit than for the letter of the books which formed the subjects of his teaching. In a little volume, *Stelligeri and Other Essays Concerning America,* published by Wendell in 1893, and named for "those that bear the stars" (the asterisks denoting death in the old Latin catalogues of Harvard graduates), there is an essay on "Mr. Lowell as a Teacher," which made its first, anonymous appearance in *Scribner's Magazine* for November 1891. In this paper Wendell tells of the prompting that came to him in his junior year, through a lecture of Norton's, to read Dante under Lowell. He knew not a word of Italian, and was firmly resolved to waste no more time on elementary grammar. Nevertheless, he applied to Lowell for admission to his course. His plea was kindly, though quizzically, heard; "and finally," says Wendell, "with a gesture that I remember as very like a stretch, [he] told me to come into the course and see what I could do with Dante." In the paragraph that ensues it is not fantastic to find a clue to much of Wendell's own later teaching: —

To that time my experience of academic teaching had led me to the belief that the only way to study a classic text in any language was to scrutinize every syllable with a care undisturbed by consideration of any more of the context than was grammatically related to it. Any real reading I had done,

I had had to do without a teacher. Mr. Lowell never gave us less than a canto to read; and often gave us two or three. He never, from the beginning, bothered us with a particle of linguistic irrelevance. Here before us was a great poem — a lasting expression of what human life had meant to a human being, dead and gone these five centuries. Let us try, as best we might, to see what life had meant to this man; let us see what relation his experience, great and small, bore to ours; and, now and then, let us pause for a moment to notice how wonderfully beautiful his expression of this experience was. Let us read, as sympathetically as we could make ourselves read, the words of one who was as much a man as we, only vastly greater in his knowledge of wisdom and beauty. That was the spirit of Mr. Lowell's teaching. It opened to some of us a new world. In a month, I could read Dante better than I ever learned to read Greek, or Latin, or German.

Thus it was not only what Barrett Wendell learned about Dante from Lowell, — and through that he became a lifelong reader and lover of Dante, — but also what he learned about teaching, that made this course of study a truly formative influence. He must have learned also the value of a close personal relation between teacher and pupil, for his remembrances of encounters with Lowell in his study at Elmwood are recorded with warm appreciation. When the Class of 1877 graduated, Lowell stepped at once into public office as United States Minister to Spain, but not until the class, torn with dissensions over its senior elections and threatened with the loss of all its Class Day pleasures, availed of the departing professor's hospitality in the use of Elmwood and its grounds for the time-honored festival. The Smith Professor of the French and Spanish Languages and Literatures and Professor of Belles-Lettres had provided the later Professor of English with a standard of relationships, individual and collective, to be applied in what was then a distant future.

For the three years that followed Wendell's graduation

from Harvard College he was a student of law, and not at all a happy one. He began his legal studies through no desire on his own part to become a lawyer but — the prospect of a business career being abhorrent to him — in conformity with his father's wish that he should prepare himself for some useful employment. In 1877–78 he attended the Harvard Law School; in 1878–79 he was a student in the New York law office of Anderson and Howland; in 1879–80 in the Boston office of Shattuck, Holmes (now Mr. Justice Holmes of the United States Supreme Court), and Munroe. At the end of these three years he presented himself in Boston for examination for the bar — and failed. "At that time," President Lowell has written, "he remarked that while all his friends whose judgment he respected thought he ought not to accept a defeat, but try again, he did not himself see why he should do so. Nor did he; and he was right. His friends had not appreciated capacities not fully revealed, or the future that lay before him in quite a different line."

For the two years between his graduation from Harvard College (1877) and his engagement in marriage (May 1879) to Edith Greenough of Quincy, Massachusetts, Barrett Wendell suffered a frankly miserable existence. The winter of 1878–79, spent in a New York law office, was perhaps the worst time of all. But all the available letters of this period — and a considerable number, addressed to F. J. Stimson, have been preserved — reveal clearly the writer's deeply discouraged outlook upon the world: this is equally true whether they are written from New York or from the Isles of Shoals, where his family was then wont to spend the summer, or from Florida, which he visited in the spring of 1879 in company with another lifelong friend, John Templeman Coolidge. These letters to Mr. Stimson are, however, so charged with personal flavor and so significant as documents of sensitive youth, discouraged to the point of despair, yet unknowingly on the very threshold of satisfying achievement, that some passages from them may profitably be cited. Since many of them are but partially dated, their chronological sequence cannot be guaranteed.

8 EAST 38TH STREET, NEW YORK

. . . I can find no words to express the dulness of life here; and the devil of it is that I am yielding to it completely. In Gath I am becoming a Philistine. *Nunc de me tacendum.*

My cousin Lilly Wendell is staying here — having what she describes as a pleasant time. All I know about it is that I have in no way contributed to her pleasure. The Upham girls dined here the other night. . . . Miss Olla . . . talked about Matthew Arnold, and I became feebly interested in that poet and bought a volume of his effusions. They are horribly pedantic and priggish, to my mind; but the fellow means something and knows what he means. I don't like his way of putting things as a rule, but I understand the things he means to put better than I expected to. I have come across several ideas of my own — not original, but favorite — badly embalmed in artificial poetry, but still recognizable. So on the whole I am rather glad that I bought him — particularly as the book happens to be bound in cloth of a most delightful color — a rich dark peacock blue-green — and is extremely ornamental and correct upon a somewhat chromatic library table.

I am deep in the *Divine Comedy* again. After all, Dante is the only book which carries me away. I manage to lose myself in the smoky depths of hell for half an hour or so every evening; and I am beginning to incline to the opinion that, whatever my own views may be on the existence of that locality, it is a matter of congratulation that the people of the Old World entertained strong convictions upon the subject. Hell has certainly given me more pleasure during the past two years than Heaven and Earth combined. . . .

8 EAST 38TH STREET, *Sunday*

. . . I was greatly amused yesterday at the contrast between your letter and some remarks addressed to me by the boss. You accused me, as of a crime, of being able, after all, to become excited from time to time. The boss stated with deploring gravity that he had never seen a person of my age who showed so little power of caring for anything. On the whole, I might as well keep on with law; he did n't know that anything else would bore me less; but unless I roused myself to a little more enthusiasm than I at present showed for anything, he did not promise me any great chance of success in life. Then he said some civil things about no need of work and the management of family estates, that were mildly amusing, and our tête-à-tête ended. . . .

49 Nassau St., New York, January 7,1879

Dear Fred, — I have tried with utter lack of success to do the writing you ask for. You can form no idea, in your present Kingsley state of mind, of the utterly ruinous condition of my character. I have lost every atom of self-control I ever had. I am growing duller, and stupider, and weaker, and more of a Philistine every day. I shall not be surprised if you do not answer this note for a dozen reasons. It is rude to write on office paper. It is contemptible to leave Lampy in the lurch after having pledged myself to help him. It is doubly contemptible to see a sane, healthy-looking man of three-and-twenty who ought to be a gentleman, and as a gentleman to have something approaching a respectable amount of character and determination, fading out into a miserable limp paper-doll, which has not even the recommendation of being dressed in the fashion.

Believe me, Fred, I do not know how to help myself. My life is a succession of fits of indignation at my own weakness, and of fits of complete *abandon* to that weakness, in which I grow weaker and weaker. I will try to do something for you, and for myself; I am beginning to fear — I have been beginning to fear for some years, I believe — that while man proposed that I should be something, God in his infinite wisdom is disposing of me as a mere copyist in a bad hand — with an ultimate view to the fertilization of the soil.

*[At the end of an undated letter from Appledore, Isles of Shoals]*

## LA TRISTEZZA DI APPLIDORO
### Opera Tragica
### PERSONE
#### IMMORTALI

MR. BARRETT WENDELL: handsome, accomplished, genial, beautiful, foolish, studious, literary, sentimental, and unhappy.
MR. —— : ugly, ponderous, intellectual, appalling, bugbear *pro tem.* to B. W.
—— : musical, smiling, slightly under the influence of liquor.
H. I. BOWDITCH, M.D.: elderly, dovelike, fresh from an operation on the l-g of a young woman from parts unknown.
SANTA CELIA: patron goddess of the island.

#### MORTALI

White men: none.
MISS —— : dark-eyed, Oriental, voluptuous beauty from New York. Bad musician, goodish flirt. Slow mother and fast brother.
MISS —— : jolly, noisy, and at a loss for somebody to flirt with.
LA MARCHESA DI INFERNO E FIAMME: sister to the foregoing.
MISSES BOWDITCH AND SISTER, LONG, KATE WENDELL, JONES, ALMY, AND WEISS: walking ladies.

#### DIABOLI POVERI (i.e., cads)

A family named ——, and a whole lot of people with other names.
Old women, old men, young women, young men, noisy children, etc., by a large company, which for a wonder is destitute both of accomplishment and talent.

JACKSONVILLE, *February* 27

... No one can know better than I the damning sense of uselessness which saddens the lives of men like you and me when we find ourselves, as we find ourselves too often, with leisure to think and nothing in particular to think about. Life for its own sake is not to us worth living. Whether it be our national dyspepsia, or our unused muscles, or a hateful

fact makes very little difference. To us eating, drinking, living, and breathing — even if we breathe this delicious Florida air — are delights which we shall not be very sorry to say good-bye to. Yet something or other deters us from being the first to speak the farewell word. In my own case, it is half a regard for the feelings of people whose lives I do not help to make happy, and yet who have a certain fondness for me which can be explained upon no rational ground; and half a feeling that it would be a confession of weakness at which men whom I think not so strong as I would laugh. If other people can bear life until its end comes, I ought to be able to bear it too. At any rate, if I can carry through the world these wretched nerves of mine, that quiver with pain at things which make other men's nerves vibrate with pleasure, I can at least feel that I may leave the world without the fear that it will pry into my secrets. As a cynical character in one of my comedies says, "All men are fools. Those only are wise who succeed in concealing their folly." The removal of oneself from the world is a confession of folly which sets all the world which knows us to picking our follies to pieces. We are not allowed to rest in peace without a psychological post-mortem performed by very unskillful doctors. And Heaven grant that when our time for rest comes, it may come at last as peacefully and be as peaceful as our world will let it be. . . .

8 EAST 38TH STREET, [*Good*] *Friday*

. . . I went to Trinity Church this morning with Ned. The great altar, with the white reredos rising behind and a flaming window full of saints and angels above it, was draped in heavy black. A great white cross stood out against the draperies. The church was full of people of every rank in life, standing side by side with that wonderful Christian equality that we see in the old churches of the Old World. And the most glorious floods of solemn music came rolling down the dim Gothic aisles. It was a morning to be remembered for a lifetime. Ned was sorry that he could not sympathize. I did sympathize, and it was all that I could do to help myself from falling on my knees when that grim old prig of a —— —— gave a benediction as solemn as a Pope's.

The frame of mind represented in these letters, written chiefly from New York, was obviously due in large measure to imperfect health, uncongenial prospects, and a general lack of incentive to satisfactorily directed effort. Two of these three difficulties vanished with his engagement. The tone of his letters immediately underwent an extraordinary change, the reasons for which are not far to seek. Miss Greenough's father was William Whitwell Greenough, a Boston man of affairs, for many years a resident of Quincy, who enriched the life of his community by a long and valuable service as president of the Trustees of the Boston Public Library. Through her mother, Catherine Scollay (Curtis) Greenough, her New England lineage was identical at points of the seventeenth and eighteenth centuries with that of Barrett Wendell. To all the congenialities of ancestral and immediate background, there was added that fortunate divergence of temperament upon which the happiness of one so constituted, emotionally, as Wendell may depend.

The more significant passages in Wendell's letters to Stimson in the years between his engagement and his marriage are too intimate for print. To his older English friend, Colonel Robert Thomson, he wrote, àpropos of his engagement and his prospects, more appropriately for the present purpose.

QUINCY, *September* 28, 1879

DEAR COLONEL THOMSON, — Your welcome present has just been sent to me from 38th Street, where Mr. Gray left it a few days ago. I am sure that I need not tell you how much it pleased me; and indeed did I feel that there were such a need, I should not know how to do so. I have begun to learn this summer that there are real feelings in the world that conventional expressions were invented to describe, and yet which they fail to describe for the very reason that they are conventional. And so when I thank you most heartily for your kind remembrance, I am sure that you will understand that I appreciate and value your sympathy in my happiness and your kind hopes for my future.

How soon my future will assume a definite form I cannot yet say. My father does not wish me to be married until I am admitted to the bar; and Miss Greenough is an only daughter and is only twenty years old, so her people are unwilling to lose her; and although I have a hope of being married in the spring, I hardly dare to breathe it abroad and nothing is settled as yet. I have already begun my studies. I read law for four or five hours every day in a Boston office, with one of the most charming men I ever met — young Wendell Holmes, a son of the Autocrat of whom you have probably heard — and a distant kinsman of mine, although I never happened to know him until a few weeks ago. Quincy is so near Boston that I can come out every evening, however; and here I shall stay for a few weeks longer. Then I am going into lodgings in Boston for the winter. I have taken a suite of rooms with my most intimate college friend [F. J. Stimson] and we are looking forward to some delightful evenings over a great wood fire . . . .

But instead of turning to letters at this point, we may better resort to one of Wendell's own principles of composition and bring this record of his student years to a close with something like a summary of the preceding pages. This is found in his own words, written in the memoir of his father which has already proved its value to the present purpose: —

So in the autumn [of 1877] I returned to Cambridge, and began the study of law. The year was disappointing. Though I have since found that the discipline of legal study strengthened my mental habit for life, the work at the time was both detestable and depressing. An accidental physical fact probably had something to do with this. The muscles of my back have always been rather weak, so that I habitually walked with a cane ever since I was an undergraduate. The hard chairs of the Law School library therefore combined with the constant need of going to bookshelves and handling heavy volumes to keep me constantly tired. Even now, in consequence, I am aware of instinctive displeasure when I see a book bound in legal calf. The fact that my courtship looked unpromising did not help things; and in the early winter a not serious illness resulted in a permanent scar on one cheek. At the end of the year I did not take the trouble to present myself at the annual examinations, so got no credit for what work I had reluctantly done. Hardly any line of conduct could have been more disconcerting to a parent; yet I do not remember that the letters sent me by my father contained even a syllable of reproach. Instead, he found no fault with my suggestion that I had been devoting myself too long to abstract study, and might possibly find the more responsible duties of studying in an office less repugnant; and he proceeded, with no help on my part, to find a place for me.

My months of professional study in a Nassau Street office gave little relief. The surroundings there, nevertheless, were friendly. The head of the firm, Mr. Henry Anderson, had become, as he always stayed, an affectionately intimate friend of my father; they had met, I believe, as vestrymen of Calvary Church. His wife's friendship with my mother was just as close.

My work in the office was mostly the searching of titles and the indexing, with cross references, of the published reports of the New York courts — the Supreme Court and the Court of Appeals. Though an admirable discipline in the matter of accuracy, it was solitary and far from stimulating to the imagination. Some time in February or March I got to a point of nervous depression which I imagined serious. As usual when even the shadow of real trouble appeared, my father was instantly kind, and let me go for two or three weeks to Florida with my college friend, Templeman Coolidge. Called to Boston, not very long after my return, by the funeral of a classmate, I found my personal affairs taking a wonderful turn for the better, and came home engaged. In every way this happily altered the outlook.

In the frequent and prolonged intervals of my office I read, as conscientiously as I could, the subjects requisite for admission to the Suffolk bar. When the examinations came in April or May, I presented myself. Greatly to my chagrin, I failed to pass them. On general principles, I should have expected my father to be furious, and Mr. Shattuck — whose office had never before produced an unsuccessful candidate — to be resentful. Instead, though both confessed regret, neither spoke an unkind word. Just as if I deserved it, the preparations for my wedding went on. I was married at Quincy, on the first of June, 1880, to Edith Greenough.

The next week my wife and I passed together in the old family home at Portsmouth, which was destined years later to become our own, and where I am writing now. Already fond of it, I had asked Aunt Carry to lend it to me; and, doubtless at my father's suggestion, she had cordially done so, going away for some family visits. I can now see that my wish to begin my new life in his old home touched him deeply; however we might unmeaningly have jarred on one another, our hearts proved at one.

His real wedding present was a letter of credit for five hundred pounds, which gave us three months of travel in Europe. On our return, while we were still staying for a few days in 38th Street, came from a clear sky the telegram which decided my future career. Months before, I had chanced to meet in the street my college teacher of English, Professor Adams Hill. We had hardly come across each other since I graduated. He asked me what I was doing. I told him that I was reading law. He asked whether I liked it; I said no. And on his duly inquiring what kind of job I should prefer, I am said to have answered, "Even yours." Somehow the incident stuck in his memory. So early in October, finding himself in need of some one to read sophomore themes, he proposed my name to President Eliot, who was always fond of experiments with inexperienced teachers. The result was a telegram, inviting me to come on and discuss the matter. It arrived, I think, on the evening when Doctor Washburn came to dine, and I saw him for the last time; he died a few months later — some years younger than I am now. The telegram decided my career; it also gratified my father as indicating, for the first time, that somebody thought me conceivably useful. Though I began teaching at Harvard thus fortuitously and with no notion of keeping it up long, and though more than once I came near dropping the work, I was actually on the rolls there as a teacher for thirty-seven years; and a few months before my father died he was gratified by my promotion to a full professorship.

# IV

## THE YOUNG INSTRUCTOR AND WRITER
### 1880–1888

THOUGH the year 1880 marks the beginning of Barrett Wendell's definite work in the world, no excuse is needed for having devoted so much space to the years preceding that date: they were the years that determined what he was just as much as what he was not to be. His personal stars in their courses fought against the law and practical affairs quite as clearly as on the side of letters and their pursuit. The obvious means to this end was an academic post, and — for Wendell — at Harvard. His own apprehension of the grounds on which his appeal as a teacher began to be felt, was frankly expressed on an autobiographic page relating to his early years of teaching: "The work at Harvard kept me pretty busy; I did it conscientiously, and my oddities of temper and of manner chanced to interest my pupils." There can be no doubt that his marked individuality counted in his favor.

One who came to know him when he had been teaching only six years out of the thirty-seven devoted primarily to this work may be permitted to recall him, not as he appeared at any one period, as a younger or an older man, but in the singular unity of impression produced by his personality throughout his life. He stands, then, before the eye of memory, well-proportioned of figure, of moderate height, shapely of head, tawny-bearded, with quick blue eyes, alert and responsive in personal encounter, the man of the world rather than the professor in general appearance. Ready of tongue, addicted to repartee, he expressed himself in a staccato and much-inflected speech that was eminently his own — not the utterance of Oxford, yet much more English in its effect than American. Add to this distinctive characteristic such an easily imitable habit as the twirling of a watch-chain while addressing an audience, and it is no wonder that Barrett Wendell offered an irresistible temptation to the mimic in successive college generations.

It is a sure token of poverty when a college does not possess in its teaching force one or more "characters," the "taking off" of whom becomes a recognized accomplishment. These are generally the men who impress themselves most strongly upon the undergraduate. The superficial things about them can be, and are, imitated with mirthful results. As a rule, however, the personal peculiarities of a teacher are interesting in proportion to his own value as an instructor and stimulator of youth. The real things, — the fruits of study and thought, the expressions of intellectual and personal friendship, the intimate concern for the welfare of pupils, — these are not objects of mimicry, however they may enhance its appeal. In the case of Barrett Wendell — as many of his letters will show — such realities stood throughout his career at the foundation of his teaching and of its far-spreading influence.

In October 1885, as in February 1876, almost exactly ten years before, a new periodical came into existence at Harvard through a secession from the *Advocate*. This was the *Harvard Monthly*, in the origin of which Barrett Wendell was even more involved than in that of the *Lampoon*. An editorial article in the first issue declared, "There can be no doubt that the study of English composition at Harvard has come out of the second and into the first rank of the studies now offered," and referred particularly to Wendell's course, "English XII," started only the year before and already enrolling about a hundred and fifty men. The purpose of the *Monthly* was to establish "a magazine which shall contain the best literary work done here at Harvard, and represent the strongest and soberest undergraduate thought." The editor-in-chief of the first volume was Alanson B. Houghton, now United States Ambassador to Germany, and on the editorial board were the late George Rice Carpenter, who became a distinguished professor of English at Columbia, William Morton Fullerton, afterwards Paris correspondent of the *London Times*, and George Santayana. Carpenter was the second editor-in-chief; George P. Baker, now professor of dramatic literature at Harvard, the third; and Bernhard Berenson, the fourth. With these men, their colleagues, and their successors, — of whom the maker of this volume happened to be one, — Wendell stood in a stimulating relation of counselor and friend. The *Monthly*, an ambitious infant, needed all the help he could give it, in continuance of his sound advice to its parents before its birth, and all this help Wendell gave, without stint. He contributed the first article to its first number — a New England sketch, "Draper," based directly upon a passage in one of his diaries recording a driving trip with his brother Gordon from New York to Boston in the summer of 1885. His interest in the magazine might indeed have been taken for granted, since the *Monthly* was merely the student expression of the very concern for letters which Wendell as a teacher had begun to quicken. The immediate result was a publication which after nearly forty years bears with astonishing credit the test of critical examination. No doubt its editors — and perhaps Wendell himself — thought it more remarkable than it really was. What neither they nor he may have realized is that the teachers who throw themselves as heartily into an undergraduate enterprise as Wendell did in this instance are few. Their ultimate reward is suggested by

Professor Baker, in his reminiscence of Barrett Wendell, printed in the *Harvard Graduates' Magazine* for June 1921:

"Mine was the day when the *Harvard Monthly* was founded. It might almost be said that Grays 18, the room his name made famous, was its editorial office, for he was intensely interested in the magazine from the first day of its founding. In its second year I never knocked in vain at Grays 18 for counsel as to policy, available undergraduate work, or searching criticism. Immediately after the appearance of each number, at least a postcard and often a detailed letter of criticism would be on my desk. Nothing ever did so much to give me a sense that an art is far greater than any of its servants as Wendell's praise and blame of those successive numbers."

In the period covered by the dates above this chapter, Wendell made and abandoned his attempts to become a novelist. His juvenile efforts as a playwright, his continuance in this direction through the authorship of plays for college and private theatricals,[1] bore witness to a strong bent towards creative writing. It was but natural, therefore, that while other nascent professors of English were delving into Anglo-Saxon roots, and pressing the dry leaves of higher scholarship, Wendell was trying his best to deal with human life and character through the medium of fiction. As it turned out, his best was not so good as to establish him among the younger novelists of his time, from whom much better things were to be expected. Two published novels, *The Duchess Emilia: A Romance* (1885) and *Rankell's Remains: An American Novel* (1887), were the public fruits of this effort. There is besides an unpublished novel, *Plaster of Paris*, begun in 1881, when for a time there was a break in what was to

---

[1] A farce, "Poison," written by Wendell and J. T. Wheelwright and acted by the Hasty Pudding Club at Harvard was booked for a benefit production at the Boston Museum in the spring of 1881, but never acted there.

BARRETT WENDELL AT THIRTY-FIVE, IN "GRAYS 18"

prove the long continuity of Wendell's teaching at Harvard. The occasion of this break was characteristic enough to be recorded. Near the end of his first year of teaching, it was made known to him that the finances of the College did not warrant the reappointment of two instructors in English, of whom he was one. To the other the salary attaching to the post was of far more immediate importance than to Wendell. Without hesitation, and, one may well imagine, somewhat to the consternation of his family, he accordingly resigned his instructorship. His formal reappointment was dated October 11, 1882. The writing of *Plaster of Paris* had proved, however valuable as an exercise in composition, a frail substitute for teaching as a means of support.

*The Duchess Emilia* is a story of nineteenth-century Rome before the temporal power of the popes came to an end. For its difficult theme it has the Roman experiences of a strange young New Englander, into whose body at birth passed the soul of a great but maculate Roman lady whose life ended at the moment his began. The critics of course called it "Hawthornesque." As a work of art it suffers sorely from its author's attempt to tell a complicated tale from a variety of angles, to the notable sacrifice of a sustained dramatic effect. In relation to Wendell's own life it is significant as showing to what good purpose, in his admirable descriptions of Roman scenes, he could turn observations fully recorded in his diary of 1874. But this does not make a novel, and *The Duchess Emilia*, creditable as the work of a beginner, must be regarded as an object rather of personal than of permanent public interest.

Two years later came *Rankell's Remains*, a more realistic endeavor to portray contemporary American life. The Republican National Convention of 1884, which nominated James G. Blaine for the presidency, is thinly veiled in many pages of description. In the robbing of the grave of the hard-hearted — yet romantic — merchant, Rankell, whose sinister figure dominates the story, there is an obvious reflection of the outrage, then comparatively recent, upon the grave of the New York merchant, A. T. Stewart, in St. Mark's churchyard. In *Rankell's Remains* there is something of the same element of the *macabre* as in *The Duchess Emilia;* there is also the same unfortunate resort to a method of divided narration. But there is a definite gain in directness and effectiveness — whether enough to guarantee a further improvement in later novels, had they been written, it were idle to conjecture.

In passing, it ought to be noted that, although Barrett Wendell did not attend the Republican Convention which nominated Blaine, he was present, a month later in Chicago, at the Democratic Convention which nominated Cleveland. At this time indeed he served as a correspondent of the *Boston Daily Advertiser* under the signature, "A Looker-on in Chicago." In the ensuing campaign he became a pronounced "mugwump," with scant sympathy for those who placed party regularity first in their political considerations. This was an attitude which could not escape its penalties. They are suggested in an editorial note, under the title, "A Tabooed Novel," printed in the *Boston Herald* of November 21, 1886: —

"Mr. Barrett Wendell, the author of the clever story, *Rankell's Remains*, published by Messrs. Ticknor & Co. a few weeks since, has the honor of being brought under the ban of certain party newspapers in this city. The *Journal* was put into a frame of agitation by his manner of making a sketch of a political convention, which impelled it to publish a leading editorial, in which it assumed that Mr. Wendell must have meant to describe a Republican convention here, and went into an argument to prove that the latest Republican national convention was no such body as was represented in his depiction. The *Advertiser*, it is stated, has been similarly disturbed, and the edict is said to have gone out in that office that the book shall not be noticed at all in its columns. Is this the beginning of an *Index Expurgatorius* to deal with mugwump literature? If carried out, we suppose that it will be necessary, in the future, to have all books of mugwump authorship examined, to see that no heresies which conflict with the party standard are contained in them; and, as all the authors of the country are largely infected with lack of faith on this point, the work of these censors is likely to be no light one. In the mean time, this tabooing of Mr. Wendell's book will be likely to invite curiosity to it, and should prove a valuable advertisement to its publishers."

Possibly prodded by these expressions, the *Advertiser* two days later printed a review of the book, beginning, "There is advantage frequently in delay," and, after some praise of the purely fictitious elements of the story, declaring, "If, indeed, Mr. Wendell intended an accurate portrayal of historic scenes and situations in the national republican convention of 1884, he has been grossly misinformed ... No such convention ever did take place in this country and none probably ever will." In the light of Wendell's later political views the idea of placing one of his books on a conservative *Index Expurgatorius* has an aspect almost comic.

The occasion of his visit to Chicago in 1884 was the prosaic mission of supervising the local entrance-examinations of candidates for admission to Harvard College — a task which before the days of the College Board was assigned to young instructors. Two years later, in 1886, a similar mission took Wendell to San Francisco. His capacity for intelligent travel, of which he

always made ample record in letters and journals, gave
to each of these expeditions the value of a broadening
experience. Apart from all the impressions of places and
persons so recorded, his written words give a clear impression of himself — significantly, for a single instance, in a
penciled note at the end of his Chicago Convention diary
of 1884: "Moonlight night on the seashore with news of
death. The infinite spaces of peace into which the dead
man expands open before one's eyes." The whole man
appears more distinct when one thinks of him, returned
from the turmoil of crowded halls and trains, rejoining
his little family at New Castle, New Hampshire, where
his father had a summer house, and moved to expression
by the poetry of night and death.

During the years to which this chapter is devoted the
first two of Barrett Wendell's four children were born —
Barrett, Jr., April 19, 1881; Mary Barrett, February 17,
1883. His two younger children were born in the
next period to be considered — William Greenough,
November 11, 1888; Edith, September 5, 1893. His
entire family life, of singular felicity, was centred in the
Boston house, 358 Marlborough Street, in which he and
his wife went to housekeeping in the autumn of 1880.
"We had two servants," Wendell wrote long afterwards,
"who were sisters, of spotless character and little skill.
My wife nevertheless displayed her talent for hospitality";
and so it began, the long happy domestic scene, the background of friendships, industry, and fruitful service to
the intellectual life of his time. Not that his nature
underwent any such change as to ensure him unbroken
satisfaction in life and circumstance. On the contrary,
there were the inevitable ups and downs of a sensitive
temperament. A passage in a page-a-day diary, written
in May 1884, apropos of a friend who had just taken his
own life, indicated, however, the frame of mind which by

that time had replaced the steady depression of five years before: —

Certainly suicide is an unhandsome proceeding, if you have near relatives to be troubled, and disgraced too — for people always look doubtfully at a suicide's kinsman and wonder if he will not do it too. And again, as Mr. Norton once observed, even if there were nobody to whom you owed the civility of living as long as forbearing Nature will let you, it is very bad taste to leave so nasty a mess as your body on the hands of your friends. I wonder if anybody ever reached thirty-five in New England without wanting to kill himself. Really, it rather surprises me to see how few do so — though for my part I am past the critical stage, and find life pleasanter every year.

In this chapter, as in those that will follow, the plan of assembling the chosen portions of letters and journals after introductory pages applying to the period under consideration, will be followed. To these selections themselves only such words of explanation as may seem imperatively needed will be added.

*To F. J. Stimson*
[*Written while Wendell was housed, on his wedding journey, with a depressing cold.*]

VERONA, *August* 15, [1880]

. . . I grieve that law cuts into G. G. We could get along better without law. But this infernal Yankee prejudice in favor of something that brings in cash — as if one cared for money when one could find decent amusement without it — makes law the thing to do, I suppose. In fact, a man who wants to do serious literary work, nowadays, must sacrifice not only his best hours to it, but shocking to say, he must sacrifice that still more useful thing, the general respect of other people. It is maddening to have to do one's best work in an amateurish way, if not actually on the sly — at the risk of having fingers pointed at you if you are found out. . . .

I think you have enough in your new book to feel sure that somebody will always remember your work, though. As for me, I am like a prosaic, uncourageous hero of a prosaic "Madonna of the Future" — see H. James's story. When I die of a cough or something else, perhaps some amiable fool may imagine that my empty blank books might have contained something worth having.

*To Colonel Robert Thomson*

QUINCY, *October* 19, 1880

. . . My habits of travel are too far confirmed to be broken; and a very pleasant thing has just happened to me which seems to offer me a chance of continuing them from year to year. Almost immediately after my arrival in New York I was invited to teach Rhetoric at Harvard; and in case the experiment is satisfactory to the University people and to me too, there is a very fair chance that I may stay there permanently. In this case I shall have a good three months of vacation every year. And I think that I shall very often pass them in Europe. . . .

*To his Father*

BOSTON, *April* 3, 1881

. . . I do not believe that any two human lives ever had fewer things to trouble them than ours have had this year. From the day that we were married to this day that I write to you, everything has been as bright and as happy as it could be. And really it seems to me that in this past year I have had happiness enough to make life worth living, even though the future were as black throughout as the gloomiest dreams of my most despondent moments ever painted it.

And I feel that I owe all this to you, and that I can in no way repay you except by telling you over and over again that I realize every day more and more what you have done for me and are doing for me.

For myself I can do little, so far as I can tell. I have worked hard at Cambridge, with what success I do not know. I have done nothing else, beyond my work on the farce which will probably appear at the Museum in the course of two or three weeks.[1]

Whether I shall keep my Cambridge place I cannot tell until the end of the year. In the summer I may try to prepare myself for the bar again; but in spite of the advice of all friends for whose opinion I have any respect, I cannot bring myself to approve of the plan.

Practice is pretty much out of the question. I am hardly strong enough to stand it. If I were brought face to face with the necessity of money-making, I should much rather venture myself in some business than in a profession overcrowded with stronger and abler men than I — a profession in which all but the very highest work is underpaid to an appalling extent. And from anything but the purely practical point of view, I cannot bring myself to regard the work which admission to the bar would cost me as worth doing. However, for two months more I cannot seriously think of it.

On the other hand, it is just possible that there may be something in this play-writing business. If our farce is successful, Jack and I intend to try our hand at a more pretentious comedy. If that is successful, we shall probably have received a market for our wares and an incentive to produce them. If I don't study law this summer, I mean to give the morning of every day to systematic writing, which may result in something. My Cambridge work will help me there.

If I keep my place at college, I shall continue to make something, to which I may add a little by writing. I can see no other prospect of helping myself. . . .

*To F. J. Stimson*

QUINCY, *October* 7, [1881]

DEAR FRED, — Your letter from Santander asks me what young American wives should be allowed to read. In my opinion they should be allowed to read whatever they want to. Perhaps I am too unreserved in my ways of talking and of

[1] See *ante*, p. 42.

thinking, too; but I like to say to Edith whatever comes into my head, and I like to have her talk to me in the same way. For the rest, I don't know why a married girl should not read whatever she pleases. In foreign life, which you and I are apt to read about, family relations are so different from what they are with us that unless we stop to think, we are apt to draw inaccurate conclusions about the world in which we ourselves live. To a French woman with a French husband, and the peculiar surroundings of Continental life, certain sorts of books might be pretty dangerous. They might take a serious hold on her imagination, and without really altering her character they might fill her open thoughts with hateful images, not devoid of fascination.

But it seems to me that the nature of our women is too high and pure easily to be lowered, or corrupted, or even injured. From things they ought not to think of — I mean things that you and I would not like them to think of — they turn away of themselves. Seriously, my dear fellow — for I take it for granted that you wrote seriously — it would be better if we followed their advice in our reading — or rather their example. I think we can trust them with anything with which they are willing to trust themselves. Can we say as much for one another? . . .

As for staying away, I think you do well. Conventional America says a young man should be on hand and keep looking out for a job. Of some men this view would be the only true one; but I admire you enough to believe you to be capable of setting to work with a real will, even after you have been doing nothing but hunt pleasure for some time. And such periods of life as you are now enjoying don't happen every day. As the delightful man in "Engaged" says, "You're only married once a year, you know — that is — I mean — only every now and then". . . .

*To the same*

*November* 10, [1881]

. . . I am trying to write a novel, but with little success. When you come here you can write one about me, entitled

"A Study of a Failure." A good motto for it would be the epitaph I have lately composed for myself: "He lacked the courage to do good or evil."

## To Colonel Robert Thomson

BOSTON, *February* 8, 1882

. . . We have been living along very quietly. We passed a month with the Greenoughs — my wife's people — at Quincy; and we were at my father's in New York through most of December. Then we came back here, where we are so perfectly comfortable that my old rambling instincts are disappearing. Owing to a rather disagreeable complication of circumstances I resigned my place at Harvard, with which I was more than satisfied last year. And at present I am ashamed to say that I am without any particular occupation — a state of affairs regarded in this part of the world with stern disfavor. Still I am as comfortable and as happy as mortal man can be; and I am not quite idle. I have read a good deal, and I have indulged my old fancy for writing as far as to write a short novel, which I'm thinking of sending to a publisher. If it ever sees the light, I'll send you a copy. I remember a civil speech of yours at a table d'hôte at Naples, when you expressed a hope that you might some day hear of me as a writer. Now I feel a little encouraged to hope that you may. The book I have finished does not altogether please me, though. It is a little gloomy, and tinged with a cynicism that I really don't feel. Then there are one or two incidents that I could wish out of it. But I had an idea, and the idea worked itself out in its own way. Have you ever tried your hand at fiction? I believe that your novel-writer is almost as much hampered by imaginary facts as your historian is by real ones. Things turn up unexpectedly; and you can't get away from them. . . .

Your compatriot, Oscar Wilde, has been here lecturing, and has rather puzzled good Americans. Some lion-hunters went wild over him and behaved like fools. Some respectable people, among whom is my mother, think his poems dreadfully improper, and say that he should n't be received. He is caricatured so constantly in *Punch*, and we see his name so often in print, that he must be a well-known figure in London. What do people think of him there? Is he somebody, or only a conspicuous guy? Or is he a man who has had his day — a dying lion, lacking the dignity of Thorwaldsen's? . . .

*To his Wife*
[*On office paper of Shattuck, Holmes and Munroe*]
BOSTON, *October* 3, 1882

Eliot offers me an annual appointment at twelve hundred — with rather more work than I had before. After all, there may be a chance of reappointment.

My father advised me to accept whatever Eliot offered. I thought it might be well to see Mr. Shattuck first, so I came here, only to find him closeted with some other legal swell, and inaccessible for God knows how long. I am waiting in hopes of a chance to ask him whether the *Advertiser* could possibly make it worth my while not to go back to Cambridge. . . .

I shall write Eliot a definite answer to-night — undoubtedly accepting, I think. Work will then begin immediately. Love to all at Quincy. I wish I could be there too.

*To Colonel Robert Thomson*
BOSTON, *January* 10, 1884

. . . Greek has been in my head of late almost all the time. In America it has always been the custom to prepare boys for college by teaching them Latin, Greek, and the simpler forms of mathematics. Of late there has been much discussion about changing all this. Scientific people, and people who are deep in modern languages, declare that their own fields of study offer quite as good ground for cultivating young minds as do the older fields where all minds have perforce been cultivated. And now we have before us at Harvard a proposition that we shall receive in future students who prepare themselves in science or in modern languages instead of in Greek. There are many arguments on both sides, besides the "practical" arguments with which I do not find myself in much sympathy. The great thing in education, some say, is that the student shall be taught to master something, and it is better that each man should master something which he cares about than something which he finds odious. This is plausible; at times I am almost inclined to think that it is true. Yet, whatever the reason may be, there is no doubt that the schools that I have seen where the classics are not insisted upon have not had the tone that one wishes a school to have. And then, we Americans, with strange inconsistency, hate novelty in any form with a hatred as deep as we know how to feel. We shall vote on the subject before long. I will write you how the vote goes.

Life has treated me gently this year, though it has kept me very busy. Indeed, this is the first letter that I have found time to write for a month. I have worked, and read; and I have gone out very little. I have met two countrymen of yours who have interested me — Mr. Matthew Arnold and Mr. Irving. Mr. Arnold I saw several times, with much pleasure — Mr. Irving only once, but he said so much about Shakespere in ten minutes that I have been thinking about it ever since. His acting I found very interesting; I had never seen him before. Mr. Arnold will carry home curious ideas of America. He has been seized upon by rich lion-hunters whom nobody ever heard of, and has been fed and flattered to the last degree. He capped the climax by going to visit Barnum, who tried to persuade him to give a course of lectures on "Personal Reminiscences of Eminent People I have Known." . . .

*To the same*

KILBOURN, WISCONSIN, 3 *July*, 1884

DEAR COLONEL THOMSON: — For the first time in four years I am on my travels, or something very like it. I have been to Chicago on some business for the college. I have slipped away from there for a few days, to see something of this Northwestern country of ours. In a day or two I go back again, to see the National Convention of the Democratic Party. You do not follow our politics, I suppose. At present they interest me a good deal. The Republicans have been in office since 1860. Their original policy — the preservation of the Union — was successfully carried out. For years they have had no fixed policy at all. Naturally they have been growing very corrupt. . . .

The Democrats — the Opposition — have not yet made their nomination. If they make a good one, so many men who have hitherto voted with the Republicans will support it that their candidate will almost certainly be elected. But the Democrats have a positive genius for blundering. They have had chance after chance in past years; they have always let them pass. At present, when unanimity and respectability are the two things they want, there are some signs that they are squabbling among themselves, and that men equally unfit with Blaine have a very fair chance of the nomination. . . .

In view of all this, the Convention which meets next week to nominate the Democratic candidate is distinctly the most interesting that has been held since I can remember. I think myself very lucky in being able to be on hand. I have left my wife and the babies with my people at New Castle. When I last heard from them — now a week or more ago — they were in capital condition. I have not been away from them so long since the babies have been in existence; and I am quite appalled at my own domesticity. I am as homesick as the Swiss of fiction. The truth is that this Western country of ours is terribly uninteresting. It is very fertile, but very flat. The landscape is as monotonous as landscape can be. The towns are brand new, and very ugly. The cities are the colossal works of men who as a rule know how to make money but not how to spend it. And though here and there you find oases in this desert, — such as a small club in Chicago, which is in every respect all that a club should be, — the whole atmosphere is very depressing to a man who is not too busy to stop and think. Accordingly, I am rather depressed.

To-night I am at a small town on the Wisconsin River whither I came over some hundred miles of railway because the scenery is said to be the finest in this part of the world. It is fair to say that I have not seen the scenery in question as yet. For when I arrived here it was raining cats and dogs, and when it stopped raining it was after dark. But the place is not promising in general aspect. It is fairly clean; to-night I perceive no other engaging quality.

On the whole, though, I fear that I am a little unfair to what we call the Northwest. The Great Lakes, which I have seen for the first time, are very beautiful. The tints of the water are marvelous; they are like the finest tints that you see on the Mediterranean. Unhappily, I have seen them chiefly from cities. And in the lake cities so much coal is burned that they are buried in smoke-clouds as heavy as those that hang over London. Imagine the Bay of Naples mixed with a London fog. Then you will have some notion of what Lake Michigan looks like at Chicago.

Well, I have rambled on until I find my paper almost full. I have not said much, I fancy; but I have said enough to express to you how much I prize our friendship — now ten years old. Let me hear from you when you can, how the world goes with you and yours. . . .

[*A few passages from a journal of Wendell's Chicago experiences supplement the preceding letter*]

*June* 26, 1884. — Blaine will be hard to beat here. My present points against him are (1) The bloody shirt, which is pure disunion in thin disguise; (2) His foreign policy, which I hold to be purely British; i.e., aggressive, blustering, and expensive; (3) His proposal to divide the surplus among the states; (4) The Maine machine, as shown at Kittery; (5) The total barrenness of his career in any great public movement; (6) The political company he keeps. His personal character, for honesty, etc., I hold for the moment to be irrelevant. Webster was hardly honest, though he never sold his vote. But I do not know that Blaine would actually sell his vote on a public question. And those who hold that private legislation is purely a matter of business, and legislators in so far forth pure attorneys, are too common to be damned utterly. Hideous as such morality is, it is morality of a certain kind. . . .

*June* 28. — I slipped out of the examination room for a while, and called on Sumner, of Yale, who is examining people in a neighboring street. He tells me that the independent movement in Connecticut has real strength among the better classes of the people, as well as among the college men. In regard to the nomination, he says that in all probability there was a preliminary bargain between Blaine and Logan that each should throw his following into the other's line, if the chances turned in favor of either. (Heaven forgive me, an instructor in English, for writing a sentence like that!) What I mean is this: if either Blaine or Logan showed strength enough to warrant hopes of success, the other was to support him. The Illinois delegates, personally offered to Blaine, had been voting for him for reasons of policy. Finding that there was some danger of his nomination, they came to the Logan manager and offered to cast their votes for Logan. This would have given him the whole vote of Illinois, and at the same time would have taken their votes from Blaine, who hitherto had lost none. Smaller things turn political tides. But Logan's followers would have none of it. Logan had telegraphed that they should vote for Blaine, and for Blaine they voted. I think that I have the story as Sumner told it. Possibly the state may have been Ohio. The main facts I am sure of. . . .

*June* 29. — . . . Later to the club. There I found Emmons Blaine, who was very cordial. I was really glad to see him, and he wanted to hear all about his Boston friends. All of a sudden he asked if I was engaged for luncheon to-morrow. Taken by surprise, I told him the truth — that I was not. Then he invited me. This put me in as uncomfortable a position as possible. No one can more earnestly oppose his father than I do; and though I like and respect Emmons very heartily, it seems almost unworthy of a gentleman to accept the hospitality of a man whose father you are bound to speak ill of. Yet to decline when an invitation is put in such a way, with all the frankness of old friendship, needs more courage than I can quite summon up. The dilemma is painful. . . .

*June* 30. — . . . Blaine called . . . and took me to a queer little restaurant not far from the hotel. It was apparently a wineshop. Wine boxes were piled higher than your head on all sides, with narrow paths between them. At one end of the labyrinth are a few cabinets with sliding doors. In one of these Stevens met us; and there we had a luncheon of cold beef, salad, and Pontet Canet, with cigarettes to top it. After luncheon Blaine began to speak of politics. I answered him as frankly as I could. He dilated a little on the iniquity and imbecility of Arthur's administration. With no policy, he said, the President had used all the patronage in his power to run himself in. I was unable to contradict him, and free to admit that the independent movement, in which I believed, had more earnestness in it than horse sense. On the other hand, I stated as clearly as I could my feelings about the civil service, the foreign policy, and the revenue. About the Kittery Navy Yard I spoke with more detail. I disclaimed, as I really meant to disclaim, any intention of publicly attacking the personal honesty of Mr. Blaine, who after all may have done little more than anybody would have done in his place. When acting president of the Pudding, I remember once so managing my voting that by tactics that were technically fair I managed to get Jack Brown elected — on the whole against the will of the majority. This I did because I rather liked Brown. My conduct afterwards appeared to me and to others unprincipled. At the same time it was not really so; at worst it was thoughtless. And if thoughtlessness can run away with a boy in a small matter, without really affecting his character, I do not see why it should not misguide a man in a great one. Well: Brown has thrown light on Little Rock.

However, as I wrote a day or two ago, my feeling about Mr. Blaine has stronger foundation than mere personal distrust in private matters. I hold him to be — as Everett put it — politically profligate. And though I would not say this in so many words to Emmons, I told him as plainly as I could how and why I disagreed with the policy that his father has been known by.

His rejoinder was curious. With much apparent good fellowship, he regretted the bolt in Massachusetts and in New York, because it alienated from his father just the sort of men whom he would have liked to recognize. To this I had no reply. In fact, I do not think that until this moment, when I write it down, I had any full understanding of the real meaning of it.

And so we parted. He invited me, I think, to pump me. So I am glad to have gone — I feel quite absolved from any obligation. For I told him what he wished me to tell him as frankly as I could, yet said nothing, so far as I know, which could commit anybody. And, half unmeaningly, I gave him to understand that the movement of the independents in Massachusetts was less serious than on the whole I really think it. We are not as yet *practical*, but we have determination enough to make proselytes. The brain is started; the nerves are beginning to quiver; if we do not stir the limbs before we are done with it, then we are no true men. . . .

*July* 11. — North Carolina changes her whole vote from Bayard to Cleveland. Much enthusiasm. The New York delegation now waves its flag; but arouses little applause. Georgia now gives Cleveland nine more votes. Virginia gives him ten. My figures grow doubtful. Certainly, amid vast uproar, rather of confusion than of enthusiasm, the tide is setting toward Cleveland. Missouri, I think, in the midst of great confusion, gives Cleveland her vote. This nominates him, apparently. Tremendous shouts. "Hail to the Chief!" Profusion of flags. Everybody on his legs, cheering, waving anything he can get hold of. This outburst seems genuine. Barrett[1] has prophesied this nomination all day; and is pleased, though a good Blaine Republican. Now come the cannon, speaking to the heavens, etc.

A rush about town, a dinner at Cousin S's; and off at 5 in the limited express for New York. Gov. Carroll, Robb, and P. Dana on board. Bearded New Yorker, fresh from Colorado, dines with me and orders three meats at once. He goes to Europe twice a year and believes in Blaine. I bring forward facts which shake his faith. Smoke with Mr. Carroll, who talks of his sons and of Mr. R. Phelps's dangerous illness. The Cleveland men, he says, were wonderfully organized. Poor Mr. Belmont, a staunch Bayard man, is in despair. He is a hot-tempered, kind-hearted man, politically absurd, used by Kelly as a money-mine. Passionately fond of his children. Mr. Carroll has impressed upon his sons that no gentleman drinks before dinner. A delightfully high-bred man, with bold head, grizzled mustache, and well-bred smile. To bed early,

---

[1] A Chicago cousin, Samuel Barrett.

shortly after the cars left Fort Wayne. Here a crowd was on the platform, waiting for the County Democracy which followed us in a special train. News was there that Hendricks had been nominated for Vice-President. A thin youth, of humorous inclinations, kept popping his head out of a car window, like a jack-in-the-box, and making incoherent speeches which were cheered. A compartment full of politicians, who looked their trade, played poker, and smoked cigars out of a common pile on one of the seats.

*July* 12. — A bad night. Somebody has trodden on my bag and bent the frame so that it will not shut; and having been open all night it is full of cinders. I feel rather seasick. At Pittsburgh between six and seven o'clock. Grimly smoky like towns in the Midland Counties. Commercial gent, affably disposed, tells of what Pittsburgh looked like in the riots of '77. I was too uncomfortable to attend to him; so he departed in a dudgeon. Breakfast with Mr. Carroll. Fair coffee, shaken by movement of cars like the champagne of Mansfield in the Union Square play. We pass into rather effective hill-scenery, following the course of a middle-sized stream. At places the valley is quite narrow, between hills covered with decidu-ous trees, notably dark in color. Occasional farms. Daisies, which I have not noticed in the West. The roadbed looks remarkably good, but the train, perhaps because of its speed, is very unsteady. I have a slight misunderstanding with the man who sleeps above me, because I ask him whether it was he who stepped on my bag. Later he is mollified by an apology for opening a window, on the plea that I felt unwell; and he goes so far as to give me a telegraph blank. I get some good brandy, of which I drink rather more than I mean to. It diminishes my sickness.

*To Lindsay Swift*

NEW CASTLE, N. H., 30 *June*, 1885

MY DEAR SWIFT: — I can't criticize *Richard Feverel*, but really I feel half inclined to repeat Woodberry's word and have done. I don't know when I have been so stirred by a book — hatefully, horribly stirred. Hatefully, I say, because somehow

I feel that the whole thing is too dreadful, that there is no real need of all the tragedy. There is cause and effect enough, logic enough for anybody; yet there are just those unlucky accidents which an artist may cast aside. And without them there might have been in this great symphony a final harmony. Why must the last note be so harsh a discord?

Yet, after all, my very protests show the power that this book has. These people live and breathe, and this they do in an atmosphere almost as vast as the real one. Life is a broader thing when we have known them. And life is a fairer thing for knowing such a woman as Lucy. I cannot tell where in our fiction to find her mate. I shall look to Meredith for more. I shall not leave his other books unread.

For such power as I feel in his work I cannot neglect. I don't like it, any more than I like his style, which seems full of crabbed affectation, caught, I fancy, from Carlyle. But I simply acknowledge it.

My wife wishes to read the book. When she has finished it, I will send it back, with many thanks to you.

I have sent to Turin for *Malombra*, by the way. It is not to be had nearer. If it turns out to be as like *Emilia* as your reviewer makes it, I shall be tempted to send a copy of my book to Fogazzaro.

This is a very unsatisfactory kind of a letter, I fear. Perhaps when I grow cooler I can write you a better. Now I am simply upset by the book you have given me. Let this be my claim to pardon for incoherence.

*To the same*

NEW CASTLE, N. H., 13 *August*, 1885

DEAR SWIFT: — I have to thank you for another literary treat — *Malombra*, which has been sent me from Italy and which I have just finished. Fogazzaro's method is as unlike mine as Howells's; but in his chief motive there is certainly a curious analogy, though hardly a likeness, to *Emilia*.

I have had the impudence to send him a copy of my book, chiefly for curiosity to know what, if anything, he will say in return.

Have you gone into modern Italian literature at all? I
know little of it; but what I have read has a flavor distinctly its
own. There is a boldness about it — a clearness of form allied
with a certain tentative indefiniteness of thought which I
think very promising. They have none of the over-ripeness of
the French, none of the commonplace everyday literary
decency of the rather canting English. If you want to get off
a new monograph, why not take this subject?

I have just received the Class Report. It makes me feel like
an animalcula. What a procession of jurists, and medical dis-
coverers, and mayors, and active supporters of Blaine and
Logan, and other great men flits before one! And here am I,
a beggarly little tutor, with a limited knowledge of his subject
and a bad temper — so bad that I said *Damn* when I read that
you were not a Mugwump. But then a man can't be all good
on earth; otherwise there would be no call for Heaven, and
our pulpiteering classmates would find their occupation gone.

*To Colonel Robert Thomson*

BOSTON, 31 *January*, 1886

Time flies with me nowadays faster than I can tell you.
And though I meant to have written weeks ago, your answer
to my last letter has come before my next. I have never been
so busy as now. All day long I am at Cambridge with nearly
twice as many pupils as I have ever had before. And just now
the season is at its height here. I come home to a round of
dinners and parties which take every moment of time that is
not given to my work. Writing is nowhere. At this rate I shall
be five or more years at my next novel.

The other night I was at a dinner where for the first time,
and perhaps the last, I sat near my kinsman, Dr. Holmes. He
is not a very near relative, and though I have known him in a
way for years I have never seen much of him. And now that
he is seventy-six I doubt whether any of us will see him long.
But I am sure that, hereabouts at least, it will be long before
we hear such another talk again. Two things are worth repeating: One of the men who were there told of a marriage between
a spinster of eighty-five and a bachelor of eighty. "I need not

ask," said Holmes, "if there were any children; but were there any grandchildren?" The other was very different: to him, he said, the most perfect stanza in our language is one that his mother repeated to him when past ninety-one, which nothing but old age can reveal in all its perfect beauty. It is this stanza in Gray's Elegy: —

> For who, to dumb forgetfulness a prey,
>   This pleasing, anxious being e'er resigned,
> Left the warm precincts of the cheerful day,
>   Nor cast one longing, lingering look behind?

Pleasing and anxious, he said, are to him the final epithets for human life. Somehow, this gave the words more meaning for me than they have ever had before. And what fine human optimism such words tell of in the mouth of a man past his allotted time!

As I have said already, I have little time for writing; but as I go back and forth between Boston and Cambridge, I find odd moments for reading. And, of all things in the world, I am deep in *Clarissa Harlowe*. Do you know the book at first hand? I have heard of it for years as interminable, and the copy that was given me in a dear old set of Richardson at Christmas, has seven volumes of more than four hundred pages apiece. But I do not know in all our literature so lovely a woman as Clarissa. You grow to love her, to care for every little detail of her life, until prolixity vanishes. Now and then my heart is in my mouth as I read her letters; and I am beginning to wonder not that the world raved over her a century ago, but that it has ever ceased to rave. Lovelace, on the other hand, seems to me absurd; just as Clarissa is beyond all things human, so Lovelace is a novelist's invention of no very fresh kind. Yet his name is a part of the language, and hers is half forgotten.

Another book, of a very different kind, has delighted me of late — Walter Pater's *Marius the Epicurean*. The beauty of the style, and of what I call the atmosphere of the book is exquisite; it deepens and broadens and strengthens all that Italy means to me. And, as *Emilia* must have shown you, Italy is to me more than any other part of the earth. . . .

[*Of the many letters written to Mrs. Wendell in lieu of a diary during Wendell's journey to California, in the summer of 1886, a typical specimen, prefaced by a shorter letter to F. J. Stimson, must suffice. The companionship of his brother Evert, in San Francisco, and in many excursions thence and from their westward and eastward routes of travel, played a large part in the expedition.*]

*To F. J. Stimson*

SAN FRANCISCO, 2 *July*, 1886

A telegram of my election to the Φ B K came yesterday afternoon. It was signed "Brigs Tausig Co Lidgo Orlidt." Whether or no you are "Orlidt" I am unable to determine.[1] But at any rate I want to tell you how thoroughly pleased I am at the news, in bringing which to pass — if that's English — I know you did so much.

I have a few enlarged ideas of America, and a genuine respect for the memory of Brigham Young. Apart from this, — and a growing suspicion that some rich men are only fools instead of all being thieves, — I am unchanged. San Francisco is apparently a more possible kind of place than any other to the west of the Hudson. Still, its architecture — mostly ornamented by the jig-saw — is depressing enough almost to counteract very good cookery, better wine than I expected, and the best fruit-market I ever came across. — Here Evert, who is acting as proctor for me at $1.00 per hour, leans over and whispers a polite message to you, which resolves itself into a hope that you are having a pleasant summer, and a statement that he means to look you up the moment he gets to New York. — To go on with San Francisco: they smoke frightfully strong tobacco here, and are said to have fewer morals to the block than are common in America — but then the blocks are rather longer than in the East.

Hospitality prevails. My first glimpse of California was in a Pullman car, where a quiet little grey-haired woman with

---

[1] The other names were taken, apparently with reason, for those of LeB. R. Briggs, F. W. Taussig, and J. T. Coolidge.

whom I had fallen to talking, suddenly produced from her travelling bag a couple of bottles of champagne, with which she proceeded to regale the company — in large tumblers. Then everybody you meet asks you to dine, or to visit him in the country, or in general to do something that involves financial expense for him and temporal for you.

I have fallen in, of course, rather with the literary crowd here than with the world of fashion. Stringham — who is professor at the University — and Harold Wheeler have been as kind as possible. To-night I am going to do Chinatown with Shafter Howard. To-morrow I dine with the master of the school where I am engaged in examining five Christian youths and seven Israelite. Next week we go to the Yosemite. The week after we start for home. I am looking out for the July *Lippincott*, but do not yet find it at either of the clubs when I am down. When I read it, if I like the play, I shall write again; if I don't, I shall preserve grim silence.

*To his Wife*

SAN FRANCISCO, 16 *July*, 1886

DEAREST EDITH: — This letter, I think, is the last I shall write here. To-morrow we start for the North, feeling at last that we begin our journey home. To-day we are resting after the hurry of travel and the demoralization of the Harvard dinner, which I digested a good deal better than I expected to, possibly because I took a fine hot bath before I went to bed, and read myself to sleep over the battle of Borodino. Tolstoi is certainly the greatest realist of modern literature. With none of Zola's brutality and none of Howells's timidity, he has all the qualities of both — save humor — and a power of presenting individuals which seems to me unequaled. There is more unity in the book, too, than I had looked for; the apparent confusion comes, I think, from a failure to see that his hero is not an individual or a group, but the whole nation of Russia. This cannot be presented save in such detail as we find in *War and Peace*. It is never lost sight of. As a work of art, the book seems to me far more skillful than it is called. . . .

And now, to take up my journal where I really dropped it, I want to write a little of Monterey. This is an old town, on a slightly indented bay lined with such sand-hills as you see on the coast of Holland. At this season incessant fogs float about the Pacific, now rising into clouds, now slinking off to the horizon, now coming creeping over everything. You remember, perhaps, some of the beautiful studies of mist-effects in the Japanese paintings that Percy Lowell brought home. There is a strangely fascinating faintness of line and color — a delicacy of gradation — that I used to say our paintings lacked. Here I see the reason why — our painters have not seen the Nature that on this coast of the Pacific, as on the other, affords men a chance to create such art. Well, amid this softly drifting fog and mist, full of infinite delicate variety, lies Monterey, whose buildings still, with adobe walls, red-tiled roofs, and queerly rambling balconies, give the place a Spanish look, and even an Oriental — for the characteristic Spanish building is more than half Moorish. The town is not all Spanish, though. There are many of the small gable-roofed wooden saloons, with perfectly square false fronts facing the street, that pervade the whole West. . . .

In Monterey, too, are one or two vestiges of New England architecture. I saw one real New Hampshire lean-to tacked on a crumbling adobe house. In short, the place shows, like none other I have seen, the transition from Spanish California to this enormous American shop.

At the Hotel del Monte I saw a human example of this transition — a grave white-bearded, beautifully well-bred old Don Something Ortez, who won't learn English, and his fine black-eyed daughter, a very promising specimen of the more respectable variety of piazza girl, who tried to make me buy some tickets to some tableaux she knew I could not attend. Her brother, aged perhaps two-and-twenty, was too callow to be quite a cad, but looked in danger of ripening into one. . . .

The Howards, who were unending in their kindness, took us to drive in the afternoon. The fog came in more thickly than usual, and the roads, like all here at this season, are horribly dusty; but we had charming glimpses of the ocean, about which grew fine old weatherbeaten cypresses, and the rocks, and flocks of sea birds as thick as those in Japanese painting, and queer piles of weatherbeaten boards, where Chinamen live, who hunt the rocks for those great pearly shells such as used to lie about my grandmother's parlor in West Cedar Street.

I must hurry on, for the morning draws to a close, and I have no more paper within a couple of stories. The Howards introduced us to no end of people, including Mr. Crocker, "the millionaire," and the Chief Justice of California. Crocker resembles Silas Lapham; Judge Morrison has a gray chin beard, a lineless, pink-and-white face, and a paralyzed arm. . . .

We came to town yesterday with Mr. Howard, and a most invigorating journalist named Mills, the President of the Associated Press here. I have rarely met a more delightful American, of the most national and attractive kind. He reminded me a little, in his manner, of my uncle Baker; and his range of information, while not infinitely deep, was amazingly wide. Yesterday, Mr. Howard took us through some wine-cellars here, which reminded me of Rheims. As I wrote you, we tried to shop, too, but with little success. I shall bring you no great gifts, I fear, simply because I can find nothing that seems the thing to buy. . . .

*To Robert Grant*

29 *September*, 1886

. . . And this suggests a conundrum that I might perhaps ask myself. Why don't you try an out-and-out love story? I have an idea that the times are ripe for one. I want a heroine that I can want to marry; and a hero good enough for her; and real life about them. And I have a mistily growing idea that the real cue of a good many of us who try to write nowadays lies in the simple old traditions.

My new book, by the way, is aggressively eccentric, I fear. It is a development of the body-snatching that I once read the S.S.V.[1] The few who have seen it speak kindly; I hope the world will. . . .

---

[1] A small club, pleasantly named the "Society for the Suppression of Vice."

*To Colonel Robert Thomson*

NEW YORK, 29 *December,* 1886

DEAR COLONEL THOMSON, — *Arthur Hamilton*[1] has thoroughly interested us — for my wife read it as eagerly as I. And yet, when we came to talk of it, we found that to both of us it proved one of the hardest things to talk about imaginable. For all its vividness, if I may say so without contradiction, the impression it leaves is strangely indefinable. There is no doubt that the character of Hamilton is among the most vital I have met in fiction. Indeed, were it not for the rather aggressively impossible nature of the Persian episode, I should never have dreamt that the book was not true; and even now incline to think that the hero is not make-believe, but rather a slightly veiled portrait either of the author or of someone he has studied almost as one studies himself. There is no doubt, either, of the great cleverness and suggestiveness of much that is in the book. There are dozens of phrases that set you thinking. Yet for all this, I think, the style is, like the story, not perfectly lucid.

Matthew Arnold, you remember, rang the changes on "lucidity" through a whole essay, and a very good one. If I recall this, the gist of it was that lucidity — the characteristic note of French writing — was characteristically lacking in English. We want it in America quite as much as you in England. As my efforts to write have perhaps shown you, I am passionately fond of it. Here, then, I find in Arthur Hamilton something wanting; but the want is characteristic of our literature rather than of the book.

In another respect the book is intensely English. The earnestness, the seriousness of the tone puts it, for all its religious breadth, in distinctively Puritan literature. The fastidious virginity of Hamilton's mind is so impossible in any people but ours that no language but ours has ever come near expressing such a quality. And frankly, I do not personally like it. Sexual sin I can deplore as heartily as anyone. Such stories as the papers have brought of recent *causes célèbres* in London shock and pain me as heartily as they can you. But

[1] *Memoirs of Arthur Hamilton*, the first of the many books of Arthur Christopher Benson, published in 1886.

that a man grown should not recognize and feel the full force of human temptation makes him to me a little lacking in the human part of manhood. To say that the flesh should be kept down is one thing; to work to keep it down, to shrink from any other view of life, is another. Such a criticism of feeling does not belong to a normal period of human development. In a way, it seems to me as monstrous as what I am told the papers have printed of Dilke and Campbell.

I trust I do not permit myself to write too freely. You asked me to tell you just what I thought, and so I do. And so doing, I come to the last observation I have to make about the book. It is intensely modern; the fastidious over-refinement that I have been talking about is after all only a phase of the whole life it pictures. I feel this the more because of late I have been reading a little of the Elizabethans, and thinking of them a great deal. I have some idea of lecturing on that period of our literature. What typifies the period in my fancy is the old motto of the arms of Spain: "*Plus Ultra.*" The road through the Pillars of Hercules leads to unmeasured things beyond.[1] The exuberance that passes on towards these throbs through all our literature of the sixteenth century. To come from this to the self-analytic inaction of the nineteenth is shocking. And I, for one, cannot quite feel, at all events in this great, growing America of ours, that this introspection, this idealistic inaction, is really a necessity; and certainly it is not to me an ideal. A man who goes through life without playing an active part is a failure. He may be a noble one; but his life is a real tragedy. To me there seems to be more and more truth in what I used to think the vulgar commonplaces of Philistia. The Philistines, to be sure, mouth their precepts with so little knowledge of their inner meaning that we may be forgiven for thinking them meaningless. But, just as truly as ever, action is the ideal that we should keep before us — an active struggle with the life we are born to, a full sense of all its temptations, of all its earthly significance as well as of its spiritual. To sum up in a word the place where I should put such a figure as

[1] Wendell afterwards elaborated this idea in his Clark Lectures at Trinity College, Cambridge. See *The Temper of the Seventeenth Century in English Literature* (1904).

Hamilton's, I group him in my mind with the Dudley of whom I said a little in *Rankell's Remains,* and of whom I may some day say some more.

I have written longer than I meant to, saying just as they came to me whatever thoughts your book has suggested. If Mr. Benson is a friend of yours, and you think he would like to see them, I am quite willing that he should. I like to know how what I write impresses anybody who takes the trouble to read it. And perhaps he may not disdain the impressions of an unknown Yankee. I will add just two words more. From this book I cannot convince myself that he has in him the making of a creative writer; interesting as it is, it is a book of but one character, and wanting in dramatic power. And in certain details, which catch my professional eye, the style is wretchedly careless. I found a singular verb with a plural subject, etc. He alludes somewhere to the "gift of expression," or of style, or some such thing. He does not appreciate, I think, the fineness, the delicacy of the technical art of writing, which is no more a gift than that of painting or of counterpoint.

But lastly — for I feel as if I had been fault-finding — I want to repeat that I think the book among the most interesting that I have read for years. . . .

And now I have written more than enough for once. I have delayed this letter longer than I expected, for my work is really appalling in its demands. It has grown so that I rarely have a minute to myself; and whenever I am not at it, I am generally too tired for anything but unmitigated loafing. . . .

*To the same*

358 Marlborough St.,[1] Boston, 31 *January,* 1887

Dear Colonel Thomson, — The winter is flying away so fast in this corner of the world, where one day is just like the last, that more than a month has gone by since I sent you from New York a letter that promised a sequel. Yet hardly a day has come without the intention of writing you. For what I wrote then dissatisfies me in memory.

New York is — and always has been — to me the most

[1] This was the superscription of nearly all of Wendell's letters from Boston.

depressing spot in the world. The air has a touch of fever in it, you know, not unlike the Roman; and I can hardly believe the strangely bewildering effect the city produces on me to be other than a definitely physical one. But the phenomena — the symptoms — are mental and moral. My character there is a different one from my character anywhere else. From the moment I set foot in the place I am morbid to a degree that when I am away from it seems almost inconceivable. And so I cannot help feeling that what I wrote of *Arthur Hamilton* was tinged with a morbidness that is not quite true to me. I will try in a few words to repeat what impression the book has left on me.

In brief it was this — that the writer had given us as an ideal a life of exquisitely fastidious, over-refined inaction. And just this kind of life is to my thinking a very dangerous one to think of with admiration. Over-refinement is the curse of the century — in virtue as in vice. Virility — the broad human courage that takes the world and the tasks of life as they are given to us, that knows temptations and pleasures and duties, that fights and struggles and wins and fails — is more to seek than it used to be. And the ideal we need most to keep before us is that of the man who does the real work of life as truly as he can. There is no calling so mean that it cannot be followed with a firm purpose to follow it well. And one condition of sanely vigorous life is that there shall not be too much preliminary thinking. So, in the end, Hamilton typifies to me one side of the characteristic tragedy of our times. I hardly put the matter clearly now, I fear. But if I have made you understand that what I meant to say was that the book seemed to make a heroic ideal out of what seemed to me a pitifully honorable failure, I have come somewhere near what I have wished to.

Now for a few words about my Rankell. Of course his church and his love were material and selfish; for such a nature as his could not rise above materialism and selfishness. But in them, I thought, the selfishness and materialism were less gross. In them he came nearer to the better man that under other circumstances he might have been. And so they were really to him the most precious and the best things he knew; and by consecrating to them all he left, he did the pitifully little he could to give to the world the best things he knew. And one of these things at least — his church — had a meaning far greater than he could give it. In time to come it will speak not of the founder of its stones, but of the founder of its creed. Most of the great religious structures in the world, I fancy, have sprung from beginnings and motives as base as any Rankell's. Yet what they mean to us, who know nothing of the builders, is as pure as if they had sprung like wild flowers. In short, there is in all the evil I see about me some latent germ of good; and it is the good that fructifies the most after all — even though it bear what seems but sorry fruit. And this is the motive I have striven to work out. I do not feel satisfied with my work; but I do feel what satisfaction comes from the knowledge that I did it as well as I could.

Now for an answer to your kind question about the *Duchess Emilia*. Trübner had some copies of it a few years ago, with his own imprint; and as I have no reason to believe that the book has had any sale in England, I think that he may very likely have them still. The *Saturday Review* damned it in a way that seemed to me a little unfair; and no other reviews touched it at all. . . .

*To the same*

NEW CASTLE, 30 *August*, 1887

. . . I have been most wretchedly out of sorts all summer long. If I remember aright, my last note was rather plaintive, but hoped for better things before long. The better things have hardly come. A dull sore throat and exquisitely irritable nerves have greeted me almost every morning until very lately. And during this whole vacation I have read nothing, written nothing, thought very little; and altogether nowhere. At last I begin to feel the benefit of the idleness that has been so extreme. Overwork, I fancy, was really the matter with me; and I have had to pay for it by what to us Yankees is the most detestable of pastimes — absolute inaction.

I wonder whether the feverish ebb and flow of energy that

makes up our lives here is human or only trans-Atlantic. Calm, steady, regular, healthy, normal progress from day to day seems almost out of the question. Temperance in life is a virtue almost unknown. Over-action and crushing reaction seem the rule. For all this lesson I dare say I shall be doing twice as much as I ought to as soon as the college term begins again. If so, I shall certainly do next summer what I ought to have done this year — go abroad for two or three weeks. The absolute change forced upon one by foreign surroundings is a better tonic than all the bottled remedies in the world.

Just now there is a curious craze very prevalent in New England. People who have been for years invalids are recovering full strength by what they call the Mind-Cure. The process consists in sitting still in company with a practitioner who silently thinks all kinds of benevolent things about you. The result in hysterical cases — and a great deal of modern illness is in some degree hysterical — is so extraordinary that a good many really intelligent people are quite carried away. The sanest theory is that all physical — or rather muscular — states affect the nervous system specifically; and that the nerves affect thought, whatever that may be. Every thought, many psychologists urge, is accompanied by a chemical change in the brain. Well, say the Mind-Cure people, if a muscular contraction can cause a chemical change in the brain, why can not the process be reversed? Grant this, and the other modern hypothesis of Thought-Transference, which the English Society of Psychical Research thinks it has proven, and the whole matter is clear common-sense. All of which impresses me as contrary to the common-sense which the elect declare to be Philistine prejudice.

However, I know two or three really educated people whose whole lives have been made happy and useful, instead of miserably invalid, by what seems such palpable quackery. And these cases have begun to call to the matter the attention of educated people in general. The most curious case is this: a lady well on in life was discovered to have a cancer. Her regular physician pronounced the case indubitable, and told her she might try any means of alleviating pain she chose.

She went to one of the Mind-Cure people, who treated her for more than a year. At last the cancer killed her; but from the moment the new treatment was first given she felt no pain whatever. This I believe is vouched for by good medical authority.

But after all, these matters will hardly interest you. What puts them in my head is that I have just come from a visit to a friend who has been cured of what he supposed a hopeless disorder of the spine, and is very anxious that I should try the same harmless practice; this my wife advises, and I — who hate quackery — don't want to. So just to spite them, I believe, I am rapidly growing convalescent after a good six months of depression and discomfort.

I have been here almost all summer. Early in August I went with my friend Clymer to Vermont, Lake Champlain, and the Adirondacks — a pretty trip, but quite as tedious as amusing. We ended by passing a day at Saratoga — an incredible city of monstrous hotels, with big gardens in the middle of them half as big as the Palais Royal. Here people who have more money than wit come from all over the continent to wear diamonds and otherwise pass the summer. There are mineral springs, and tolerable bands of music, and thirty or forty rainy days in the course of the season; and every known means of visibly expending money. Altogether the place is so stupendously fine a flower of plutocracy as to excite almost unqualified admiration. Perfection in kind — even though the kind be bad — is something. Lake George, which is nearby, is certainly the most exquisitely pretty sheet of water out of Italy, but over-run with summer tourists and young women of the type remarked by Henry James in *Daisy Miller*.

Later my wife and I went to Bar Harbor, on the visit which impressed on my mind the theory of the Mind-Cure. Bar Harbor is a really beautiful spot on a bay which is more nearly like a Norwegian fiord than anything I have seen out of Norway. The mountains, rising straight from the ocean, are two or three thousand feet high; and the bay is full of bold, woody islands. Twenty years ago the place was a fishing village where land was worth five dollars an acre. Now it is a fashionable watering place, where a good deal of land is sold by the foot. There are no end of gaieties there; and all kinds of society — much such as one could have in winter. A good many of the diplomatic corps from Washington were there; as was the North Atlantic squadron. The town was a constant bustle; but the house where we stayed, which happily has large well-wooded grounds, was as quiet and pleasant as house could be. And the views from the terrace are as charming as any I know. I sat there in the sunshine reading Elizabethan poetry, and generally feeling more like a human being than usual. The night before we left we went to a "domino-party," i. e., a ball where the ladies were masked. Here my wife completely deceived me by changing her domino and taking me off for a quiet flirtation. It was not until I happened to notice her hand, which is rather individual, that I had the least idea who it was that knew so much.

Both she and the children whose picture I send you have been as well this year as I have been ill. Indeed, all goes well with all of us. . . .

*To Edward J. Lowell*

[*Apropos of an article on "A Liberal Education" in the* Atlantic Monthly *for January 1888, in the course of which the author declared, "there is probably no European language whose study can approach that of Latin as mental training for an American lad."*]

SOMERSET CLUB, BOSTON, 7 *January*, '88

DEAR MR. LOWELL, — I have just been reading with much interest your article in the last *Atlantic*. Some time, I hope I may have a chance to talk about it with you. Two or three observations I shall venture to scribble.

In the first place, do you quite make out your case for Latin? Why is not Greek — a language equally logical, finer in structure, and in its literary contents almost supreme — a better subject for such prolonged study as you recommend? For my part, I am prepared to assert a conviction that the predominance of Latin in my early training was, so far as I can now detect, one of the most fatally benumbing of educational mistakes.

In the second place, while recognizing with you many of the evils of our present system, I am, whenever a discussion of it arises, confronted with perhaps the most conspicuous fact in my experience as a teacher. This is that the average man — for whom the system you advise is without doubt admirably adapted — is a statistical fact, but not a human being. Our system of English training at Harvard is by no means ideal; but it is at once the most thoughtfully developed in America, and I believe anywhere, and the constantly ripening fruit of the best thought and energies of a number of men among whom I am quite contented to rank low. Our object has constantly been to make it stimulating and practically useful to all students. In this effort we are constantly foiled by the fact that many students seem as unable to meet us intellectually as a near-sighted eye to detect a small star, or a color-blind man to read railway signals.

Yet as I scribble these similes I am conscious of their ineptitude. The trouble is not infirmity; but a certain sluggish ineptitude. The whole man is before us; but to be what he may be and what we would make him, he needs not what we have to give him but the magic word that will speak to him. And when this is once spoken, somehow he flashes into a sane completeness of being that has often seemed unattainable.

What I would say for the elective system is that, so far as I have been able, in fifteen years, to observe its working, it speaks this word — even in its present state — oftener than any other scheme of training I know. So true is this that I, for one, would be quite willing to abandon for my own work the protective system of prescription. And what masks it in great degree, I think, from men of one's kind is that the students we personally know — the men of our own class — are, as a lot, far from representative. In college as in outer life, "society" and the real world which gives our time its significance are very different things. Yet we who happen to observe matters from the point of view of "society" are apt to forget — or at least not fully to realize — how small a part it plays in the life we criticise.

From French novels one would conclude adultery to be the only thoughtful occupation of the full-grown society of France; from our general observation of our acquaintance, we should be disposed to assert a certain polite aimlessness to be the prime trait of character developed by the present system of education at Harvard. Of France I know nothing; but I am pretty sure that, by and large, our present system does more literally to educate the mass of men exposed to it to-day than anyone who has not a deeply intimate knowledge of its workings ever dreams.

Sincerely yours,

BARRETT WENDELL

*To Colonel Robert Thomson*

BOSTON, May 16, 1888

DEAR COLONEL THOMSON, — My youngest brother and I are going abroad this summer for six weeks or so. We sail from New York in the Fulda, on June 23, landing at Southampton. I suppose we shall pass a fortnight or so in England, and then go to the Continent for a scamper as far as Baireuth, where I wish to hear the Wagner operas. These I have heard only in America, where they have not been particularly well given. But somehow they take hold of me in a way quite unique. I am paradoxical enough to hold that, in spite of his undoubted complexity of method, Wagner's motive and purpose are so fundamentally simple that even a stranger to the technicalities of musical art — like me — can give himself up to the emotional effect of the work with a completeness of enjoyment not to be found in any other modern art. But I had no intention of scribbling a dissertation on the music of the future. I write just to ask you when and how we may perhaps be able to get a glimpse of you. We shall be in and about London, I suppose, during the first week or ten days of July; and again a month or so later. Shall you then be thereabouts? Or would you like us to come for a day or two to Broomford?

My journey is largely for the mental rest, or rather diversion, that is sure to come from change of scene. I am pretty well tired with eight successive years of college work. Still, I have, now that this year is almost at an end, the satisfaction of feeling that what I have accomplished is on the whole respectable. They have just made me an assistant professor — a rank of no very great importance, and one that alters neither my work nor my salary; but one that gives me a slightly increased academic dignity. . . .

# V

## THE ASSISTANT PROFESSOR AND SCHOLAR
### 1888–1898

WHEN a man enters upon the duties of an assistant professor at Harvard — as Barrett Wendell did in the autumn of 1888 — he may be regarded as beginning the period of probation on which his elevation to a full professorship will depend. Through the ten years of his assistant professorship Wendell worked hard not only at his teaching but also at "productive scholarship." In 1888 — at thirty-three — he had already shown himself a teacher of rarely provocative power, one of the distinctive personalities in his academic circle. As an author, he could credit himself merely with two novels which had met with no great success. By 1898, when he became Professor of English, he had produced his *English Composition* and his *Cotton Mather*, each in 1891, each a book of marked and lasting importance in its own field; his *Stelligeri and Other Essays Concerning America* (1893), a little book with qualities both sound and brilliant; his *William Shakespere, A Study in Elizabethan Literature* (1894), a direct outgrowth of his college lectures; and had written the first two of the three pieces of dramatic poetry contained in his *Ralegh in Guiana, Rosamond, and a Christmas Masque*, published in 1902. These books, taken together and added, in token of achievement, to his chief work of teaching, place his academic advancement in 1898 beyond any need of explanation. To each of the books in turn a few words must be devoted.

In *English Composition* Wendell gave to the general public a series of lectures which he delivered as a Lowell

Institute course in November and December 1890. "My excuse for offering a new treatment of the subject," he wrote in a note for the printed book, "is that I have found none that seemed quite simple enough for popular reading." This book proved simple enough to command a wide popular reading, and sound enough to deserve it. It was written with an enthusiasm for the teaching of English composition, and a confidence in its value, which, unhappily, appeared to diminish in Wendell's later years. Whether there really was such a diminution or not, those who used to hear him lament the time he had wasted in teaching the unteachable were never quite sure. They knew that his work had been a piece of genuine service to his generation, and that the book embodying it took its proper place beside Hill's *Rhetoric*, the earlier contribution of Wendell's beloved senior and chief, Professor Adams Sherman Hill, to the cause of good English. They would doubtless subscribe to the definition of *English Composition* in the minute on the life and services of its author presented to the Harvard Faculty of Arts and Sciences by a committee of three of which Dean Briggs was chairman, as "probably the most suggestive book ever written on that subject." It would, moreover, gratify them to know that in the last month of Wendell's life, a correspondent previously unknown to him sent him from Arkansas a copy of his *English Composition*, which he had studied at the State University under a former pupil of Wendell's, asked him to autograph it, and declared: "I would not take $50 for this book, for it has been my constant companion for fifteen years. They have battered it up some as you can see by its looks. When I went away to war I only took three books — Wendell's *English Composition*, Stevenson's *Essays*, and a *New Testament*. I told my wife that I intended to teach the Germans English out of that Composition book."

Of Wendell's *Cotton Mather*, written "to order" as a volume in the "Makers of America" series, the same "faculty minute" already quoted says that it "was a surprise and delight to students of New England life and thought." The surprise was that one who seemed so remote from Puritanism in his own person could write so sympathetically of its high-priest; the delight, that he performed his task with thoroughness of research and a mastery in the arrangement and presentation of material, which made the book enduringly notable among American biographies. In this volume, as again in later writings, he stated the case of Calvinism and the resulting Puritan theology and life, with a comprehension and clarity altogether remarkable. For the pains he took with it all there is good evidence in a letter he wrote to his classmate, Lindsay Swift, soon after the publication of the biography: —

My book makes no pretense to exhaustive research. But this I can say for it: I examined everything I could find mentioned; and I do not believe that any further material would in an appreciable degree alter the features of the character I made it my business to portray.

In the light of autobiography the book bears a definite relation to the keen interest which Wendell, at about the time of writing it, was taking in the whole question of psychic phenomena. The activities of Richard Hodgson, American Secretary of the English Society for Psychical Research, in connection with the trances of Mrs. Piper, were then absorbing the attention of a considerable circle in Boston, with which Wendell had many contacts. His whole treatment of the Salem witchcraft tragedy in his *Cotton Mather* was accordingly, and most intelligently, colored by his knowledge of psychical matters under modern investigation. This interest of his was reflected further in two short stories — "The Last of the Ghosts," published in *Scribner's Magazine* for February 1888, a tale of the supernatural, with the old Wentworth house at Portsmouth, New Hampshire, for its setting; and "How He Went to the Devil," published in an excellent but short-lived Boston periodical, *Two Tales,* for April 30, 1892. This long short-story of the moral disintegration of a fine fellow who took to spiritistic séances, practised his psychical powers on his wife, and ruined both their lives, may be taken to represent Wendell's own conclusions with regard to the personal consequences of dabbling in the supernatural. It should be said of it, moreover, that within its compass it reveals a mastery of the technique of fiction that was beyond his grasp when his novels were written.

In an essay, "Were the Salem Witches Guiltless?" in his *Stelligeri,* Wendell speaks of himself as "one who has tried to make himself a man of letters." This book, containing seven essays written from 1891 to 1893, is a clear manifest of that attempt. Besides, it foreshadows distinctly one of his most important later works, his *Literary History of America,* not only in its historical, biographical, and critical topics, but in more concrete terms. Here— for example — is found, I believe for the first time, his definition of literature as "the lasting expression in words of the meaning of life" — a definition to which he reverted, with amplifications, both in his *Literary History* and in his *Temper of English Literature in the Seventeenth Century* (1904). Here, too, are such characteristic bits as the allusions to Whittier as "the least irritating of reformers" and as "one generally troubled by that sort of robust poor health which frequently accompanies total abstinence."

The Introduction to Wendell's *Ralegh in Guiana* yields a significant item of autobiography: —

Certain disputes about a work of art,[1] at that time [1896] exciting local interest, had led some friends, in the warmth of

[1] The "Bacchante" of Macmonnies, offered but not accepted for the courtyard of the Boston Public Library.

discussion, to inform me that I was temperamentally inartistic. Stirred by this intimate frankness, I found myself eager to express, as well as I could, sentiments which had long been gathering about the thoughts concerning the character, the fate, and the historical significance of Sir Walter Ralegh. . . . I made of his story some such free version as I had previously made of Percy's ballad about Rosamond. Having completed this, I proposed that it be performed at a small club [the Tavern Club, Boston], where the dispute which provoked it into being had arisen. There it was so far successful that we were invited to reproduce it more publicly. On March 22, 1897, then, my essay in chronicle history had the honour of a University performance, at Sanders Theatre, Harvard College.

Produced under the conditions of the Elizabethan stage, *Ralegh in Guiana*, in its Harvard performance, made a memorable impression. In refutation of the charge that its author lacked the artistic temperament, it stands beside the dramatic poem, *Rosamond*, now to be found in the same volume with it and to be read as the piece of writing to which, perhaps more than to any other, Wendell imparted a positive quality of beauty.

Wendell's *William Shakespere: A Study in Elizabethan Literature* (1894) gave to the public what he had been giving to his pupils in college lectures. It was thus primarily a teacher's book, and, in its appeal to non-academic readers, was a disappointment to its author.[1] Still more definitely in the field of textbooks stood an edition of *As You Like It* (1896) for which Wendell supplied the Introduction, and William Lyon Phelps, his assistant through the college year of 1891–92, following immediately upon the studies which won Professor Phelps

---

[1] Apropos of this volume, it is worth noting that after Wendell's death A. T. Quiller-Couch wrote of him as "my star among Shakespearean scholars," and that he dedicated his own *Notes on Shakespeare's Workmanship* "To Professor Wendell, in gratitude for many pleasures of insight directed by his illuminating common-sense."

BARRETT WENDELL IN "RALEGH IN GUIANA"

his Master's degree at Harvard, provided the notes. A prefatory sentence, signed with the initials of the two editors, read: "At a time when such differences as declare themselves between the two oldest colleges of New England are unduly emphasized, it is a singular pleasure to bear part in any work which shall help to show how truly Harvard and Yale are at one."

So much for the books that Wendell produced in the period now under scrutiny. It was in this period also that he was establishing the foundations on which his whole work as a teacher rested. At this point therefore it is peculiarly fitting to read the more general statements in the "faculty minute" presented by Dean Briggs, from which two brief comments on specific points have already been quoted: —

"For many years he taught English composition. In this subject, as in every other, his method was his own; and in this subject he made himself felt through the whole country. He invented the 'daily theme,' as the result of his own practice in training his pen. For criticizing themes he devised a system of analysis which, in hands as skilled as his, proved invaluably specific and efficient. He himself was never satisfied with his results, and in his later years maintained that the subject had no place in the curriculum of a university.

"As a teacher he showed himself from the first no ordinary man. He did his own thinking and expressed the results with uncompromising courage. Few men have been more persistently misunderstood by the outside public and even by the general college public than Barrett Wendell in his earlier years. His eccentricities of voice and manner, his humorous epigrammatic exaggerations, his willingness to shock the straitlaced with what they could not but regard as levity and irreverence, the facility with which he was imitated, the frequency with which some trifling or ill-advised remark of his in the classroom was torn from its context, colored by reporters, and sent broadcast, produced in many places the impression that he was a light-minded aristocrat whose conduct was quite out of keeping with his official position. Yet when he said, 'I believe that a great part of whatever success I have had as a teacher is the result of my indiscretion,'[1] he was right. His pupils knew that he kept nothing back, that he was never warily on his guard, that they had whatever was in Barrett Wendell's mind, and that the mind was fertile, original, and bold. It was also discriminating. Whatever he read, from a sophomore theme to a great classic of the world, he characterized in itself and in its relation to other works with a penetration incredibly swift, with a judgment which stimulated even those who would not accept it, with a phrasing which could not be forgotten. It is doubtful whether any teacher or writer in America has equaled him in the quick and clear perception of literary relations, in the power of generalizing.

"Slowly and steadily he won with his colleagues and the reading public the place that he had long held among his pupils. Men began to see in him a touch of genius; from his writing they learned that he knew both literature and history, that he threw light on whatever he discussed, that he who understood the Cavaliers understood also the Puritans, had in him much of their spirit, and could write of them with unexampled discernment. Along with his deep-thinking seriousness men discovered his open-hearted simplicity, his genuine humility, and his singular lovableness. He died a man who had given new and just distinction to the University and to literary scholarship in America."

---

[1] "A faculty of committing judicious indiscretions" was counted to Wendell's credit in the official report of his death to the Colonial Society of Massachusetts.

Few of the men who studied under him could have made so penetrating an analysis of Wendell's qualities as a teacher. But one of his pupils, who afterwards became one of his assistants, Mr. William R. Castle, now of the United States Department of State, writing of Wendell in *Scribner's Magazine* for July 1921, gave a glimpse of him in the classroom which adds a line and color of its own to the portrait of him drawn by his faculty colleagues: —

"It would not be true to say that all students liked Professor Wendell as a teacher, yet as a teacher he probably exerted his greatest influence. Young men of flabby intellect generally gained comparatively little from his lectures. Prigs were shocked. A very few never recovered from the first surprise at his high-pitched voice and explosive speech, his nervous manner as he strode heavily up and down the platform, twirling his watch-chain. They chose to consider him affected, thereby missing at the start one of the profoundest realities of the man — his contempt for affectation. I have watched class after class as it became accustomed to him, the first general attention, based on nothing more than interest in the eccentricities of a new teacher, giving place to individual reaction in the various types of student. The plodders took notes with indefatigable zeal, a little bewildered at the paucity of mere book-facts and pleasant platitudes such as fill the pages of all too many lecture-notebooks. The mentally lazy frankly gave it up, settled themselves as comfortably as possible for an hour, and tried to think about other things. Sometimes they went to sleep. Wendell did not like this, and when it occurred he stopped his lecture abruptly and stared at the offender. When the dead silence at last woke the delinquent, he laughed aloud, the class invariably joining in his mirth, and then the lecture proceeded.

"But not all boys who sat under him were dull or lazy.

It was a joy to watch the others as they sat quietly, their notebooks often closed, listening intently, sometimes agreeing, sometimes struggling not to agree, but thinking for themselves, thinking hard and constructively. To such students he was an inspiration; to all but an insignificant few he was a vitalizing influence, because he taught them how to use their own brains. He never filled their minds with useless lumber to be checked, filed, brought out at examination time and then forgotten. On the contrary, he taught them one of the vital facts of education — that knowledge must be a part of life, that it must be used, wrought into the texture of being, and become the source of impulse."

Of his relations with students outside the classroom many pages might be written. The college room — Grays 18 — which served as his office was the scene of scholastic and friendly counsels of which the memory and the benefit extend beyond all reckoning. At his house in Boston, in his summer correspondence, his readiness to lead into profitable paths of thought and study pupils whom he believed he could help found ceaseless expression. The personal concern, the open-handed expenditure of pains and time which he put into all this, carried the effect of his teaching, as a lasting influence, into the lives of man after man through a long sequence of college generations. Twenty-five years after graduation, one of these pupils writes from the world of affairs: —

"I have again and again, when telling a story of his peculiarities or merely thinking of him, tried to imagine him on a bank board, or at a managing editor's desk, or on a crossbeam of a new skyscraper directing the construction. His figure so thoroughly connoted the academic environment that, in these imaginings, he was always a bit out of place. But, one thing — if his lot had fallen in finance, journalism, or engineering instead of Grays

18, every last detail of his work would have been well done."

In 1898 a piece of administrative work at Harvard in which Wendell took a special interest and pride came to its culmination in the formal report of the "Committee on the Relations between Harvard University and Radcliffe College," of which he was chairman. Late in his life (22 May 1919) Wendell deposited a copy of this report in the Boston Athenæum, together with a reprint of an article on "The Relations of Radcliffe College with Harvard" which he contributed to the *Harvard Monthly* for October 1899. On the fly-leaf of the reprint he wrote:—

The Report I leave with this article, based on it, was the result of much discussion in the committee. At the time I was disposed to think — I now believe mistakenly — that the Radcliffe authorities were deliberately trying to make Harvard coeducational, by slipping Radcliffe into closer and closer relations. This tendency, which really existed, was probably a matter more or less of accident — or of following lines of least resistance. The Report, and my comment on it perhaps too, had the result of preventing any further unobserved encroachment by Radcliffe on Harvard. So I have always felt that my work on this committee, by saving Harvard from coeducation through at least twenty years, was perhaps the most far-reaching I ever did there.

From the *Monthly* article itself a few paragraphs must be given here, in token of Wendell's deep-rooted feeling about his college, the profession of teaching, and its relation to coeducation — important topics all: —

What may happen in future is of course a matter only of opinion. My personal opinion is that unless a strong public sentiment declares itself against the principle of coeducation at Harvard, complete coeducation will slowly establish itself here. To this I strongly object. My grounds are partly sentimental. Were Harvard merely a factory of scholars, the case might be different; but to me Harvard seems, even more profoundly than it seems an institution of learning, a traditional school of manly character. Its past history in this respect is too precious to be risked without better reason than has yet been shown. Were the higher education elsewhere closed to women, their plight might excite chivalrous sympathy; but, as every one knows, most colleges in America already receive women on virtually equal terms with men. The question, then, really becomes one where men are justly on the defensive: shall we do our best to preserve one spot where men, if they choose, may be educated by themselves, just as women may at Bryn Mawr, or Wellesley, or Smith, or Vassar? At this moment Harvard has not gone too far to recede. By the express terms of the votes of the Overseers which opened our courses to women, the privilege is still revocable, either by the Faculty or by the governing boards. If not revoked, however, it may soon be claimed to have acquired the authority of established usage. Unless revoked, I believe, it will permanently do away with the pure virility of Harvard tradition.

In at least two ways, I may add, Radcliffe has worked perceptible harm to Harvard instructors. The first is incontestable. Harvard salaries are necessarily low, particularly during the early years of service. Harvard instructors who are not fortunate enough to possess independent means are therefore compelled to do outside work or to leave their bills unpaid. The kind of outside work most valuable to them as scholars, and most valuable to the reputation of Harvard, is undoubtedly original research and publication of its results. Radcliffe meanwhile offers them some hundreds of dollars for mere repetition of college lectures, and the like. If they did not yield to such a temptation, they would not be human. Neither would they be if the yielding, which involves just so much more of the drudgery inseparable from teaching, did not tend slowly to diminish their scholarly vigor. They tend more and more to become mere schoolmasters. So while Radcliffe has undoubtedly helped Harvard instructors to increase their scanty earnings, there can be as little question that it has on the whole impaired their original power. It has thus tended to diminish the reputation which they might have won both for themselves and for the old college to which they owe prime allegiance.

To this objection, there is an obvious answer. Double-daggered courses[1] involve no extra teaching. But double daggers stab both ways; neither do these courses involve any extra salary whatever. The little money paid for them goes not to the instructors but to the corporation. The only thing which they necessarily involve is coeducation — violation, as I have said, of the one tradition which until five years ago Harvard had preserved inviolate.

The other injury which Radcliffe teaching has worked to Harvard instructors is far more a matter of opinion. My own opinion about it, however, is decided. The profession of teaching presents to a man who enters it a danger which few characters prove strong enough to resist. A mature man, to preserve and strengthen his powers, needs manly opposition. To put the case colloquially, he ought to pass a good part of his time in vigorous contest with men of his own size. When a young teacher begins his work, the real state of affairs does not appear at once. His pupils are near enough to him both in years and in power to give his life a little of the wholesome element of resistance. But teachers grow older with each year; and each year their pupils seem younger and younger. More and more, then, the profession of teaching tends to develop that arbitrary self-confidence and impatience of contradiction which has long been recognized as probably the most insidious failing observable in the somewhat kindred profession of the ministry. Now this danger, inevitable in any teacher's life, is increased when his pupils are girls or women. Whoever has taught both men and women must be aware of the comparative lack of mental resistance which he finds in a class composed wholly or chiefly of the latter. To some temperaments the consequent relaxation of mental muscle may be healthily unwelcome; to many others it is rather luxuriously agreeable. In brief, a man who likes to teach women is in real danger of infatuation.

[1] Courses in Harvard College open to Radcliffe students. — EDITOR

To prevent coeducation, then, to increase the original scholarship of Harvard instructors, and to preserve them from probable danger of slowly enfeebling infatuation, I could wish to see arise here a state of public opinion which should forbid further encroachment on the part of Radcliffe.

There was another piece of work for Harvard College which Wendell began but, unhappily, did not continue. This was the writing of a journal on Harvard affairs. Under the heading "Private," the first page read as follows: —

26 *September*, 1888. — In what slight efforts I have made to find what Harvard College was like before I knew it, I have been impressed with the purely official character of what records exist. It has therefore occurred to me that an informal journal of what goes on in the faculty may ultimately have interest. At this moment, just as I am beginning my term of service as assistant professor, I start this book, with the purpose of noting in it, from time to time, anything that occurs or that occurs to me. The record will be thoroughly desultory, thoroughly informal, perhaps unduly personal. I shall try to make it a current account of college matters as they present themselves to me. If I can manage incidentally to describe some of my colleagues, I should like to. Obviously, such matter is not suitable for publication until a considerable period has elapsed. Thirty years I believe to be the conventional limit. If it ever gets into print, then, I shall never see it. And perhaps I should write down distinctly here that what value it may have lies wholly in the fact that I shall try to make it a sincere record of my personal impressions — which means that it avowedly states things not as they are but as they appear to a man who has some reason to believe himself eccentric.

For about fifty pages — the last entry is dated 3 May 1889 — the journal preserves a lively record of faculty meetings and discussions, with many observations upon the participants. In its entirety it would make a disproportionate demand of space upon these pages; and there are passages in it for which the time of publication is hardly yet ripe. A few specimen fragments from it should nevertheless be presented.

16 *October*, 1888. — Shaler, I think, doubts my sanity. He is chairman of our committee on special students, and professor of geology. A thorough Southerner, he has all the enthusiasm imaginable, which makes him at once the best of teachers and the best of fellows. You cannot see him without being stimulated. But he is very loth to believe ill of anyone whom he has not caught lying; such as he has, he would like to shoot. . . .

10 *November*, 1888. — Family matters have kept me so busy that I have not written a word here or anywhere else for days. I am driven from my library by a nurse, now calmly waiting for her services to be needed. What has happened at college is this: The Republicans called a meeting to rebut the Free Traders. It was more genuine than the other, more successful, more vulgar. I did not manage to get there; but the list of names was curiously inferior to the other — good fellows enough, but almost all of notably inferior fibre, or else — like Hale and Hallowell — hereditary foes of everything south of New England. What this meeting is notable for is the letter that old "Fanny" Bowen wrote to Governor Long. Bowen is the Nestor of American Protection, having taught it and written of it for years so vigorously that J. S. Mill called him an obscure American metaphysician. Long sent him a line, asking for a letter to read at the meeting. Bowen answered in an open letter, published in the *Post*, exposing and denouncing the lying dishonesty of the Republican campaign, and explaining why he, and all honest Protectionists ought to vote the Democratic ticket. I saw him walking across the yard, the day the letter came out. He is a typical pedant — a bag of bones with thin white hair and beard, spectacles, and an incessant habit of sniffing with a funny distortion of feature. He always wears an old felt hat, shapeless loose clothes, and nowadays, cloth boots. But his eye is still keen at well on to eighty; and that day he had a look of almost boyish vigor and

content. He does little or no teaching now; he gave up coming to the faculty shortly after the requisition of Greek for admission was made in a sense voluntary. I shall never forget the gallant fight he made, almost alone, for the rigid old system. He read a speech, that lasted through two or three meetings, to a room full of bored modern professors, who could hardly restrain their ridicule and impatience. But on he went with his quavering old voice, shaking his shining old head, with the gas-lights gleaming in his spectacles. "Ultimus Romanorum" was his phrase for himself, I think. And so he was — game to the last. There was a torchlight procession; and then came the election, in which every conceivable prejudice and superstition beat honest government and common-sense hollow. And now, five days later, nobody knows the difference. . . .

23 *December*, 1888. — The latter view [on a matter of college discipline] prevailed — an interesting fact because, as is often the case, the president was voted down. Clymer remarked a little later that nothing has impressed him so much in the faculty as the president's attitude: popular belief has it that Eliot has surrounded himself with a company of followers who do what he tells them to, with almost religious devotion; in fact, there is a body of men so independent as to be almost unmanageable — fifty or sixty Mugwump parties of one, each one of whom votes on every question precisely as he pleases; and the president is simply a debater, so well equipped with facts and so able in debate that by sheer force of argument he is apt in the long run to carry more points than he loses. But his attitude throughout my knowledge of him has been scrupulously fine, impartial, on the whole even unprejudiced. What he demands of the faculty is that they teach for all they are worth; then each man, provided he vote honestly, and I know none who do not, may vote about anything however he pleases. . . .

A few nights ago I went to a dinner of the graduates of Andover, as a guest. No wine was served; and expecting as much, I had brought a flask along with which I tinctured my ice-water — previously asking leave of Ropes, the president.

In consequence, I am told, the report is abroad that I drank raw whiskey and got dreadfully boozy. In fact, I made so lame a speech — for I cannot talk after dinner — that I don't much blame the gossips. . . .

[*Apropos of an investigation of Harvard teaching and discipline under the elective system.*]

2 *February*, 1889. — One thing that interests me now is to determine how far the matter is genuine on the part of the malcontents; and how far a half-unconscious organization of a wish to smash Eliot. As I told Frank Lowell, few things bother me more now than radically to disagree with the president: for after eight years of service at Harvard I have seen him so generally in the right — so far-seeing, so honest, so disinterested, so wise — that as a simple matter of experience I am forced to admit that whoever disagrees with him is apt to prove mistaken. Yet nothing could be further from truth than the vulgar notion that he imposes himself on his subordinates, either by brute force — like McCosh, who used to pound the table at Princeton until opposition was silenced — or by a more subtle exercise of his power. He simply reasons — and more convincingly than anyone else I know. In his conduct to individuals, I have never known him to depart from the finest standards of justice and honor; and his devotion to the college is so deep, so earnest, so passionate, that one cannot think of it without a throb of loyalty both to the college itself and to the president, too, for the very loyalty with which he leads us.

28 *February*, 1889. — On Friday, the 22nd, the Tavern Club celebrated J. R. Lowell's seventieth birthday at a dinner no one who was there will forget. Norton presided: Lowell spoke delightfully; Dr. Holmes read a poem; Judge Hoar spoke, and Wayne MacVeagh, and Gilder of the *Century*, and Mr. Henry Lee. What makes it worth noting here is that all the speakers who were Harvard men kept referring to their college life — to all of us the dearest memory we have. After dinner I told Mr. Lowell how much his teaching had been to me. He grasped my hand rather impulsively. Such a thing, he said, he liked

to hear best of all; for he often wondered whether in his years of teaching he had not wasted rather fruitlessly time he should have given to literature.

"The days of journeying," Wendell wrote in his chapter on Milton in *The Temper of the Seventeenth Century in English Literature*, "are not generally days of harvest; but the seeds which fall in those pleasant times are apt to sink deep." Between 1888 and 1898 he himself made three journeys to Europe; in the summer of 1888 with his youngest brother, Jacob Wendell, Jr. ("Jac"); in the summer of 1891 with his dear friend and classmate, W. B. Shubrick Clymer, at that time an instructor in English at Harvard; and in 1894–5 with his wife and children. For eight months of this time the Wendell family established itself in Italy, spending the winter in Rome. Thence, with his younger friend, Gaillard Lapsley, recently graduated at Harvard, now a Fellow of Trinity College, Cambridge, Wendell made a journey to Egypt and Greece. It was a period but scantily recorded in his letters. In September of 1893 he made the nearest American approach to European travel by visiting with his friend Clymer the World's Fair at Chicago, to his great enjoyment and profit.[1] His letters from abroad yield more than one evidence that when he wrote of the seed-time and harvest of travel he was writing whereof he knew. Wagner and Bayreuth, described in a letter of 1888, reappear in his *English Composition;* a letter of the summer of 1891, picturing the funeral of an ecclesiastic which he happened to witness at Bourges, has its fulfillment in a poem, "The Dean of Bourges," published in *Scribner's Magazine* for January 1893. Thus the broadening horizon of his personal experience was constantly

[1] An article, "Impressions at Chicago," published in the *Harvard Monthly* for October 1893, recorded vividly the effect of the World's Fair on Wendell's sensitive observation.

revealing itself in his work. In the last of the ten years to which this chapter is devoted, on May 21, 1898, the death of Wendell's father made the first break in the intimate family circle in which his affections were extraordinarily centred.

His letters, again, may now proceed to autobiographic purpose.

[*Out of the summer letters of 1888 from England, — where Wendell and his brother visited Colonel Robert Thomson in North Devon, — from Holland, Germany, and France, one passage, preserving the impressions produced by* Parsifal *and the* Meistersinger *at Bayreuth, must suffice.*]

*To his Wife*

NUREMBURG, *July* 28, 1888

It was on Wednesday we heard *Parsifal*, and on Thursday the *Meistersinger*. Now it is Saturday night, when I steal from bed a little while to try to say what I think of them. *Parsifal* puzzles me. It puts itself in two distinct ways. One phrases itself in French; "*Il y a un monsieur qui ne veut pas s'amuser. On danse. On célèbre l'Eucharistie. Voilà tout.*" In short, from one point of view, nothing could be more absurd. Carpenter says that Tom Perry ticketed it as decadent German romanticism, with an expression of somewhat bored satisfaction with his opinion. All of which means that, unlike what I am accustomed to think the highest type of art, it seems to me rather to demand sympathy than to command it. In a work not essentially great, — in one that has not a significance that cannot quite express itself in any other imaginable form, — such a quality as this is fatal. That it is not fatal in *Parsifal* seems to me a very certain indication that *Parsifal*, while not so perfect a work in its full effect as others of Wagner's, — as *Siegfried* or as *Tristan*, to go no further, — is at once a nobler effort, and would prove itself, could one study it at leisure, perhaps the most profoundly interesting of all.

The great truths of life are so great that most people forget they are more than commonplace. People who call themselves clever, and despise what they define as Philistine, accordingly disdain all truths but such imperfect little ones as are true only day by day and hour by hour. The great men look with calm eyes at the eternities; and however great they be, their eyes are by and by dazzled. When they try to tell, with pen or pencil, through sound or form, what they have seen, the greatest of them grow inarticulate. And after all, the truth they fail to articulate is only the commonplace that good is good, and evil evil, and one or the other bound to prevail. Which no one can know; sometimes the evil seems bound to overcome all else; but the men we call greatest speak forth a belief, all the more stirring because, like all beliefs, it cannot prove itself, and demands a loyal sympathy, that what will prevail is the good.

That is all that Wagner tells us in *Parsifal*. But he tells it with such a sense of all it means — of the infinite power in evil, the infinite vitality of good, the infinite complexity of which the infinite simplicity of truth clothes itself for human minds, — that he, who with all his perversity and what seems deliberate eccentricity had, I think, more consummate command of expression than any other man of our time, finds himself here almost at a loss. The mystic allegory that from beginning to end bewilders the spectator as much as the unveiling of the Grail bewilders the witless Parsifal, is not, I think, as deliberate as it seems. In the strangely fascinating poetry of mediæval Christianity, Wagner finds at last what better than anything else he can see helps him to phrase his last message.

Just how didactic all this is I cannot tell. At first sight it seems like an incarnate sermon. Perhaps it may be. But I incline rather to think that the profoundly ethical quality that makes this opera as stirring as the grandest ceremonies of the Church, is due rather to its essential truth than to any more vulgar trait. Like the great men before him, and those who will come after him, Wagner looked at life asking only what manner of thing this was — though, like many another great man, I dare say he was small enough never to recognize this fact, and even honestly to deny it. Like all of them, he saw that life was and must be this endless struggle I have spoken of between good and evil; and that somehow, no one has ever told us why, the good is best, and always must be. And so he wrote Parsifal — in a different sense from the old plays it so often recalls, truly a mystery. With this Mystery of Mysteries his work closes. Just what it means beyond this commonplace, no one, I think, can tell. Yet no one, I think, who will give it his sympathy, can fail to feel, ill articulated, within himself, a growing belief that it is a great work and a good. . . . The inevitable inarticulateness of such work as this is perhaps more aptly expressed by a performance that comes a little short of what it might be than by one which seems to leave nothing to seek.

Quite the reverse of all this was the *Meistersinger*. A light work for Wagner, — with no deeper thesis than that pedantry is everlastingly feeble in trying to treat the living truths of art as if they were as dead as a classic grammar, — it is from beginning to end as finely, definitely articulate as human work can possibly be. The libretto is on paper perhaps the heaviest in existence; evidently it is meant to be funny, but how it can actually be so is more than you can see. If the whole thing were not given to absolute perfection, it would be, I conceive, simply intolerable. But it was given to absolute perfection. From the moment the curtain went up, barring a few stretches of intensely German length of wind, it was perfectly delightful. Orchestra, singers, actors, stage effects, audience and all combined to make it, in a word, perhaps the most perfect work of dramatic art I have ever seen. And I doubt if any could ever be more so. I am perfectly sincere, I think, in putting this down as my own impression. Certainly it was confirmed by all I heard next day from critics better able than I to pass an opinion. On the whole, many seemed to think, it was, if one may so grade such things, the best operatic performance ever given.

So I have written, largely for myself, but by no means little for the people I send these notes to, what I found at Bayreuth. It will show, I hope, why I begin to feel as I write that my two days there were an experience that will not pass away. When

I began this note, I was eager to go back again, and hear *Parsifal* once more. It is out of the question; I cannot get tickets before Wednesday, and cannot wait till then. On the whole I am content with what I have had. And now to bed. We start early to-morrow, and wherever we go are on our way home.

*To Colonel Robert Thomson*
[*On the occasion of the engagement of his son Remington*]

BOSTON, 20 *October*, 1888

. . . As I grow older, such news as this has far more meaning than it used to. Before long I shall have been married nine years; and when I stop to think of what I was nine years ago, I am lost in wonder that so mere a boy dared to marry at all. But, after all, what has chiefly made the difference, is that very married life, which has so unspeakably completed life for me. It has meant some sacrifices, of course, and not a few trials. It has brought me face to face with a good deal of petty economy and such-like that I never dreamed the sense of before. But, taken for all in all, it has meant a depth of happiness that without it I should never have known in this world. Indeed, I find myself saying now and then, that, whatever may chance now, I can have no right for a word of complaint; for in these years that have passed and are passing I have had more than one man's share of what all men crave — thoroughly, profoundly sympathetic happiness with a wife whom every year has made nearer and dearer. It is without affectation, then, that I send Remington, as my most cordial message, my earnest hope that his life may be as complete as mine. . . .

*To Edmund Clarence Stedman*

BOSTON, *December* 3, 1890

DEAR MR. STEDMAN, — I had been meaning to send you some word of my lectures anyway. They take better than I expected. The audience began with about three hundred, and instead of falling off has increased. Mostly school teachers, I fancy.  They are earnest females, I mean, who take notes, and don't take jokes.

As for length, I find that I was mistaken.  I have had to cut each talk ruthlessly.  My pages, you remember, average a little above 200 words.  To get forty-five of them into an hour requires fast reading; it gives little time for emphatic pauses.  From eight to nine thousand words can easily be made to fill the hour; and even fewer I think, might be managed.  I had a funny experience with my second lecture.  I had bracketed a number of passages, which might be skipped if necessary, and finding fifteen minutes past, before I was quarter done, I began relentless skipping.  To my horror, I suddenly discovered that I had thus brought myself within ten pages of the end of my MS. when there were still twenty minutes to spare.  I slackened my pace, and assumed an air of unusual authority; and came out on the minute.  I can't get at *Mather* until after Christmas.  So he will not be ready till late in the spring.  With cordial messages to all of you, in which my wife joins,

Sincerely yours,

BARRETT WENDELL

*To Robert Herrick*

[*Mr. Herrick, a senior in Harvard College, had just become
editor of the* Harvard Monthly]

MARLBOROUGH STREET, 14 *October*, 1889

. . . Your leader I liked, in spite of the slightly editorial emphasis on the importance of the *Monthly*.  Why can't people who puff things keep quite clear of the notion that they have found the panacea?  Modesty, my friend, is the best policy; but I hasten to admit that you are n't palpably immodest.

Last, not least, for your story.  It is full of suggestion, and decidedly, I think, the most distinct and firm piece of your work that I have seen.  You don't lose an inch, which is saying a good deal.  But before you do what you might do, we must have something more real still.  The function of the novelist to-day — if indeed he have any — is to interpret the life he lives in — the life that throbs all about him.  So-called realists try to, and fail. They photograph when they should paint. But they are on the right track. One can't afford to disregard the tendencies of his day. Who yields to what is bad in them, of course, is swept away to nowhere. But who fails to grasp and do his best with what is best in them is left behind. Does all this mean anything to you, I wonder? Or is it all flat Philistinism? I don't feel over wise to-night, but I really mean something. . . .

## To his Wife

LONDON, 11 *June*, 1891

. . . Shubrick has never been to the Tower, so we had planned to go there; but Winchester took so long that we gave it up and went to the National Gallery instead. I have lost my critical sense of painting, but not my delight in it. Two such hours as are found there were worth all the bother I have had to get them. It seems to me that if I were utterly broken in spirit — bereaved, tortured — I should crave most of all some great masterpieces of painting. In looking at them, even as blindly and uncritically as I must look now, I find an absorbing interest that makes me unconscious of other things. To-day it was a whirl of impressions I cannot disentangle: from some strange old fresh portraits discovered since I was last here through all the schools of Italy, and the Netherlands, and France. Nothing stands out: everything was fascinating, delightful.

We had to hurry home, to prepare for lunch with Henry James. He has charming rooms in Kensington, with a western sunlight that to-day was glorious. No one else was there; and no one could have been more delightful. He surprised me in many ways. In the first place, of course, and above all — which is not surprising — he is a consummate man of the world, with manners and address so perfect that you hardly realize how good they are. Then he has a great deal of the personal quality that seems in William so individual. Turns of phrase and tones of voice constantly reminded me of his brother. But the individuality that surprised me was his astonishing combination of almost feminine intuitiveness of feeling with almost boyish frankness and decision of expression. His mouth is in its lines among the most sensitive I have ever seen; and now and then actually quivers as he speaks of something that touches his feelings. And there is in his talk not a trace of the analytic lack of self-committal which is often so irritating in his writing. Altogether, he seemed a man that one would grow heartily to care for, which was the last character I looked for. And at the same time you felt, as you always do with people thoroughly of the world, that he regarded you, and expected you to regard him, simply as a passing incident of a single day. The talk turned on all manner of things unliterary. Books we did not touch on. . . .

At this hotel I found the Thornton Lothrops, who were to all appearances much pleased to see me. But Shubrick and I had to hurry off to dine with Andrew Lang, at the Oxford and Cambridge Club. He had Saintsbury, and Boyesen of New York, to meet us. And really we had a most funny time. Lang is a languid, thin person, with dapple-grey hair, thin whiskers, and slightly unkempt aspect. He has a single eyeglass attached to a cord that has been broken so often that it looks like a string of knots. Saintsbury is a conventional Englishman, with very red nose, steel spectacles, and a cravat — concealed by a large beard — which he had not taken the trouble to tie at all. Both of them seemed in disposition all that could be asked, but perfectly unable to talk of anything outside the ways of London. So they talked incessantly to each other. Boyesen occasionally broke in with anecdotes of Turgenieff and other people he had met; but to no avail. Such a revelation of the insularity of England I never had before. What added to the fun was that both Lang and Saintsbury — but particularly Lang — spoke English with so curious an accent that we could not understand more than half they said. . . .

*To the same*

Eton, *Sunday,* 14 *June,* 1891

We came down here at one o'clock yesterday. Earlier in the day I had been again to the National Gallery, where I stumbled on Bôcher and Miss Grace Norton, who are staying at Hampton Court. At the moment they were attached to a party of well-dressed women, of high apparent respectability, who were following about a short-bearded youth, who was lecturing on the pictures most intelligently; and who proved to be Bernhard Berenson. He seems really at work in earnest, having two or three such classes on hand, and being engaged in a critical study of the pictures at Hampton Court. These are good, but have got hopelessly mixed up — being attributed now to all manner of people who could by no possibility have painted them. If he disentangles them, he will have done a notable work.

Altogether I was so well pleased with his looks and with what Bôcher said of him that I gave him my address and asked him to look me up. . . .

*To the same*

LONDON, *June* 16, 1891

*[From a letter containing an account of a luncheon at which Austin Dobson was a fellow guest]*

. . . Berenson had asked us to breakfast this morning. I could not get there in time; but found my way to him just as Shubrick and he had finished their meal. He has rooms in a little house as old as Queen Anne's time, just behind Westminster Abbey. I have rarely seen so charming an interior. An angular little staircase, much like those in the older houses in Portsmouth; rooms wainscoted from floor to ceiling; colors dark and very harmonious. All as simple as possible, and on a very small scale, but in perfect taste. . . . He has mastered his subject, he is thinking hard, and working, and writing; in short, I think he has gone very far to justify the rather exorbitant demands he has made on his friends, in these years when to many of us he has seemed so idle. We stayed there until noon. . . .

Dobson is a rather short, stout, good-humored, plain man, not very well dressed, with hair and beard dark and not lately trimmed, and no little finger on his right hand. Unaffectedly far from nonsense, one would say of him first of all — a man who would be the last to over-estimate himself; and father of thirteen children. You would never for a moment guess him to be author of the sort of thing he writes. You would actually like his work the better for knowing him. We had a very simple luncheon; and afterwards strolled in a private garden behind the club, [the National, in Whitehall] not unlike my father's in New York, except that you could lean against the rear wall and look across the Thames embankment at the river, covered with boats and tugs. . . .

*To the same*

LONDON, 17 *June* 1891

. . . We have been out of town for the whole day. Grant Allen, to whom Blathwayt gave me a letter, lives at Dorking, thirty miles or so from town. It is where Keats wrote "Endymion," and Disraeli, *Coningsby* — or something; and where Mr. Pickwick met Sam Weller, and where old Weller drove the coach, and his wife kept the Marquis of Granby and entertained the Reverend Mr. Stiggins. Incidentally it is in the loveliest part of Surrey, which is one of the loveliest country districts in England. Allen had written us to lunch with him to-day. I was quite unprepared for what sort of person he might be. He has written no end of second-rate novels, and a lot of popular stuff about evolution. I had an idea I should find a shallow person, who took himself in comical earnest.

Instead of this he turned out to be distinctly a gentleman, of rather unusual cultivation, and the most unobtrusive personality. A slight man, evidently something of an invalid, a little like Mr. Quincy in aspect, he does this popular writing to support himself. Meanwhile he is, in his own ideal way, a tremendous radical and democrat. On the whole, he is the ideal of a gentle idealist, looking for an earthly millennium that can never come. He has a charming little house — a villa — on a hillside; and a remarkably vigorous, active little wife, who seems more like a well-bred American than an English woman. They were, like everybody we have met, cordiality itself. It came out that they did not know exactly what kind of beings to expect us to be. Blathwayt, of whom they spoke most kindly, appears to be a journalist who has, with excellent intention, described his private friends in print with more enthusiasm than discretion. I related the anecdote of your experience with good Mr. Snell, which appeared to amuse them, and established us in Mr. Allen's good graces. So when we talked of going they would not hear of it; and kept us for four good hours.

After a very good, simple luncheon we sat under their trees for a half hour. Then Allen took us for a walk, mostly across fields, up a delightful hill, where we lay on the grass, looking over half Surrey and Kent, and lazily talking of all manner of things. They are great friends of Meredith's, who lives near by, but who seems to be overwhelmed with strangers. They suggested that we might call on him; the manner led us to protest that we would much rather stay with them, which seemed to please them. They had been in Boston, and knew the Jameses, and Norton, and Howells, and the Shalers, and poor Mrs. Lodge. Altogether, we got along capitally. As Shubrick said on the way home, their radical idealism was sophomoric. They spoke of girl friends who had left home and set up establishments for themselves, etc.; evidently the Pownalls are not unique. But altogether their notions of what is and what may be are more like what our boys and girls amuse themselves with than like what our mature people consider sane. Allen is in this respect more delightfully dreamy than his wife, who, like all good wives, has good sense enough for both. . . .

*To his Father*

BOSTON, *Sunday*, 18 *October*, 1891

DEAR PAPA, — . . . I heard a queer theory the other day about the Yankee Puritans, whose religious views were so strongly Hebraic. They came chiefly, it seems, from Norfolk and Lincolnshire. These counties, some two or three centuries before the Reformation, had been the chief strongholds of the English Jews, who were finally expelled from the kingdom by one of the Plantagenet kings. At the time of the expulsion, many changed their faith and remained to be absorbed in the native population. It is wholly possible, then, that the Yankee Puritan, with all his Old Testament feeling, was really, without knowing it, largely Jewish in blood. There is in the Yankee nature much that would give color to the theory; but of course it is very far from being a proved fact. . . .

*To Edmund Clarence Stedman*

BOSTON, *December* 25, 1891

DEAR MR. STEDMAN, — I took you at your word for the moment, and left unanswered your very kind letter, and unacknowledged the very interesting clipping. But I appreciated them all the same, just as I heartily appreciate your kindness about *Cotton Mather*. Hereabouts, if I may judge from what I hear privately, the book is distinctly successful. The Historical Society likes it, and much to my surprise so do the Orthodox clergy. Objections come only from one professor of history, who says it is "nothing but literature," and from a very radical Unitarian divine who thinks my last chapter unjust to the clerical character. . . .

We had a most interesting time at the Tavern Club last night. Bates, with infinite pains and study, reproduced Elizabethan Christmas games — Yule log, Court of Misrule, mummers, morris dances, etc. Paderewski played for the morris dancing! It lasted from 7 till 12 — I mean the sports, not the dancing. And oddly enough, I have no headache, after all. . . .

*To the same*

CAMBRIDGE, 7 *January*, 1892

Few things have ever gratified me more than the notice of *C. M.* in the *Critic*. It is just the sort of thing that stimulates one to constantly better work. The book has done for me what my novels never began to do, in making people take what I do seriously. I am conscious of this in numberless ways; and feel, all the time, that I owe no small part of the recognition to your kindness. . . .

You know better than I how much sympathetic recognition means to one who has tried to do his best. To outsiders, relish for praise seems fatuous. I don't think it so. It is really a longing not for commendation of work done, but for stimulus at a moment of temporary relaxation and despondency, to help work that is to come. . . .

### To his Father

BOSTON, *Thursday morning*, 10 *November*, 1892

DEAR PAPA, — . . . As I have told you, the gist of my feeling since the McKinley Bill passed has steadily been that — whatever its real merits — it could not possibly be made to look like anything but an enormous grant of privilege to certain classes — of whom we are part. To persist in maintaining it, then, would endanger all our holdings, exposing us, as soon as bad crops happen to coincide with an election, — to absolute free trade. In defense of your own property, then, I am for the moment a blind Democrat. To insist on privilege seems to me to be as blind as the old slaveholders.

Incidentally, as I have told you often, I should in your place endeavor, as far as possible, to place my investments where changes in tariff legislation would not immediately affect them. They are in less danger now, in my opinion, than before Tuesday — inasmuch as the election prepares the way for a gradual, instead of revolutionary, withdrawal of privilege. In general, I welcome this change, believing that just so far as business can be kept free from government interference it will grow healthily. To tie up commerce and State is almost as bad, in the end, as to mix up Church and State. The big corporations and Wanamakers are politically as dangerous as —— and not much more or less so, either, than the Catholics.

You see I'm not a thoughtless Democrat. . . .

### To Colonel Robert Thomson

BOSTON, 3 *February*, 1893

. . . Since the first of January no less than nine people whom I knew more or less intimately have died. The most notable, of course, is Bishop Brooks, whose end came with no general warning at all. I happened to be passing his house one morning, saw a little movement about the door, inquired of a friend what the matter was, and heard that the bishop was just dead. He was distinctly the most eminent figure in New England; and his death affected the city in a way I have never seen anything do before. You felt in every corner of the town that some serious thing had happened. There was a sort of hushed solemnity about people and places usually noisy. What was most striking, perhaps, was the strong feeling evinced by people whom one would never have thought touched by the Church. In public conveyances, in the street, everywhere, you heard people say "It's too damn bad." When such spontaneous profanity is evoked by such an event, it really means, to my mind, very much indeed. Even the morally vulgar felt as much as anyone that there had been a great public loss.

The bishop was a man of wonderful enthusiasm and purity. His purity made him, I think, underestimate the evil that is in human nature; and in his teaching to over-insist on the authority of conscience. This, combined with his somewhat lax churchmanship, and a lack of personal sympathy, had made me, I think, fail quite to appreciate the full nobility of the man himself. As I think of him, now, I feel that for honesty of purpose, for purity of thought and word, for enthusiastic energy, for constant effort to help men to be better men, he was — at least hereabouts — unique. Not a great thinker at all, he was a great poetic religious enthusiast, conveying his message to every Gentile he met.

My brother Evert was very fond of him — in fact always stayed with him when he came to Boston. And the family made him one of themselves at the funeral. I did not go, as there was so great a crowd that every unbidden guest seemed in the way. There was an open-air service, after the regular one, however, on the steps of Trinity Church. The coffin was borne out by the pall-bearers, the rector made a prayer, and literal thousands of people, gathered in the square, joined in a hymn that had been a favorite of the bishop's.

It is significant that among his contemporaries and the younger generation in New England there are no figures of eminence left. And when I came here to live we had Longfellow, and Lowell, and Whittier, and Emerson, and half a dozen more, as well as Dr. Holmes, who survives alone. We are vanishing into provincial obscurity. . . .

*To the same*

BOSTON, 17 *December*, 1893

. . . When you get this it will be well on to twenty years since I first knew you. I have just been looking at my old journal. I went aboard the Mongolia at Gibraltar on the 21st of January, '74. We reached Malta on the 24th. My first note of you is on the 25th, mentioning that I had met you a day or two before. It was in the late autumn of that year — November or December — that I met my wife, then just past fifteen. I hardly recognize myself in the old journal. My whole life has taken such a different turn from any I expected. I supposed — as far as I supposed anything — that I should be a lawyer or a man of business in New York; and had rather an idea that I should not marry anybody, based on profound distrust of my personal attractions. And here I am a rapidly middle-aging professor, with four or five unsuccessful books against my name, and a flourishing family of four very firmly settled in the more conservative part of Boston. I have just joined the most conservative of clubs here — one that has met every Wednesday evening in the season since 1777. There were originally four clergymen, four lawyers, four physicians, and four gentlemen of leisure. The last class they have meantime enlarged to eight; the numbers of the other three classes remain fixed. As most of the men are old enough to be my father, it is a bit slow. And democracy has quite destroyed the actual influence the club used to have. But to my taste there is a distinct charm about the tradition of the thing. We meet at one another's homes. They come here for the first time on the 27th.

I am very glad you like *Stelligeri*. In a way, as the essay indicates, I feel that we Yankees are as much things of the past as any race can be. America has swept from our grasp. The future is beyond us. And we have not the great background of European tradition to console ourselves with. Our best memories are that we have tried to fix ideals for other folks to live by. We have done our best — not greatly, but honestly. At this moment, very often, I feel a certain regret that I had not the fortune to be born fifty years earlier. Then I could eagerly have joined in the expression of faith in the future which made New England literature promise something. Now I find my temper doubtful, reactionary.[1] Such moods as mine are not things that literature demands. I begin to feel sure that what I may write will never be widely accepted. It is a bit depressing; but I have more to the good in life than t'other way. . . .

## To Robert Herrick

BOSTON, 27 *January*, 1894

DEAR HERRICK, — Don't be afraid of boring your correspondents — or better, whoever has the luck to get so welcome a letter as came to me a month ago. You blaze away on paper, and the paper sparkles with real life. Damn figures of speech, of course — I've damned them unremittingly since the autumn of '80. I wish to goodness, though, that I could let my pen go, as sometimes I can let my temper.

After all, your great bewildering surge of what one shrinks a bit from — if only for its endless energy — is a stimulating thing to think of. Shut up here in New England, and getting less and less discontented with its daily repetition of things no one outside cares for, I find myself, as I read your letter again, wishing to goodness that at your time of life I had had at once the luck and the pluck to give and take in a world where something was a-doing. Muscularity is n't my trait, now, I fear; so I love the trait far more than it may be worth by the standards of the eternities. And, while I don't love crude material, and coeducation, and such like, and behave like the devil when I get foul of such things, I can't help feeling that this is the stuff whereof — if of anything — our future is to be made.

[1] This temper — perhaps a little deliberately nursed — became more pronounced as time went on. Even as early as the summer of 1896, Wendell wrote, with characteristic hyperbole, to his wife from Bar Harbor: 'I begin to feel sorry for '84, deeming Bryan, on the whole, the fruit of reform. Hereafter let us all try to preserve the decencies of comfortable corruption."

Whoever can give it, then, a living leaven from the past is lucky. A vulgar person, whom you would n't approve, sat next me at a club dinner not long ago. Talk falling on the horrors of democracy, he declared a solemn sense of duty. Power, he averred, was bound to reside in the masses. The obligations of a gentleman, then, were plain — namely to breed into those masses as much decent stock as he possibly could. It's pleasant to think that remnants of New England conscience — and Puritan manners — thus survive. Play your part, then, metaphorically. God knows what may become of the seed thoughtlessly sown. Herndon says much of Lincoln in this matter. And I'm really very abominable. The Colonial Club encourages one's infirmities, you see. We don't get enough to drink, and have to stimulate ourselves, if so may be, by intellectual excess.

The year passes blamelessly. Harvard is unusually like itself. I've abandoned the faculty as hopeless, much to the benefit of my temper. Unreminded of the manifold follies of my colleagues, I begin to forget them, and sometimes to imagine that the world I live in is not altogether deluded — which is comfortable, if not wise.

If you want to see what I am capable of meanwhile, keep an eye on your Chicago *Dial*, to which yesterday I dispatched — "as per request" — an account of the Teaching of English at Harvard worthy of a John-shopkeeper. You know that bit of slang, I take it — dear to M. le Baron Briggs. It is comforting, in a whisper, when the vote goes against you. Meanwhile, as we are above all else a nation of shopkeepers, to some variable and expansive degree ennobled by lack of the corruptions and standards of autocracy, it is subtle, and a beautiful tribute to the broadly rational excellence of the ideals so admirably embodied in the whiskers and the utterances of President Gilman.

Do you know that when I began this letter I had no idea of being nonsensical. God is disposing of me, I fear, with more justice than mercy this morning. It all depends on your mood, though if you have read thus far you 'll have forgiven. If not, why truth is truth, and just now my pen reveals me happily unwise. The truth is, I suppose, that a serious event has really disturbed my usual pose of phrase and temper. I had the grip, by way of occupying an otherwise puzzling Christmas vacation. I got up in a severely moral state of mind, and have abstained from inhaling the smoke of cigarettes since just one month ago this evening. The abstinence greatly enhances my relish of a pipe; and by increasing my consumption of cigars patriotically does its best to relieve the dreadful pressure of these hard times. . . .

*To Henry Copley Greene*

ATHENS, 26 *March* 1895

DEAR HARRY, — As you would n't come with me, you see, I had to come without you. Your place is taken — *pro tem* — by Gaillard Lapsley, who joined me in an attack of influenza at Rome, and subsequently in a particularly serene trip to the Nile and here, which is drawing to a close. We were about a week at Cairo, and ten days on the river, going as far as the ruins of Thebes. Here we have now been a little above a week, and have about the same time before us. Then we return to Italy, where I hope Edith will meet me at Naples. Beyond that as yet, I have no plans.

This outing has proved perfectly tonic. For the first time since I left home, I begin to feel like myself at last, and to see that during all the first months of my vacation I was pretty near nervous prostration. Such a work as I did last summer on *Shakespere* was beyond my strength. D. V., I will do such no more. Incidentally I feel still unable to do any serious writing. I have n't even kept a journal. My hand, though, at last begins to forget its cramp, which I had begun to fear might be permanent. . . .

As you see, I am more like myself again than my letters have shown me since I actually saw you in the flesh. Egypt was most curious — vastly more barbaric and remote than I expected, impressive in a different way from that which books and pictures had prepared one for. The modern life is just a squalid, decrepit reproduction of the outward forms set forth in Genesis and Exodus. To read them there with dawning certainty that their god-like heroes were such beings as now crowd about you, swarming with flies and lies, cringing for baksheesh, is a very notable literary experience. Meanwhile the ruins, vast and mysterious as they are, seem as far from any humanity one can think of as common as are the sculptures of Central America; while Mohammedanism is such a blow between the eyes for whoever swears by conservatism and authority as knocks one silly. To phrase the thing a bit adequately, I should have to be as dithyrambic as I was about Chicago. I don't know that I shan't be. One never knows where one's impulse of expression is going to break out.

Greece is simply the most beautiful thing to look at I ever saw. The ruins, and all that sort of thing, are what one expects. The loveliness of natural form and colour on every side goes quite beyond words. Yesterday we went to Marathon — an amphitheatre of rocky hills, so bold in shape, so admirable in proportion, that you never think of their size. Between them and the narrow sea which runs between the mainland and the equally stirring mountains of Euboea is the plain, flat, covered with crops and vineyards, and yesterday alive with great wild anemones dancing in the cool wind, gleaming with all sorts of tender colour above the glittering white of dainty little daisies. From amid the vineyards rises the barrow raised over the Athenian dead and unchanged until Schliemann's time. He and Greek archæologists between them have almost destroyed it; really so undermined it that a few years of rain may wash it level; but enough is still left for you to climb, and sit on, watching the most marvellous hazy colours you can imagine brightening and fading over land and sea alike. Really, you see, I grow in my own way ardently Grecian. . . .

*To Colonel Robert Thomson*

[*On his defeat as a Conservative candidate in a parliamentary election*]

NEUCHATEL, 5 *August*, 1895

. . . In my extreme inaction of the past year, I find myself growing almost absurdly cynical. Democracy, in old world or new, seems little better than a caricature of government.

Power, wherever it reside, seems bound to develop the hateful traits of human nature — tyranny, dishonesty, petty baseness, corruption. In a government of the better classes, at least those traits are balanced by certain external graces and dignity, and often by some sense of personal consequence which is at least impressive if not admirable. In any democracy they are at their worst. In America generally the better classes have renounced public life altogether — with certain exceptions, of course. The country is doubtless the worse for it; individuals, I rather think, the better, for they are freed from almost inevitable temptation to swerve from ideals, and from truth of word and deed. After all, I often think nowadays, the best comment on democracy ever written is *Coriolanus*. The pity of it all is that we can't escape the evil. . . .

*To the same*

BOSTON, 18 *October*, 1895

. . . Harvard opens this year, by an odd chance, with exactly the same number of students that were there last year. A slight loss in one department — of 28 — is counterbalanced by a gain of 28 in another. My work begins rather more pleasantly than usual, and is certainly less oppressive in quantity. Our department of English, however, has just had an irreparable loss in the death of our oldest professor — Child. He was a scholar of wide reputation, and a man whose character — though a bit eccentric — made him to all who knew him not only admirable but lovable.

The children grow like weeds. Barrett, Jr., who is about as tall as I, has suddenly begun to show signs of a mustache, which fill me with sentiments of longevity. Mary, about the same time, shows corresponding signs of a waist — which phenomenon is that which visibly makes the final end of childhood. She is distinctly taller and larger than her mother — and if it were not that her hair is not yet done up in mature fashion, she would be in appearance altogether grown up. William has turned from an amusing child into an awkward little boy. The baby — little Edith — is a delightful person who does not realize that I understand English; so she preserves the French she learned abroad, in her talk with me. As French, I fear, it leaves something to be desired; but it keeps alive her familiarity with the sound and the vocabulary of the thing.

Politically our summer has been very anxious. The election is now only two weeks from us; and every sign points to the defeat of Bryan. McKinley is not in all respects what we could wish. His faults, however, are rather faults of limit than worse. He is a sincerely excessive protectionist. He is personally a man of admirable character, however; of the highest political integrity, too; and profoundly determined to save us from the terrible danger of national repudiation with which the mob has threatened us. The circumstances of the summer have been such that this matter is paramount. No minor differences of opinion can count with me. Though heretofore a Democrat, I shall vote this year the straight Republican ticket. As a party, the Democrats seem to me either gone to pieces or quite beyond the pale of sympathy. . . .

### To James Ford Rhodes

[*Wendell used to say of Mr. Rhodes that he had "dined with him on three continents — and never a poor dinner." They first met in Cairo in 1895, and soon formed a friendship which remained close through Wendell's life.*]

MATTAPOISETT, 30 *July*, 1896

DEAR MR. RHODES, — I am so grateful for your two kind letters that it seems a poor acknowledgment to write you another. Don't trouble yourself to answer this; I write it only to explain myself.

In the hasty line I scribbled with the clipping about Russell, I did not make myself clear. It was not that for a moment I doubted McKinley's sincerity about the tariff. Really, I incline to think there are few more vulgar errors than that which makes us so often pretend to ourselves that public men are inhumanly designing. The fact that his economic convictions are so sincere is one reason why I for one — though not convinced of their finality — shall gladly vote for him.

Neither did I mean that I should wish him for an instant to

disguise his convictions. What I meant was rather this: His views on the tariff are known to everybody — so well known, perhaps, that every new emphasis on them is in effect excessive. His candidacy, meanwhile, has involved this other question of financial stability which to many people seems for the moment paramount. His election, then, becomes in my opinion the most desirable political result which has been possible in my voting life. The one practical question, for me as for him, is how he may get the most votes. Under these circumstances, as I said at Beverly, I believe that public interest demands the judicious use of every known engine of electioneering. Among these engines, however, the public utterances of the candidate have importance.

Had it been possible to make him also the candidate of the sound-money Democrats — as Bryan is of silverites and populists — it seems to me that his position would be stronger to-day than it is. This is clearly impracticable. The precise question now seems consequently to be what line of utterance on his part will be most apt to hold the greatest number of doubtful votes — thereby making the sound-money Democratic ticket weaken Bryan more than it weakens him. To my mind, the sound-money Democrats are mostly of two classes: men who wish to retain the political organization of an opposition, and doctrinarians (idealists or cranks, if you like). The former class are beyond reach, but would naturally vote for Bryan if not diverted. The latter class are naturally rather Republican than Democratic, or at least, will never vote for free silver, and by judicious treatment may, I think, be kept in line. This judicious treatment would involve no insincerity on Major McKinley's part; it would involve only the perfectly just assumption that his views of the tariff are too well known to need further emphasis; and in addition to this a distinct statement, now and then, that the question of sound money has become so important as to warrant, for the moment, the neglect of other differences of opinion. Such a speech as that to the glass-workers won't help a bit, I think — it will hold no one not already held, and will strengthen, among doubtful men who would not vote for Bryan anyway, the

Third Party movement. I heartily hope that Major McKinley will get and hold every vote he possibly can.

*To Sir Robert White-Thomson*
[*On his creation K. C. B. at the Queen's Jubilee, 1897*]

14 *July*, 1897

MY DEAR SIR ROBERT, — Only a line to-day to tell you how heartily glad we all are to hear of the "Jubilee honour" which has come to you. It is not long since I wrote you how sincerely even the American people seem for the moment to feel the dignity and the greatness of the reign, and the sovereign, that will probably pass into history as the most memorable in the whole story of England. This share of yours in the commemoration of this year, then, seems to me a thing one would value more than if it had come at any other moment, earlier or later. It makes one's life permanently a part, in sentiment, of one of those rare moments when worthy good-will, and care for what is good, have for a little while dominated the baser things.

I need not tell you what personal pleasure your new dignity brings me. You know already, how, during these twenty-three years of our correspondence, I have grown to feel that whatever concerns you concerns me, too. In a way, then, which is very grateful to me, this honour given you brings to me a certain sense of personal share in the seriously delightful moment through which England is passing. What is done for those whom one cares about becomes a matter of one's personal pleasure, hard to express, perhaps, but surely, deeply felt. . . .

*To the same*

BOSTON, 23 *October*, 1897

MY DEAR SIR ROBERT, — I have so far presumed on your friendship again as to give a line of introduction to my dear old friend Professor Hill, of Harvard, who may perhaps be in Devonshire this winter. He is the head of the Harvard department in which I have taught for so long. His wife's illness has suddenly called him to England; and this has left unexpectedly on my hands a good deal of his work, which is why I write now, a fortnight after he sailed. I have been busier than I can tell you.

Professor Hill is in aspect an elderly man, and has been so since he was really a young one. In temper, on the other hand, he is one of those who cannot grow old. For years he has been one of the kindest and most intimate friends I have ever had, and one of the most entertaining of companions. I am sure that if he comes to Devonshire, and if you manage to meet, you will all like him.

His absence, as I said, has made me very busy; and as usual occupation proves tonic. I am quite recovered from the lax depression of the summer. We are at home in town again; and all in good condition.

This afternoon we have been to a small reception for Lord and Lady Aberdeen, who are passing through Boston. For my part, I merely bowed; but Lord Aberdeen impressed me queerly. If his eyes were not too close together, he would be a notable looking man. As it is he looks wrong somehow; sincere, enthusiastic, kind, but distorted. I never saw a face which so expressed the limits which one would look for in a radical peer — a man who does not quite understand that he is engaged in destroying his own foundations. As for Lady Aberdeen, what I chiefly remarked were enormous clustered pearl earrings — of smallish pearls. That ornament is so utterly *démodé* hereabouts as to make it salient. A large, kindly-looking woman; but somehow excessive. It was really an odd ten minutes, to look at these people, and remember, with an effort, that for a while they are vice-regal. . . .

*To the same*

BOSTON, 19 *December*, 1897

. . . I am just at present deep in an effort to reproduce, from various documents, an old memorial window, destroyed in 1805, in which my emigrant ancestor, in 1656, had what purported to be his arms painted. Mrs. Greenough has offered, as a Christmas present, to give me a book-plate; and I naturally prefer this old Dutch design. There are various bad copies of the window, and worse of them. By comparing these, however, one of which is a faded hatchment of about 1750, which belonged to Dr. O. W. Holmes, I think I have got pretty near the real thing. Instead of having the arms engraved as if indubitable, I am going to have a small picture of the window,

with its bold old Dutch scroll-work, and its original inscription and date. When a church was built at Albany in 1656, the emigrant Wendell was "Regerenden Dijaken" — which I take to be Ruling Elder — of the Dutch congregation. So the window, which he gave the church, bore his name, his office, and the date. Where the arms came from, we have no further record; they have an analogy to those of the contemporary Dutch admiral Jan Evertsen, whose family name, apart from this mere patronymic, I can't find; and as my ancestor was commonly called, after the Dutch fashion, only Evert Jansen, I think there may have been a relationship. This is all guess-work; but the window was a fact, nearly 250 years ago. And very few American families have heraldic records so old. When the plate is done, I will send you a copy. . . .

*To his Mother*

BOSTON, *3 March*, 1898

DEAR MAMMA, — ... Bob Grant came in late yesterday afternoon, to tell me that the overseers, of whom he is one, yesterday confirmed my appointment as professor. It was not in last night's *Transcript*. This morning's papers I have not seen. The news, then, is not officially public; it may fairly be held final, however, and I think will be welcome to papa.

Last night I went, as I had been engaged to do for some weeks, to a dinner given to M. René Doumic, a French critic now lecturing at Harvard, by young Hyde of the senior class. Hyde, whose father is head of one of the large insurance companies in New York, has given a fund of $80,000 to establish an annual lectureship at Harvard for eminent French men of letters. Doumic is the first of these to come. He is a funny little man — incredibly thin and pale, and totally free from English. My French is not excellent. We managed, however, to exchange commonplaces. . . .

You asked me the other day about Norton. He is now seventy-one years old, and feels, I believe, his power of holding large classes not what it used to be. He will be made Professor Emeritus — whatever that means; keeping the title, and a pension, I suppose. He will not give up his small classes in Dante. A serious loss he will be to Harvard, at best. With obvious limitations, he is by far the most accomplished of our surviving teachers, and almost the last gentleman of the fine, distinguished sort which the last generation had, and which mine does n't. But he grows old, retiring while he can still do so with grace. . . .

*To Sir Robert White-Thomson*

CAMBRIDGE, *4 April*, 1898

MY DEAR SIR ROBERT, — ... For a month the country has been in great suspense over the troubles with Spain. At this moment, it is impossible to foresee from day to day what may occur. I cannot too warmly phrase, however, my admiration for the conduct of President McKinley, in whom I was not prepared for either unusual discretion or unusual firmness. From the beginning he has stood with dignity, decision, and broad-minded humanity at once for national honor and for all that civilization means, in its best sense. He has proved himself, whatever happens, one of our great men.

Should war come, our coasts will feel insecure. New Castle, for example, I should feel to be in danger. At Portsmouth there is always stored coal enough for a good-sized fleet; and the Navy Yard is an admirable place for naval repairs. Meanwhile, the place is virtually undefended; and would be so useful a base for operations against Boston, or even New York, as to attract Spanish attention. In New England, I dare say, we are unduly alarmed. We really fear, I think, that in case of war, our coast — almost everywhere accessible — may be attacked by privateers. Spain, I think, like ourselves, refused to agree to that provision of the treaties concluding the Crimean troubles which abolished privateering in Northern Europe. . . .

The most welcome phase of our own troubles, meanwhile, has been the extraordinary change in our popular feeling about England. The diversion of national hostility to Spain, with a blundering realization of what war might mean, has made people, far and wide, suddenly feel, as never before, how closely our principles and those of England are allied. Should trouble come to either country, one almost begins to hope, the other would give it full sympathy, after all. . . .

*To the same*

NEW YORK, 26 *May*, 1898

DEAR SIR ROBERT, — I send you to-day a paper with a brief notice of my father's death. . . .

How clearly you were impressed by his character I do not know. Really, it was one of almost childlike simplicity. I have never understood how he chanced to achieve material success. As I knew him, he seemed rather of too trusting, unsuspicious a nature to grapple with the ruder facts of life. He came of the oldest gentry of America. From the emigration, about 1640, his ancestors had always married into families who, foolishly or not, held themselves bound by their blood to maintain the traditions of a gentle past. His father, however, had met with utter financial misfortune; and he was compelled, when a mere boy, to leave his home, and to make his own way unaided. The very pride which was his moral safeguard in boyhood kept him, in a way, singularly solitary until late in middle life; and bred in him some of the superficial eccentricity of personal isolation. My grandfather's period of misfortune, which came just when my father was old enough to remember it, had involved some cruel hardships of a personal nature. My father, I think, never quite forgot them; he was never the first to seek a friendship. Those which came to him — and toward the end they began to be very many — were for that very reason perhaps all the more tender.

In the few days which have passed since he died, there have come literally hundreds of kind letters, not one of which would have failed to gladden him. None of us suspected either how widely he had come to be personally known, or how constantly the simplicity and sweetness of his personal nature, revealing itself unchecked in the mellow days of his maturity, had endeared him to people of whom we had hardly thought as knowing him at all.

To me personally his affection and his generosity had been unfailing. He thought, and I believe rightly, that I had not quite the robustness of temper which is demanded for success in the stress of American life. He unstintingly gave me, then, the means which were essential to whatever I have been and done. And, in overestimating what little I have accomplished, he took a simple delight for which I shall always feel thankful. . . .

I write all this because I feel sure, after our twenty-four years of friendship, of your deep interest in me and mine. Before long, I will write again, answering your last kind letter. To-day, my heart is too full to speak of anything but this, I was going to call it this great grief; but even as I write I begin to know more and more that, in memory, these days will not be so much days of sadness as days of wonderful, deep tenderness, which will make life mean more of good than one dreamed was in it.                      Always sincerely yours,

BARRETT WENDELL

*To the same*

MATTAPOISETT, 12 *September*, 1898

. . . The war was constantly in our minds at Portsmouth, when the prisoners from Cervera's fleet were confined on an island in the river. The kindness with which they were treated, and the cordially superior feeling they seemed to show, were very striking. It was a needless war at the moment, I think; but part of a world-movement as old as the time of Queen Elizabeth, and thus inevitable. It has brought us grave political perplexities; but it has united our national feeling in a way which has gone far to check sectional misunderstandings, and it has certainly done much to make our people feel the true community of our national life and purpose with those of England. The neglect of our own armies by incompetent "political" soldiers, resulting in much actual starvation as well as mortal illness, is the worst phase of it all. The spotless conduct of our navy is the best. . . .

*To William James*

[*James delivered at Harvard, in 1898, the second of the "Ingersoll Lectures on Immortality," then recently established by a kinswoman of Wendell's in memory of her father.*]

BOSTON, 5 *November*, 1898

DEAR JAMES, — I am really grateful for your Ingersoll lecture — both because of the friendly thought it betokens, and for a reason quite personal to me. Miss Ingersoll was a cousin of my mother's, and when she died, I think, had no nearer kinsfolk than we. She was a queer little gentlewoman, very mysterious in her migrations to unexpected, though never very remote, places. Until the last months of her life, I had thought mostly of her oddities, which did not invite alert human sympathy. Then, one day, lying sick with cancer, she unexpectedly sent me a farewell gift — an old mahogany chair left in Boston by a Tory uncle "to be kept till these unhappy troubles are past," in '75. I wrote a cordial line of thanks. A little final correspondence followed, mostly messages on her part, together with queer, miscellaneous additional gifts — a wooden panel from where my great-grandmother was married, in 1790, etc. And before the end came, I found myself rather unduly caring for this old cousin whom I had never cared a bit about before. We found that we both loved the old traditions — little traditions almost ours alone — that had come sifting down from the century that neither of us had known.

Your lecture, then, bringing what had seemed her whimsical foundation into serious vitality, is touchingly welcome to me. Whatever else, it is a fine bit of thoughtful literature — a thing so good that, once possessed of it, we should be the poorer without. And in its ardent foresight of other worthy words to come, as the years pass, it justifies my dear old cousin's life in a way I had not quite looked for. Were my threshold lower, I feel now that grateful words would come from her — if so be it there is really a beyond. So let me speak them in her name as well as in mine.

### To Sir Robert White-Thomson

BOSTON, 25 *December*, 1898

DEAR SIR ROBERT, — Just a line of Christmas greeting from all of us to you and yours. By the time this gets to you it will be almost, if not quite, twenty-five years since I knew you first, somewhere between Gibraltar and Malta. There is no memory of that quarter century which I find more constantly pleasant to think about. . . .

The day is a hard one, I fear, for my dear mother, at home in New York, where everything is so full of association with the past. For a good many years now I have kept my Christmas here, with my own little people. So I don't realize the great change quite as fully as if there were an actual absence here. But, as the months pass, I find my sense of my father's personality growing more and more vivid. For the first time, I begin to understand what the world-old sayings mean which have asserted from furthest time that human consciousness bears in itself something which should evidence immortality. Not that we can believe it without revelation; but that the instinct thereto is so strong that, to simple minds, it must be overwhelming. . . .

# VI

## THE PROFESSOR: HARVARD, ENGLAND, FRANCE

### 1898–1907

In the years from 1898 to 1907 Barrett Wendell, whose appointment as Professor of English at Harvard College was confirmed March 2, 1898, exemplified to the full the term *fructuosus*, which he had found "the final word" for Cotton Mather. He was fruitful in his teaching at Harvard, in his lectureships at Trinity College, Cambridge, and the Sorbonne, in his production of books, in the extension of his studies from letters to life, so that more and more his writings in the field of criticism and the history of literature came to bear the stamp of an individual social and political philosophy. In this period his personal experiences and his published writings bore, in general, a close relation each to each. Let us look at them as a single series of facts, and then draw upon the abundant correspondence of the time for his own chronicle of all that was passing.

In 1900 he published one of his most substantial and valuable books, *A Literary History of America*. In its relation with his own life this may be said to have sprung from his routine work as a teacher rather than from any departure from the beaten track. It was, however, anything but a routine book. In its critical survey of American literature through the seventeenth, eighteenth, and nineteenth centuries, it kept steadily before the reader's mind the close interrelation between the history, political and social, of England and America with the history of American literary production. This was accomplished in a highly individual manner. Believing firmly in the early and continuous existence of definite social classes in American life, Wendell, in his entire honesty, made no pretense to any other belief, and was capable of writing so frankly of one group of writers as "socially of the better sort, either by birth or by achieved position," that he brought inevitably upon himself the condemnation of those who held the more traditionally American view of "democracy" and democratic principles. Wendell's own view of democracy — developed more fully in such later books as *Liberty, Union, and Democracy: the National Ideals of America* and *The Privileged Classes* — was less a social attitude than a philosophic position. In stating and defending it, he obviously indulged himself at times in the peculiar pleasure he took in exciting the antagonism of the literal-minded; but his general position — that in a democracy, involving, like every other structure of society, the existence of classes, the important thing is that no class shall enjoy privileges at the expense of another class — he was constantly ready to maintain with all seriousness. If the implications of this view did color his *Literary History of America*, it would be magnifying their importance quite out of scale to let them obscure the essential value of the book. This consists in its fresh and vital interpretation of American literature in its intimate relation with English and American history, its unmistakable showing of first-hand thought and appraisal, often so individual as to provoke dissent from this reader or that, but always so honest as to command respect.[1]

The broad extension of Wendell's reputation which followed the appearance of his *Literary History* must have contributed directly to the demand in which he

[1] An abridged edition of the book, prepared in collaboration with Chester Noyes Greenough, now Dean of Harvard College, appeared in 1904 under the title: *A History of Literature in America*.

found himself, during the next few years, as a lecturer away from Harvard. In this capacity he went to the Pacific coast in the summer of 1901, to England in 1902–03, to France in 1904–05.

The first of these expeditions, undertaken for the conduct of a course in English composition at the summer school of the University of California, was memorable chiefly for an episode which brought upon Wendell a newspaper notoriety quite foreign to his taste. A clipping from the *Fresno* (California) *Republican* for 4 July, 1901, records the circumstance, with appropriate comment: —

"Professor Wendell of Harvard, who is teaching a class in English at the summer school in Berkeley, asked his students to state in writing what they expected to get out of the course, intending, no doubt, to find out the mental attitude of his students and at the same time to see what sort of English they could write. One feminine student wrote that she had 'come to the university lured by the fame of the great professor from Harvard,' whom she had long worshipped from afar off, 'to sit at his feet and gather inspiration from his gifted lips.' This extraordinary effusion Professor Wendell characterized as 'disgusting slop,' and said that he had never known a woman to make such a fool of herself on one page. Very impolite of the Herr Professor, to be sure, and probably injudicious. But, really, what was the stuff but slop, and what did the writer do if not make a fool of herself?"

This was not an episode calculated to increase Wendell's respect for women as college students. But one of the Harvard legends of the period to which the California story belongs should be recalled, for its reminder that young men are not invariably satisfying as pupils. This tale, with some basis of truth, is to the effect that a band of runagates in one of Wendell's larger courses conspired to give him a miserable hour on a certain day by bringing into his lecture-room a number of alarm-clocks carefully set to go off at intervals as the exercise proceeded. I hope the story is true that, after standing a few of the bombardments of sound, Wendell gathered up his books at the outbreak of a third or fourth and stalked in silence towards the door. I hope also that just before he crossed its threshold — for this is a part of the legend — still another alarm sounded forth from a clock within his easy reach; that he snatched it up, and once outside the building, hurled it against the wall with a vehemence which put its rousing powers to an end. The serious shortcoming of the story is that the language with which these actions were accompanied — the language of a master of English — has not been preserved. If it were a story at all typical of the discipline maintained in Wendell's courses, it would be told only to his injury. As it is, it may be taken to represent an ingenious but unsuccessful undergraduate attempt to discover what Wendell would say in a situation so disconcerting, and how he would say it.

A second excursion from Harvard into other academic surroundings occurred in 1902–03, when Wendell was appointed by President Eliot to represent Harvard at the celebration of the Tercentenary of the Bodleian Library in Oxford and at almost the same time received an invitation to deliver the Clark Lectures at Trinity College, Cambridge. This Clark Lectureship, established through a bequest of a former Senior Fellow and Vice-Master of Trinity, provides for a course of not less than twelve lectures in one academic year in the literature of England from Chaucer to the present time. Wendell possessed rare qualifications, both social and professional, for the post of Clark Lecturer. Accompanied by his wife and his two younger children, William and Edith, he established himself in Cambridge in the autumn of 1902 and, after a midwinter journey to Egypt and Rome, again in the spring of 1903, taking up old and making new friendships, giving — in the vernacular — as good as he got, in the multiform social relationships springing from the cordial reception of an agreeable American into the inner circles of English academic and domestic life.

Near the beginning of the book, *The Temper of the Seventeenth Century in English Literature* (1904), which embodies the substance of Wendell's Clark Lectures, there is a brief passage which lends itself well to the presentation of the author "on his own terms." It reads as follows: —

Having grown to think of literature not only as a lasting expression, but as a lasting expression of the meaning of life, I have grown to care for it mostly, not as an historical fact nor yet as an æsthetic, but rather as a temperamental. The literature of any nation may be likened to the talk or to the letters of men we know. What we come to care for in our friends is not their circumstances but themselves; we feel that we confidently know them not when we can glibly state facts about them, but when, with such indefinable certainty as assures us of the savor of a fruit or the scent of a flower, we can instinctively recognize in each the qualities which are peculiarly his own. So a literature seems to me most interesting, and most significant, when we consider it as the unconscious expression of a national temper.

It was to the sympathetic study of English literature in the seventeenth century in the spirit of this statement that Wendell devoted himself throughout his Clark Lectures. The spirit of another statement, found in the preface to the book, animates its pages: "Loyal Englishmen can never be Americans, nor loyal Americans Englishmen; but no patriotic loyalty can ever affect the truth that Englishmen and Americans are ancestrally brethren." Revealing an intimate familiarity with English letters from the Elizabethan period to "the age of Dryden," and a gift of generalization which would have rendered any of the apparatus of pedantry foreign to the book, it is notable particularly as a milestone in Wendell's progress along the road which led him in his studies of literature, always in its relation to history, more and more to the consideration of life and human society in the large.

After the year at the English Cambridge, Wendell's teaching at Harvard was resumed for a year (1903–04), and this was followed immediately by the year in France which may be counted as the most fruitful in all his life. At this time Mr. James Hazen Hyde, a young graduate of Harvard, — in the Class of 1898, — had already proved his devotion to the cause of a closer intellectual relation between France and America by providing for visits from French scholars as lecturers at Harvard. It was a natural extension of this plan to set up a reciprocal provision, under which Harvard scholars should visit France. Thus the system of French Exchange Professorships came into existence, and Barrett Wendell was chosen as the first of what has become a distinguished line of Harvard professors to represent American scholarship in France.

Before he sailed on this pioneer mission his fellow-members of the Tavern Club in Boston gave a farewell luncheon in his honor. His capacity to see the humor of a situation involving himself was never better illustrated than when, in his few characteristically inflected remarks about the lectures he was soon to deliver at the Sorbonne in English, he declared the French so familiar with the written word of our tongue that he had of course been chosen to address them as the most typical exemplar of the spoken word.[1] To illustrate his further capacity to meet the French on the terms of their own *esprit*, a single anecdote should be related. Asked by an academic Frenchman — not in Paris, but in Cambridge — to tell why Yale had taken for its motto *Lux et Veritas*, Wendell is said to have replied, as if providing a joke for a *Lampoon* drawing, "*Parce qu' à Yale la vérité est toujours un luxe.*"

Whatever his hearers in France may have made of his diction, there is no question that his lectures were conspicuously successful. At the first of them the attendance was so great that it was necessary to move the audience from a smaller to a larger lecture-room; and the interest in the Paris course was notably sustained. At the provincial universities — for his work included a tour of these — he met with the same enthusiastic reception. In Dijon, the pupils of the Lycée Carnot, under the direction of Professor Charles Cestre, gave, on May 25, 1905, a performance of Wendell's *Ralegh in Guiana*, at a *Matinée Anglaise, Dramatique et Musicale, donnée par la Société des Amis des Études Anglaises et le Club Anglais*. Everywhere the visiting American, his wife, and younger daughter — his younger son being established at school in Geneva — were welcomed to the intimacies of academic and family life in a manner which conferred upon month after month the value of an extraordinary social and intellectual experience.

The general subject of Wendell's lectures at the Sorbonne was defined as "American Ideas and Institutions." They were based largely upon a chapter, "The American Intellect" which he had recently contributed to the Cambridge Modern History. This, in turn, was

---

[1] In a note to Mr. Hyde, written from the Cymric, 13 October 1904, the day after the Tavern Club luncheon, Wendell said: "I just discover that the club has crowned its kindness by sending aboard for me a case of champagne. It will be interesting to attempt at once the doing of justice to this hospitality, and the preservation of superficial sobriety."

an outgrowth of his *Literary History of America.* The
Paris lectures were indeed a broad survey of American
literature and life, with topics ranging from individual
authors to such subjects as Colonization and Education.
In its more general aspect, the substance of the Paris
course is to be found in the volume, *Liberty, Union and
Democracy: the National Ideals of America* (1906), of
which the immediate basis was a course of Lowell Institute
lectures delivered in the autumn of 1905. This is a
thoughtful, suggestive book, testifying to its author's
devotion to the principles of American nationality, as
he interpreted their expression in 'the Revolution, the
Civil War, and the resulting order. For the meaning of
democracy to him, as an American, one portion of a
passage dealing with Abraham Lincoln may be regarded
as representing the core of Wendell's thought: —

Our people of America are not the rich, nor yet the poor;
they are not the learned, nor yet the ignorant; they are not the
wise, nor yet the foolish; not the good, nor yet the erring.
From the beginning to this day the true people of America has
been composed of all alike — rich and poor, learned and ignorant, and all the rest together, each in his place, none unworthily
secure, however high his place, none undeservedly oppressed,
however low. And what makes Lincoln our most magnificently
comprehensive man of the people, in whose name he spoke so
earnestly, is that among all the varied and changing classes of
which that people has been and shall be composed, there was
none which he could not meet on equal terms as one of
themselves.

"Each in his own place, none unworthily secure,
however high his place, none undeservedly oppressed,
however low": these words command a special emphasis for their honest statement of Wendell's essential
feeling with regard to democracy in America. They
embody a doctrine applicable to all the world.

The book from which this passage is taken might have been written if Wendell had never served as "First Lecturer on the Hyde Foundation at the Sorbonne and other French Universities." So he described himself on the title page of *The France of To-day* (1907), a book which owed its origin entirely to this experience, and came into being in the form of a series of Lowell Institute lectures — Wendell's third course on this foundation — delivered in November and December of 1906. The selection of "best books," one or a hundred, in any category is a perilous business; yet the reader of Barrett Wendell's writings who assigns the first place among them to *The France of To-day* cannot possibly go far astray. In this work he had a subject on which, through personal experience enjoyed by one peculiarly qualified to profit by it, he was well informed. Setting out to tell simply and sympathetically what he knew about this subject, he produced a genuine contribution to knowledge, definitely flavored with his own personality, but more straightforward, less marked by little excursions into the deliberately startling — which sometimes seemed the indulgences of the "bad boy" in him — than almost anything else he wrote. The pages are filled with felicities — for a single example: "The French are given to writing things which they would not say; English-speaking men are given to saying things which they would not write." For the larger content of the volume let the titles of its chapters speak: "The Structure of Society," "The Family," "The French Temperament," "The Relation of Literature to Life," "The Question of Religion," "The Revolution and its Effects," "The Republic and Democracy." In dealing with these topics one by one, Wendell explained the Frenchman to the Anglo-Saxon in a manner which made the France of 1914–18 more intelligible than otherwise it could possibly have been. The book, excellently trans-

# Université de Paris

## FACULTÉ DES LETTRES

Paris, le 12 Mars 1921

Madame,

La Faculté des Lettres de l'Université de Paris a été profondément émue par la mort de Monsieur le Professeur BarrettWendell. Dans la première réunion de son Assemblée qui ait eu lieu après que cette nouvelle lui fût parvenue, le 19 Février 1921, elle a décidé d'envoyer à l'Université Harvard et à la famille de l'éminent professeur , l'expression de sa respectueuse sympathie. Elle est fière de penser que c'est chez elle que le Professeur Barrett-Wendell a brillamment inauguré la série des cours que n'ont pas depuis cessé de venir faire en Sorbonne les Maîtres de la grande Université Américaine. Désireux de donner un témoignage durable de sa reconnaissance envers l'homme qui par son enseignement à Paris et par son mémorable livre sur La France d'Aujourd'hui a ouvert une ère nouvelle dans les rapports intellectuels des deux pays, elle a décidé à l'unanimite de donner le nom de Salle Barrett-Wendell à l'une des salles de conférences de la section de langue anglaise de la Faculté.

Le Doyen, en vous transmettant cette délibération , vous présente Madame, ses respectueuses sympathies.

*Ferdinand Brunot*

OFFICIAL NOTICE OF THE NAMING OF "SALLE BARRETT-WENDELL"

lated into French by M. Georges Grappe as *La France d'Aujourd'hui* (1910), was hailed by thinking Frenchmen as a faithful interpretation of their national life and genius.[1] The editor of the *Revue Politique et Parlementaire* introduced an article, "Le President Roosevelt," which Wendell contributed to the February 1905 issue of that periodical with the words: "*La lecture de cet article montrera que l'honorable M. Barrett Wendell n'est pas seulement l'un des professeurs de belles-lettres les plus distingués de son pays, mais qu'il est aussi un des hommes qui en connaissent le mieux la psychologie politique.*" This editor may well have felt conscious of a certain prophetic instinct when he came to read *La France d'Aujourd'hui*. It is no wonder that the French approved the book so highly as they did — or that after Wendell's death the authorities of the Sorbonne paid him the unique honor of naming one of its lecture rooms "*La Salle Barrett Wendell.*"

To return to Harvard: In the year after the death of Barrett Wendell's father, the Jacob Wendell Scholarship was established (1899) under his will in Harvard College. It provided an annual stipend of $350 to be awarded without regard to the financial need of the contestants for it. Both the source and the nature of the foundation made it an object of peculiar interest to Wendell himself. This interest had a characteristic expression in a practice he adopted soon after the establishment of the scholarship, and maintained throughout his life — the practice of giving a dinner each year in his own house to the latest winner of the scholarship, its previous holders, and a few

[1] It should be recorded that M. Emile Faguet, reviewing the French translation of the book in three issues of *France-Amérique* (July, Sept., Nov. 1910), challenged its title and some of its statements on the ground that Wendell had seen intimately only a single class — the academic — of French society, and declared that the book might better have been called *Étude sur la bourgeoisie française*. At the end of his final article, however he wrote: "Il a écrit sur notre pays un livre qui ne le cède guère à celui que Taine a écrit sur l'Angleterre."

sympathetic older friends. Among these guests from time to time were counted President Eliot, President Lowell, and Archbishop (now Cardinal) O'Connell. It was a quiet symbol of his belief that "the gentleman and the scholar" should be something more than an ancient phrase.[1]

For nearly twenty years the Harvard College Catalogue has contained, in the pages devoted to "Degrees with Distinction," a statement of the provisions for winning one of these degrees in the field of History and Literature. The terms on which it is now awarded represent a very bulwark of "humaner letters" in a modern university. It ought to be recorded, to Wendell's credit and in illustration of his manner of doing things, that the establishment of the History and Literature degree at Harvard had its origin at a dinner party in the Tavern Club, to which he invited a few students chosen by his son William, then an undergraduate, and a few congenial younger members of the College faculty. Thus a project of real and lasting importance was launched. In its full development it constitutes a most fitting memorial to Wendell's own devotion to the intimately related studies of literature and history.

The chief domestic event in this period of Wendell's life was the marriage of his daughter Mary, September 8, 1902, at New Castle, New Hampshire, to Geoffrey Manlius Wheelock of the Harvard Class of 1901, whose business in China obliged the young couple to establish themselves immediately in Shanghai. Even before Wendell visited the Far East — nine years later — the horizon fixed by his closest affections was thus vastly extended.

For the presentation of Wendell "on his own terms" we may now turn yet again to his letters.

[1] The practice of the annual dinner to the Wendell Scholars has been continued by Barrett Wendell's sons.

## LETTERS
### 1899–1903

*To Sir Robert White-Thomson*

BOSTON, 25 *March,* 1899

. . . My project of running abroad this summer seems a little less hopeful. One reason is that I do not need an outing as much as I thought I should — having grown steadily stronger in general condition for some months past. Another is that I don't feel sure that the expense of a foreign journey would yet be prudent. My affairs have turned out much more comfortably than I feared last summer. My income from my father's estate, which has been admirably settled, will be rather larger than the variable allowance he made me while living; and will suffice, with my salary, to give me somewhat more than I have generally spent in the year. But the margin is inconsiderable, and there is no indulgent parent to fall back on, and my expenses are almost at their highest — with B[1] in college, and Mary in the finishing stages of education. So I hesitate to spend a thousand dollars or so on myself.

Have you met Mr. Choate, our new Ambassador? He was a friend of my father's, and one of his pallbearers. By chance I have personally known every ambassador to England since Mr. Lowell. They have all been good men. Choate is full of wit, and really full of kind feeling. I had some very sympathetic meetings with him last spring. But he is a queerly impulsive man in speech. I do not feel quite sure that he will be so well understood in England as Mr. Bayard was, or Mr. Phelps, or Mr. Lowell. As a professional lawyer, he is abler than any of them, though. . . .

*To his Mother*

BOSTON, 13 *May,* 1899

. . . I went to Cambridge on my bicycle. Edith, with a lot of girls, came out after luncheon, to see the freshmen play Exeter. I went for an inning or two; but they chattered so abominably on both sides, with a view to disconcerting the

---

[1] The constant nickname of Wendell's son, Barrett.

other, that I came away in utter disgust, and took a ten-mile ride to heat my feet and cool my temper. I wish B had taken to some sport which would allow him to behave in public like a gentleman. . . .

*To Sir Robert White-Thomson*

MATTAPOISETT, 14 *August*, 1899

. . . I am writing very constantly this summer on a *Literary History of America*, which I think I have mentioned to you before. A publisher wanted the book; and I agreed to write it some time ago. The work has proved so arduous and tedious that I am trying to make a resolve never to write a line to order again. What makes this job worse is that I am trying to use a stenographer — to dictate rather than write. One gets ahead at a tremendous rate; but in such appalling style that pretty much every sentence must be recast. There is an advantage, however, in having the work all blocked out. And blocked out it will be, from beginning to end, by the middle of September. . . .

*To the same*

[*Wendell had just received news of the wounding of Sir Robert's son Hugh in the Boer War.*]

BOSTON, 17 *December*, 1899

. . . At last, then, this anxious war takes for me a really personal character. Throughout, however, as you will have known without the assurance, I have felt the deepest sympathy with your cause, eagerness for its success, and sorrow for the reverses which for the moment bid fair to prolong the contest. In this feeling I happily find myself at one, I believe, with all that is best in my own country. The last two years have awakened the better intelligence of America to what seems to me the great political fact of the future. As the world grows, the older systems of thought and government which used to exist independently are forced into struggle with one another for dominant survival. Europe, which long ago mastered America — our civilizations do not differ — must equally master Asia and Africa.  And among European ideals there must be another struggle, in which the moral conceptions and the Common Law of England must be pitted — to stand or fall — against all the rest.  Herein the British Empire and our own United States seem to me indistinguishable.  Whatever their family differences, their common language, their common law, and their common ideals of righteousness distinguish them from all the rest of the world.  The success of either means the advancement of what is noblest in the other, too; the misfortune of either is a danger to a common cause.  A while ago, in this deep feeling of mine, I was not always sure of sympathy hereabouts; now, I think, it grows constantly deeper and deeper.

In no way, perhaps, does one feel it more certainly than in the assurance everywhere that what to any powers but England's or ours might mean defeat is no more than a terribly sad check.  Even among those who preserve to some degree the old unhappy tradition of mutual hostility, there is not a shade of doubt that nothing can break the spirit of your people and your arms.  The moral strength behind them, then, appears all the more potent and inspiring in its hour of trial.  To your country, as well as to you, I send earnest hope that the worst is past. . . .

*To the same*

BOSTON, 23 *June*, 1900

. . . Let me express my sympathy with your loss in the death of your old friend . . . This comes to me the more to-day because one of my dearest friends — Mr. Augustus Lowell — suddenly died yesterday morning.  His sons — Percival Lowell, whose astronomic work is well known; and Lawrence Lowell, whose writings on Parliamentary Government are authoritative — have been among my intimates from boyhood.  For years, then, I have stayed at Mr. Lowell's house almost as one of the family.  He was a man of such strong self-assertion that many people found him repellent.  This very strength of personality endeared him to those with whom he was on affectionate terms.  The sense of loss which comes to my wife and me, then, is poignant. . . .

*To Robert Herrick*
[*After commenting on his novel,* The Web of Life]

St. Andrews, 11 *August,* 1900

. . . As to Chicago and New England, I think you fall into the "vulgar error" of forgetting that the New England which you and I have known has been a region past the zenith of its maturity. In two centuries and a half, a remarkably homogeneous race, with strong characteristics, was geographically isolated. A sudden, great accession of wealth and material activity — East India trade, cotton-spinning, and railways — suddenly waked the region into conscious life. Then, amid Unitarianism, Transcendentalism, and Reform, came a surprisingly fine flowering of ripe national character. And now the region is virtually extinct. Chicago, on the other hand, is new, and won't reach its true ripeness for ever so long to come. But other seeds are planted there, I believe, than those of Alcibiades and Creon — the two flowers of great materialism. It takes long to raise flowers anyway. Remember what Dante wrote of Florence:

> *La gente nuova e i subiti guadagni*
> *Orgoglio e dismisura han generata,*
> *Fiorenza, in te.*

Yet, in Dante's day, almost all the true splendors of Florence were to come. The dawn shows blemishes; but if Dante had had Shakespere's gentleness of temper, he would have been too great to emphasize them. And anyhow, he wrote the *Paradiso*.

"*In la Sua voluntade e nostra pace*" sometimes seems to me the biggest line of all. Evil itself is divinely willed; and when we can so perceive it, our setting forth of life harmonizes with the deep music of eternity. Only then is it all we can make it.

*To Sir Robert White-Thomson*

Boston, 4 *November,* 1900

. . . I have asked Messrs. Little and Brown to send you, from me, a copy of the life of Parkman which has just appeared. The author — a certain Mr. Farnham . . . had been, I think, a sort of secretary of Parkman's. . . . In my opinion, the book is among the best biographies I ever read. Parkman was a man of very marked individuality. This Mr. Farnham has so justly recognized and so faithfully set forth that, as I read the book, I was constantly aware of an almost uncanny sense that Parkman himself was hovering about. You can trust the book, then, in the matter of fidelity. And knowing how much you have valued Parkman's work, I thought you would be glad to glance at this pen-portrait of the man. . . .

*To the same*

BOSTON, 23 *January*, 1901

DEAR SIR ROBERT, — The death of the Queen comes to the whole world with such an overwhelming sense of personal bereavement that, in writing you this expression of sympathy in what would have seemed only a public sorrow, I feel rather as if I were trying to express much more tender and intimate emotion as should arise from the loss of a dear and trusted friend. In all human history, it seems to me, there has been no other character like hers — from girlhood to extreme age unfalteringly, simply faithful to every ideal of duty. And, so far as every record goes, it would seem that in her private life, among those with whom her relations could be such as exist between human beings in the little group of kinship and of friendship, she was as true, as kind, as steadfast as she showed herself in that public life which was surely the most noble of modern times. So, as the years passed, she had insensibly become — far beyond her own dominions — the chief earthly embodiment of what is sweetest, and best, and most trustworthy in human nature. There are myriads of us who had no direct share in her beneficence, yet who had come to feel confidence that her presence in this world made all the world more safe, more stable, more justifiable in the eyes of the eternities. I, for one, have found myself to-day literally moved to tears for the loss of her. And throughout this country, which has so often felt itself almost inimically hostile to the mother-country — at once misunderstanding and misunderstood — the stars and stripes, on public buildings and on private alike, are generally, spontaneously, at half-mast. Your loss is not yours only; it is that of all the unperverted world.

I am glad that you found Farnham's *Parkman* so interesting. To me it seems a wonderfully faithful biographic portrait — disguising nothing, and so revealing in the end a personality which, with all its infirmities, must remain among the most admirable I have had the fortune to know with intimacy.

You ask about the Divinity School of Harvard. The official school of the University began as a seminary of orthodox Calvinism, Congregational in discipline. It became Unitarian about 1805. Of late years it has called itself non-sectarian; and has developed, or degenerated as you will, into a very unspiritual, useless school of religious history and philosophy. The Episcopal School, of which Dean Gray was head, and later Lawrence, — our present bishop, — has no official connection with the University, beyond certain library privileges, and so on. It is extremely liberal, but not heretical. . . .

*To the same*

BOSTON, 24 *February*, 1901

During this past week two welcome greetings have come from you — the *Post*, with the admirable mention of Hugh's gallantry, who will always stay first of all in my memory as the very little boy of the Broomford Harvest Home in '74; and, what touched me most deeply, the *Times* and the note which you sent with it. That you found what I wrote you worth such commemoration is at once a surprise and a great and grave pleasure. I am glad, however, that my name did not appear.[1] Not that I would for a moment hesitate to acknowledge anywhere the sentiments which I wrote you; but that it has always seemed to me obtrusive for one of no wide fame to name himself in connection with persons or with events which are of great significance. When Mr. Lowell died, you may remember, I did not at first sign the record of my memories of him which

[1] Neither Wendell's name nor that of Sir Robert White-Thomson appeared in the London *Times* for February 7, 1901, in connection with the greater portion of the preceding letter, published there as from "a well-known professor in the University of Harvard." Nowhere else in his correspondence did Wendell express with such emotion his feeling for the mother country and the Victorian order.

appeared in *Scribner's Magazine.* I afterwards included them, to be sure, in my little volume, *Stelligeri,* because they really formed part of the lines of thought which I there attempted to bind together, and the volume had, in its very existence, a kind of assertion of my personality which rendered the anonymous nature of the original publication no longer needful. In the case of this little tribute to the memory of the Queen, on the other hand, there could have been no just reason why any stranger should care to know from what unknown pen it proceeded; the fact which the words carry — that it came from a human heart here across the Atlantic — seems to me the only germane one.

I find myself, indeed, apt to shrink more and more from personal publicity. My occasional work as a man of letters compels me now and then to publish my name. But my actual life is so quiet, so remote from any public activity, that any mention of me in the public prints always seems a bit impertinent. It amounts to troubling people with a name which, to most of them, must stand for nothing else than the letters which compose it.

Did I write you that I am going for the summer to California, where I have agreed to give some lectures at the State University? I long for a change of scene, which is there offered me at no personal expense. I hope now that my wife, or B, or both, may come out and join me, travelling home through the Canadian mountains. . . .

*To the same*

BERKELEY, CALIFORNIA, 30 *July,* 1901

Your welcome letter of June 23d came to me here a week or ten days ago. I left home on the sixth of June, and came hither slowly. Two days at Niagara, to begin with, made me feel the beauty and splendor of the falls as never before. The Pan-American Exhibition at Buffalo was disappointing. Then I visited Malcolm Greenough at Cleveland, where I took a steamer on the Great Lakes, which brought me to Chicago in three days more. Then my friend, Morse Stephens, joined me — an Oxford man who used to lecture at your Cambridge, and is now Professor of History at Cornell, where Goldwin Smith used to be. We have been together ever since. We stopped for a week in Arizona, to visit Percival Lowell at his observatory in Flagstaff, where he is studying Mars; and to see the wonderful Grand Cañon of the Colorado. So to San Francisco, and out here, across the bay, in full sight of the Golden Gate, where I have been lecturing ever since June 27. The work has proved unexpectedly tiresome; but the region and the people one meets are delightful. This is my last week of duty. My wife and B arrived here a few days ago. They are now gone to the Yosemite. On August 5 we all start for Alaska — Stephens with us; and it will take us, I imagine, till mid-September to stray home through the Canadian mountains. I wish you might have been able to join us. The journey has proved even more interesting than I expected. . . .

*To the same*

St. Andrews, 18 *September*, 1901

. . . When I wrote you last, I think, we had almost ceased to be anxious about the President, from whom the official reports were at first so reassuring. His death, then, came with a suddenness almost as appalling as if the murderous shot had been instantly fatal. In this remote little Canadian town one can tell what is happening at home only from the newspapers. From them it seems as if our people were bearing this national affliction with a simple, grave dignity and solemnity, which is deeply reassuring concerning our national character. McKinley, whom I never saw, impressed me more and more in his public life. From mistrust — years ago — I grew first to indifference, and finally to almost unqualified admiration. Thoroughly honest and patriotic, he had a wonderful tact in feeling what was the best popular sentiment at any moment, and so embodying and making potent the best will of the people. Thus he was the most efficient and the most truly representative president of my time. Roosevelt, who succeeds, is an old personal friend of mine — a man of admirable character and incredible energy. In talk he has often been a bit hot-headed; but never, I think, in conduct; and the tragedy of his accession has evidently affected him tremendously. His name, by the way, is pronounced in the Dutch manner — Rōse, the oo = *w*. . . .

*To the same*

FROSTFIELDS, NEW CASTLE, N. H., 24 *September,* 1901

My very last mail at St. Andrews brought me your letter of sympathy in our great national sorrow and tragedy. I have written you already, I think, how the news of it, coming to me across the border, was strangely benumbing — like some sharp sudden physical shock. Our president, of course, can never present himself personally to our feelings quite as a sovereign. He is more like a premier, who passingly represents the power of a party or a constituency. As an individual, he cannot so possess himself of our imagination and our affections as a life-long and devoted ruler, like the Queen, possessed herself of everyone's. But this does not affect the cruel horror of that dastardly crime. McKinley was a simple-hearted, honest western gentleman, devotedly patriotic, sincerely trustful of our institutions, and tactful to a degree which gave him more power of influencing our national policies than any other president has had since Lincoln's time. Our immense national growth in his time, and our great material prosperity, have given rise to much honest, as well as to much partisan, attack on him, and to great manifestations of discontent — attacks on organized capital, strikes, and the like. The phrase which constantly comes to my mind is that of the Litany: "From envy, hatred, and malice, and all uncharitableness, good Lord, deliver us!" These world-old views are what have found expression in the most wicked act of murder I have ever known.

And already, I think, one can feel that something far from evil is springing from the sacrifice of a good, true, earnest life. In his last moments, they say, the President repeated that simple, trite old hymn, "Nearer, my God, to Thee"; and murmured, "It is God's way, not ours; His will be done." And there has come over the whole country, for a while, a deep sense of simple, solemn faith. There has never been, in all my life, a time when I have felt such certain faith in the essential health and strength of our people as I have felt during these days when, united by common sorrow, they have held themselves in grave and gentle restraint, at once repeating, each in his own tongue, the simple words of faith which the dead man taught; and resolute, at least for the consecrated moment, that each would strive all the more to do his duty. It has been a period of true communion, purifying the past, sanctifying the future. No act of a living man could have had quite such depth of significance as has come from this heroic death.

As to anarchy, it cannot be crushed by force. It is a spiritual disease; or rather it is a madness which would strive by material means to avert disorders and discontents of the spirit. All we can do is to make the right-minded see and know its shameful follies. And, just for the moment, there is hereabouts such deep and just horror of it all as must be the surest preventive of its spread. . . .

*To Robert Herrick*

[*Apropos of his novel*, The Real World]

CAMBRIDGE, 20 *November*, 1901

. . . Every step you take is a step forward; and this is the longest of all.

And yet the old regret lives still, that you can't yet free yourself from the bitterness of youth. Humour, as such, one does n't ask or wish for. What one does long for is some deeper touch of sympathy — of pity, of loving-kindness. Your Elsie is so real, so true, that I put down the record of her, more than once, to ponder — for the instant — on the pity of it all. I don't mean that you should preach; perhaps I mean rather that you should preach, in mood, a little less. But, for God's sake, don't forbid the years to teach you tenderness! When that comes, such work as yours will turn — of an instant — into such work as those who care shall know and shall feel lasting. . . .

*To Mrs. John L. Gardner*

[*Apropos of the completion of her house and private museum,
Fenway Court*]

BOSTON, 2 *March*, 1902

DEAR MRS. GARDNER, — . . . May I add, however, a few
words of how deeply I am moved by what I hear of your house
and of its purposes. More and more, it seems to me that the
future of our New England must depend on the standards of
culture which we maintain and preserve here. The College,
the Institute, the Library, the Orchestra, — and so on, — are
the real bases of our strength and our dignity in the years to
come. Such things as these — everything of the kind which
we have had in the past — are in their nature inevitably
corporate, coöperative. None of them can possibly have that
touch of final distinction which can come only from a plan
controlled by consummate individual intelligence. And what
you have so quietly and so surely done seems to me not only a
thing in itself beautiful and admirable beyond anything else
in our country, but also a kind of public service, which would
have been done by no other human being, and of which the
influence must remain increasingly, incalculably great. Quite
apart from all feeling of personal regard — a feeling of which
you can need no assurance — I wish thus to express to you
how deeply I am grateful to you, as a citizen of New England,
who loves his country.

*To the same*

BOSTON, 23 *March*, 1902

DEAR MRS. GARDNER, — I have tried, more times than I
dare confess, to write you this word of what a wonderful impression stays with me from that afternoon, two weeks ago.
You must have thought me, when I was there, stupidly silent,
but the silence came from a kind of wonder that would not
confine itself to any form of words — that will not yet.

For the work you have done could be done only by a genius
of which I have never known quite the like in kind. It has
chanced to be the lot of these great imaginations which leave us

works of art that, almost always, they must begin with no other riches than those of tradition making, each for himself, some fresh and living thing of beauty. Now, in a way all your own, with the power of summoning all these beauties of the past, you have put each one in the place for which it seems as if the centuries had preserved it. You have combined in new, living symphony melodies which seemed complete each in itself; you have given each and all a new meaning; and with a power, it seems to me, which can make you feel the masters only your fellows. And I am lost in wonder that, even in our own times, such power of imagination may still be.

Above all, as an American of New England, I feel, as I wrote you before, glad beyond words that this work of living beauty has been wrought here, where I had felt that the glories were only of our own little past. Now that I have seen, even in these passing glimpses, what seems to me the most nearly perfect work of art which has grown anywhere in the years of my own time, there comes from it a great, measureless surge of happiness and of stimulus. One must do one's own best, to merit right in a world and a time when such standards may still be.

I am inarticulate, no doubt, and perhaps comically ethical. But believe me that no work of human imagination which I have ever seen has touched me in quite the same way as this work of yours.

*To the Rev. L. H. Montagu Butler, D.D., Master of Trinity College, Cambridge*

BOSTON, 23 *March*, 1902

MY DEAR SIR, — I have great pleasure in accepting the kind invitation of the Council of Trinity College to give the Clark Lectures next year. No invitation could have been more welcome or more timely. I have long wished to see something of university life in England, to which I am thus called under the pleasantest of auspices; and before I had any inkling of this, I had already made plans to go abroad next year. Apart from the gratification which such an honour would bring in

any event, I have the unusual personal satisfaction of finding
it in complete harmony both with my wishes and with my
domestic and professional arrangements.

Dr. Cunningham, in the letter sent with yours, suggests
that the most convenient times for the lectures might be the
autumn and the spring. Since I wrote him the other day, the
President of Harvard College has kindly made me a delegate
to the Bodleian celebration in October. As I shall thus be in
England during that month, then, Dr. Cunningham's suggestion seems to me happy. I am disposed to propose four lectures
during the Michaelmas term, and eight in the spring, at what
dates may subsequently prove convenient.

The subject which now seems to me most interesting is the
English Literature of the Seventeenth Century; and this
because of the conspicuous change of temper in English
literature between 1600 and 1700 — a change more marked
than that which has occurred in any other hundred years.
The subject, too, would lend itself to the division of the lectures;
in the autumn I could discuss the decline of the Elizabethan
spirit, and in the spring, what ensued. May I ask whether this
subject would be acceptable to the Council?

My wife joins in every cordial acknowledgment of the kind
personal cards which come from you and from Mrs. Butler.
The American friends you mention chance — some of them —
to be friends of ours, too. Mrs. Bayard we have known well
for many years; and Mrs. Choate was a friend of my father's.

Sincerely yours,<br>
BARRETT WENDELL

*To Sir Robert White-Thomson*
[*After the marriage of Wendell's daughter Mary*]

NEW CASTLE, 10 *September*, 1902

. . . I have been ill for some three weeks; and got up for the
wedding only by judicious use of stimulant. . . . So yesterday
I was down again, and wondering whether I should ever be
able to get away. To-day I am free from pain for the first
time in three weeks; and the doctor assures me that I have
turned the corner. We have been obliged, however, to put off

our departure a second time — until the last moment which will allow me to meet my engagements at Oxford, for the Bodleian celebration. . . .

*To the same*

51 JERMYN STREET, 18 *October,* 1902

. . . Your very kind letter was waiting me here on our arrival yesterday afternoon. We find these lodgings extremely comfortable — far more so than those we formerly had at Wedderspoons, and, if I am not at fault in matter of memory, no more expensive. My old friend Professor Goodwin, the Greek scholar, has stayed here while in London for many years. As friends of his we are received with flattering respect. The situation, of course, is not particularly quiet; but for sightseeing visitors to London none could be more convenient. . . .

London, as is always the case, rather overwhelms me. I feel what Baedeker rather comically calls "the first oppressive feeling of solitude and insignificance." In fact, I think, if one is not constantly engaged, a great city where one is virutally a stranger proves the most chastening environment which can be imposed on self-esteem. At Oxford, we had — or found — many friends. This afternoon I must leave a few cards; and Sir Samuel Way writes me that he has kindly arranged that I be made an honorary member of the Athenæum. But the bustle and rush of it all makes my head swim. . . .

*To the same*

RÖNAVINA, [WEST ROAD, CAMBRIDGE], 15 *November,* 1902

You will be glad, I fancy, to hear of our pleasant fortunes here. The solitude of London — with all its Byronic depression — lasted only a few days. Then Edith and I left the children there, with our friend Miss Ogden, and came for a Sunday, and my first lecture, to Trinity Lodge, where the Master and Mrs. Butler were most kind. We had supposed that we could easily find lodgings in Cambridge, to which we could move on Monday. But there were none to be had, and the Newmarket races had literally filled every hotel in town. So they most kindly asked us to remain for several days at the lodge, while we were looking for quarters.

We found at last this comfortable small house. It belongs to Mr. Tucket, a fellow of Trinity, who is away for the term, and who had left in charge a responsible and energetic cook. There are just the number of bedrooms our party needs; of course, we brought down the children at once; and nothing could be more comfortable. So, for this month of November, we are as thoroughly at home in Cambridge as we should be in Marlborough Street. People have been most cordial, too. The card-plate is overflowing. We have many invitations to lunch and dine out; and so on.

I particularly like Cambridge, which — rather to my surprise — is far more like Harvard in its temper than Oxford seems. Except for one day at Ely, where we went to lunch with the Bishop and Lady Alwyne Compton, and for another in London, when I went to meet Dr. Parkin, the Rhodes Scholarship agent, and found myself in the midst of the Lord Mayor's Show, I have not been away since the 24th. My lectures are going quietly — the audience containing few men. English literature — here as at home — is a subject which appeals chiefly to the feminine mind. The whole surroundings are resting me wonderfully. In fact, as somebody put it, I am demonstrating the hitherto unremarked possibility that Cambridge has value as a health resort.

My last lecture comes two weeks hence. Early in December we shall start for somewhere — probably Egypt; returning to England at the end of April, when we shall probably take another house here. Edith has been looking at one in Brookside, occupied for this term by Professor Westlake. . . .

*To F. J. Stimson*

TAORMINA, 14 *March*, 1903

. . . We had two lazy months in Egypt, and have had a delightful week here. I know no other place which so combines sea and mountain — immemorial humanity and inexhaustible beauty. The shepherds actually play folk-tunes on the heights, miles away, as one walks. And the faint music swims in the air, like true bird-song. . . .

*To the same*

PALERMO, 24 *March*, 1903

. . . We have been here two or three days, and shall linger two or three more. I like Sicily immensely. Eight years ago, when we were so long in Rome, I lost my Italy. Here I have found it again — an experience like making up with some old love with whom one thought one had quarreled for good. There is a touch of Greece about the country, too — something deeper than the mere accident of history. Even if there were no ruins at Girgenti, the very landscape would make one feel — in that impalpable, unmistakable way — as one feels in Argos or in Elis. And again, the older buildings hereabouts make backgrounds so romantic that I remember how, in '68, my first glimpses of Europe set me to scribbling wild melodramas.

*Robert le Diable*, with that delightfully absurd ballet, seems sober history in the cloisters of Monreale. I don't a bit wish to go back to England, though it will doubtless be pleasant when I get there.

*To the Master of Trinity*

12 BROOKSIDE, [CAMBRIDGE], 2 *May*, 1903

MY DEAR MASTER, — Though unable to go so far as Khartoum last winter, I asked a friend who was going thither to bring me for you — if it could be found — something which should be a true memento of Gordon. It seems that in the palace garden, or thereabouts, is a rose-tree, which he is believed either to have planted or to have cared for. And from this my friend picked a bud — the only thing she could find there which seemed to touch him personally. Very likely the story of the rose-tree may be a mere legend; but this little flower surely grew near the spot where he met his heroic end. And I have thought that perhaps you would like to have it from me, in token of the feeling which has sprung within me, from all the kindness you have shown me and mine. For the only token which could express the nature of that feeling must be one whose value springs from the heart.

*To the same*

AMSTERDAM, 4 *July*, 1903

My wife wrote an instant answer to your letter of farewell. I tried to; but somehow I could not. And even now it is hard to send you any word which should not seem either too formal or too free from restraint. On the whole, though, I am almost glad that by chance we had no definite and conscious parting at Cambridge. My dear old grandmother used to tell me of an uncle of hers, who lived in Paris, eighty years ago and more. He came home to New England only once, where everybody welcomed him. At last, one day, he was not to be found; and it turned out that he had slipped away to sea, and so back to Louis XVIII's France, without a word of good-bye. The tale always seemed to me odd. But now I can understand it. I came — with more self-distrust than you can perhaps have guessed — to a strange world. Your kindness, and the kindness of so many others which ensued, have made that world seem to me like another home. I have left it now, and finally, with some such tug at the heart-strings as would come with the knowledge that I was going away from the regions which are really and immemorially my own. It is better to go without formal farewells to those whose kindness has meant most. There is no need of words, when one's heart is sure and confident. . . .

With every cordial and grateful thought of you both, I am always,

Affectionately yours,

BARRETT WENDELL

*To the same*

THUSIS, 20 *July*, 1903

. . . This is a mere friendly line, to tell you of our journey so far, and to send you a Harvard poem which seems to me memorable.

It was delivered at the annual meeting of our Phi Beta Kappa Society — an association to which some fifteen or twenty of the highest scholars of each year are admitted. For nearly a century now, the society has held an annual meeting at which an oration and a poem are given. Usually, of course, these are rather perfunctory; though the men invited to deliver them are apt to be people of distinction. So sometimes they are memorable.

This year my colleague, Professor Briggs, Dean of our faculty of Arts and Sciences, gave the poem which I enclose. It seems to me a delightfully simple and sincere expression of the spirit we like to believe that of Harvard; and certainly it is the most delightful celebration of Harvard written of late years. I add here a few notes — numbered on the copy.

1. John Harvard, the founder. An Emmanuel man who died very young, leaving most of his property to the lately established college, which was consequently named for him. Nothing is known of him personally. An ideal portrait of him, in bronze, was given to the college some twenty years ago; and sits, facing westward, before the western gate of our great — or large — Memorial Hall. My wife and I gave a small plaster copy of it to Emmanuel, while we were at Cambridge.

2. A few years ago a large field was given to the college, for open-air sports. The giver requested that it be called "Soldiers' Field," in memory of dear friends of his, Harvard men, who fell in the Civil War. Their names, here repeated, are inscribed, with a beautifully simple dedication, on a stele, under a tree at the entrance of the field. The two Lowells were nephews of the poet — and their heroic deaths had much to do with the fervour of his Commemoration Ode.

3. Henry Higginson, the donor of the field. Perhaps the most generous and hearty benefactor of his time in New England. A man of large means, he has not only given freely to the college, but he has virtually established in Boston, at his own charge, an orchestra of excellent quality. Personally he is the embodiment of generous bravery, and of what we used to call "quality." A direct descendant of Francis Higginson, one of the principal emigrant ministers to New England, in

the earliest days. Higginson was severely wounded when serving as major in our Civil War; and his grave face is deeply scarred.

4. Ralph Waldo Emerson
5. Phillips Brooks
6. (probably) James Russell Lowell
7. Theodore Roosevelt
8. Charles William Eliot, President of Harvard College. Whatever one may think of his policy, no one can question his devotion to the ideals he believes in, nor yet the extraordinary energy and courage with which he has advanced them. He came into office in 1870. Since that time, both the numbers and the endowment of Harvard have been quadrupled.

I think you will like Briggs's lines. Do not return them. Two other copies have been sent me. I had no idea that I should become so prolix a scholiast. . . .

LETTERS
1904–1905

*To James Hazen Hyde*

NAHANT, MASSACHUSETTS, 25 *July*, 1904

MY DEAR MR. HYDE, — It was only on Friday that I could see President Eliot, who alone could tell me enough about your kind invitation that I lecture in France to make acceptance possible. I need not tell you how deeply the plan interests me, nor how heartily I hope that my work may prove useful.

May I ask now for information which will help me in preparing it? I assume that I am expected to give about forty lectures at the Sorbonne, concerning literature in America, and that selections from these are subsequently to be given at provincial universities; that the method will be impromptu speaking from notes, such as I use at Harvard; that the ordinary rule of work will be two lectures a week; and that no other systematic instruction, such as personal conferences with students, or the conduct of examination, will be called for.

My precise questions, accordingly, are:

1. Am I quite free to choose my subject, within the general range of literature in America, a subject which may naturally include reference to American history, and to other than literary aspects of American expression, such as architecture, for example?

2. Is it possible for me to know the precise dates on which the Paris lectures are to be given, with any occasional recesses or vacations, such as our Christmas recess, which may occur? It is my custom to make a complete plan of any course I deliver at Harvard, before I begin it at all; and making this, a fixed calendar is essential.

3. Do the social probabilities involved make it desirable that I look for quarters in any particular part of Paris? I have lately been apt to stay there at rather small family hotels pretty well up toward the Arc de Triomphe. The last, I think, was in the Avenue Kléber; and was fairly satisfactory.

4. My wife and my youngest child, a girl of ten, will go abroad with me. For various domestic reasons, it will be

convenient for us to delay starting as long as may be. What is the latest date, in general, which we may prudently choose?

5. At what time in July will my engagement end? I may probably desire to return home for as much of the summer as remains.

*To the same*

NAHANT, 4 *August*, 1904

. . . By October I will have ready a sketch for the Sorbonne course. The subject, so far as I am informed, is pretty comprehensive. At present, I incline to develop the sketch of American characteristics which I published, about two years ago, in the seventh volume of the *Cambridge Modern History*.[1] There it had to be compressed within thirty pages; but there is enough in it for as many lectures, or more. Should you chance to have time to glance at it before we meet, I should be glad to know whether you think my plan good.

I need not add how deeply I feel the seriousness of the task before me; and how heartily I appreciate the friendly words with which you welcome me to it.

*To Robert Herrick*

[*Wendell had been appointed Chairman of the Section of English Literature at the Congress of Arts and Sciences at St. Louis in August, 1904.*]

NAHANT, 25 *July*, 1904

I am delighted that you consider coming to St. Louis. Choose my section — English Literature — by all means. You could have no better topic than "Tendencies of Modern Fiction," which will give you scope for all your heresies. Personally I know little of the plans for the Congress, my information being derived wholly from three or four circular letters bearing the autograph of Münsterberg. The real truth seems to be that

---

[1] This substantial contribution of nearly thirty large octavo pages to the *Cambridge Modern History* (Vol. VII, 1903) had for its title "The American Intellect." In the letter from G. W. Prothero — one of Lord Acton's three successors in the editorship of the History — asking Wendell to write this chapter, it is interesting to note that the editor was "encouraged by Principal Eliot" to extend the invitation.

one must bear one's own expenses. The consideration is really the chance of meeting, at once, a remarkable number of noteworthy people.

Since I saw you, all my plans have been turned upside down. I have decided to go abroad, on leave of absence, for this coming year, to give lectures in English at the Sorbonne, concerning literature in America. Do you desire me to consecrate one of them to you? If so, what are your terms for such services?

Don't preserve this important inquiry. It might be taken seriously in years to come, when your life and letters are prefixed to your sadly complete works.

*To James Hazen Hyde*

NAHANT, 18 *September*, 1904

. . . Various inevitable distractions have prevented me even till now from making detailed notes for my lectures; but this does not disturb me. While I shall be unable to prepare everything completely now, there is in my *Cambridge History* article quite material enough for the task now before me. The only real question becomes one of proportion; and that can best be determined, perhaps, only when I am confronted with the actual situation in Paris. I purpose, in brief, conducting this course precisely as I conduct my courses at Harvard, making a broad general plan, and considering matters of detail from week to week, as the lectures develop themselves in delivery. . . .

*To F. J. Stimson*

HOTEL COLUMBIA, 16 AVENUE KLÉBER, PARIS[1]
13 *November*, 1904

DEAR FRED, — Except for the touch of suggestion that you are n't pulling together as quickly as I had hoped, your letter of the 27th was a complete delight. It came last Tuesday, just as I was starting with William for Switzerland. I stayed there for two days — one at Vevey, where I saw the Dwights in delightful rooms, happy as human beings can seem; and one

---

[1] The Paris letters are all written under this heading.

at Geneva, where I have left William to speak French in the home of two delightful old gentlewomen, and to study various things with a competent tutor across the way.

Here I am in a real whirl. I have a lot of letters, which are already beginning to involve no end of correspondence of a friendly kind. I foresee endless distraction from the main work in hand, which will begin on Saturday, the 19th. It has been postponed for two days, on account of the engagements of the Dean of the Faculty of Letters, on whom apparently falls the duty of introducing me. . . .

*To James Hazen Hyde*

PARIS, 17 *November,* 1904

. . . M. Liard[1] has kindly offered to procure for the library any books I may desire. I do not feel sure that I shall need any — certainly I shall not immediately. But I think that, when I have time to breathe, I shall prepare a list of books concerning literature in America, and leave it at the library as a suggestion of what they should procure if they desire to be fairly supplied with authority on the subject.

As to ourselves, we came rather stormily to England, and had a delightful week of visits at Cambridge. Then we came on here where we put up at this small hotel. Though not ideal, it is on the whole more satisfactory than anything else I have found. We have a small apartment of five rooms, quite apart by themselves on the fourth floor. It is remarkably sunny and full of fresh air as well as of steam heat. One is tolerably fed. The terms are reasonable. We came within an ace of taking a really good apartment on the Avenue du Bois de Boulogne; but it proved pre-empted from New Year's and so I think that we shall quietly stay here.

I will write again when the lectures are under way. . . . I am constantly more and more impressed with the importance of this work I am charged with — as well as with the extraordinary work you have accomplished in bringing together the intellectual and academic life of America and France.

[1] Louis Liard: Recteur de l'Académie de Paris, from October 1902 to September 1917.

I am to speak at the Thanksgiving dinner of the American Club; and M. Peixotto is desirous that I should write an article on Roosevelt for a French review. . . .

## To F. J. Stimson

PARIS, 20 *November*, 1904

DEAR FRED, — Well, as Paul Bourget said to me at luncheon, I am momentarily "le lion de Paris." So many people — including at least one tenth of the Academy — came to my opening lecture that they had to adjourn from a hall that would seat three hundred to one three times as big. And there was no standing-room left at that. And everybody listened as if it were Gospel. And what it was God knows — I hope — in the actual case, as we are sure He does in the hypothetic. And Hyde fixed all the papers. And I am equally civil to legitimists and radical Jews. And I find a certain difficulty in writing English. And Croiset says my French letters are quite remarkable for a foreigner. And we have been to a big dinner at René Doumic's, with a lot of *Revue des Deux Mondes* people. . . . And we have just come from a cozy little dinner of six at the embassy. And old Madame Taine has captured my heart. And, not having slept — for excitement — over night, I am now going to read myself to sleep. . . .

Affectionately yours,
BARRETT WENDELL

## To James Hazen Hyde

PARIS, 27 *November*, 1904

DEAR MR. HYDE, — Many thanks for your telegram of congratulations. The lectures begin with astonishing success.[1] At the third, yesterday afternoon, the crowd was larger than ever. The hall seats eight hundred; the aisles were packed with people standing; and they listened like a model congregation. Apparently too, there were more French, and fewer Americans, than before.

[1] General Horace Porter, U. S. Ambassador to France, 1897–1905, wrote, December 1, 1904, to Mr. Hyde, apropos of Wendell's first lecture: "The audience had to adjourn from the Salle Turgot for more room and even then hundreds were turned away; and the last man that got in had to leave his cane outside."

If the course were to be no longer than the French ones with us, there would be no question of its effect. Whether the length of it will not necessarily involve anticlimax when the novelty is great, remains to be seen. One thing I think certain: viz., that a regular foundation here for lectures in English, or American, would command sympathetic attention and alert interest, to a far greater extent than anyone anticipated. The only trouble would be the choice of lecturers who should at once be reasonably solid and have the knack of holding their audiences; in the latter respect, I find myself a fairly good man for this opening course. As to the former, I am less content; but nobody has been too critical so far. I am eagerly interested in the work, and more and more impressed with the admirable international intelligence of your plans and your execution of them during the last ten years.

Meanwhile, I am assiduously attending to the social duties involved — very pleasant, but somewhat absorbing in the matter of time. Mme. Taine has been particularly kind, introducing us to a number of her friends. Then we have a few friends apart from those to whom you presented me, particularly the Paul Bourgets, whom we knew through their intimate friends, Henry James and Mrs. Wharton.

M. Liard kindly told me, as I wrote you, that the Sorbonne would buy any books I needed. A cursory review of the catalogue shows the condition of the library, in American authorities, very bad. For example, they have no Henry Adams; no Rhodes; of Franklin they have only the old Sparks edition, now known to be both incomplete and garbled; of Washington, nothing; of Daniel Webster, nothing; of Emerson, only one volume in an English reprint; and so on. The only sensible thing to do in such a case is to give them a fair general bibliography, indicating what they might get, if need be. . . . It is not a matter of supreme importance, anyway. My notes, I find, go a long way to serve my actual purposes this year. It is clear, however, that a respectable collection of authorities on America at the Sorbonne would be made only by a really considerable donation. A few odd books here and there would not help things much. . . .

*To Charles Knowles Bolton*

PARIS, 29 *November*, 1904

. . . You will see me, in all my eloquence, covering half a page or so of the last *Illustration*. The image is not beautiful, but sincerely expresses my present attitude as it appears to the eyes of these friendly French.

They are far more hospitable than I had been led to expect. They ask one to dine like Englishmen. And I am now coquetting with the editor of the *Revue Politique*, who desires me to write him ten pages on Roosevelt. . . .

*To the Master of Trinity*

PARIS, 1 *November*, 1904

MY DEAR MASTER, — The weeks since our idly pleasant days with you and near you at Cambridge have been for me the busiest I ever remember. There could be no sharper contrast than that between my Cambridge lectures, of two years ago, and the lectures which I now find on my hands here. At Cambridge, all I had to do was once a week to read before a quiet little academic audience some carefully written comments on matters three centuries old: I hope, by the way, that you have by this time received the copy of them which I asked my English publishers to send you, in my name. Here, I have twice a week to improvise, from rather elaborate notes, before a public audience of more than a thousand people, comments — any one of which may give rise to criticism — on the actual state of affairs in my own over-sensitive country. At Cambridge, our many kind friends after all formed part of one tolerably united society. At least, so far as I could discern, they were not incompatible; or at least, whatever their personal differences, they might be mentioned to each other. Here, at an extremely confused political moment, the duties of my office compel us to meet an extraordinary variety of people — all kind, all hospitable, all interesting — half of whom, I more than suspect, really believe the other half deserving of the guillotine.

Tact has not hitherto been thought my most salient quality; but I am now trying to develop it with all my might. . . .

*Le Professeur Américain, M. Barrett-Wendell, faisant sa première conférence dans l'amphithéâtre Richelieu à la Sorbonne*

*Croquis d'après nature. — L'Illustration, 26 novembre, 1904*

*To F. J. Stimson*

PARIS, 18 *December*, 1904

So far as occupation goes, this is the time of my life. People of very various kinds are more than hospitable; so we lunch and tea and dine out at a rate which makes my head whirl, and gives my eccentric digestion no leisure to desist from duty. My oddities tend to stomachic concentration. I collapse, internally, when exposed to the test of domestic repose. Sixty miles an hour in an automobile, luncheon at a chilly country inn, with no change of knives, a nice drenching on the way home, and a diplomatic dinner of which the simplest incidents are foie gras and sweet champagne, prove complete tonics. Incidentally I am trying to learn that the one thing I can't do is to get physically tired; wherefore, God help me, my waistband is four and a half inches longer than it was in August, 1903. My tailor says so; and his books are gospel.

The lectures have really succeeded. The ninth came yesterday, — which makes about a third of the whole course, — and the audience still fills a big hall, all but the back seats of the gallery. It is a queer experience, to be taken seriously. I don't know how good the things are; but they are an honest attempt to set forth, in various ways, the queer fashion in which a half-recognized idealism has been, from the beginning, characteristic of native America — at once its motive and its salvation. It interests Frenchmen: a lot come regularly, with no suspicion that I am not as serious a fact as Eliot, or you, or Roosevelt, or Curtis Guild, or Bryan, or the Rev. Dr. Rainsford, or Henry van Dyke, or Mrs. Eddy, or Mark Twain, or George Fred Williams, or Gompers, or Andrew Carnegie. God help me, I don't want to be a humbug; but I can't help the accident which now compels me to pretend to an importance almost as imposing as that even of J. J. Roche — whom I reverence as ethically and morally uniquely our better. It will go on till March. Then I shall swing round the circle of the provinces.

And I shan't be at home again much before September.

The French people we have met have been really hospitable, till I understand what they mean by *foyer*, and have a conception of their literature quite different from my old one. On the other hand, as is the case at home, I am queerly out of it academically — having hardly any relation with the Sorbonne people. There was never a more queer career than this solitary, blind one of mine, flapping wings skyward through mists which distract my eyes, and those that look at me as well. . . .

*To the same*

PARIS, 28 *December*, 1904

. . . I envy you — under these grey winter skies — that marvelous California. It seems to me, more and more, the region from which fine art in America ought to come. Incidentally, as you have not remarked, it is the first spot on earth where English-speaking humanity ever bred on the same soil with sound wine — wine which fulfills an old definition of yours, constantly dear to me as settling what one should gulp: it is pure, and cheap, and makes you drunk.

Here the days pass like dreams, and pleasantly digestible ones. It is a fact that I can't sleep on plain cooking any more; but truffles and champagne are ambrosial. The chief trouble with this quiet inn is too much omelette and steak, not for my appetite, but for that to which my appetite entrusts them. There is no doubt about the actual success of the lectures. The twelfth came yesterday, just between Christmas and a week of vacation; yet the audience was well on to five hundred. I think I have given them sound stuff, too. In perspective, the essential idealism of America, peeping through all kinds of material surface, surprises me more and more. What is to come thence, God knows; but then He knew in the *Federalist's* time, when all looked darker than now. Imperial democracy is a tremendous fact. I think I believe in it here more confidently than amid the actual impressions of it at home. But the racial agony in which we are being strangled by invading aliens, who shall inherit the spirit of us, grows heavier with me, as the end of me — and of ours — comes nearer. . . .

*To the same*

PARIS, 21 *January*, 1905

. . . It is harder to write from abroad than from home; particularly as the conditions of life here, now that they become habitual, are so pleasantly monotonous that one hardly remembers which week is which. Work on the lectures fills every morning. Almost every afternoon, except when a lecture is due, I gravely take a *fiacre* with Edith and make calls. It seems absurd; but this kind of airing, I find, tires me less than any other. And, with the fifty years which are to round next August, I find myself comically subject to purely physical fatigue. Exercise more and more — even afoot — behaves like poison. I positively need a well-appointed stable. Saddlehorses I could dispense with; but not a proper variety of vehicles, grooms, and animals adapted to several services, day and night. Motor cars, too, begin to present themselves as matters less of luxury than of necessity. And, with my beggarly pittance of an income, I have to rest discontent with cabs; content only with the scriptural assurance that poverty on earth will probably involve celestial affluence. . . .

*To C. K. Bolton*

PARIS, 24 *janvier*, 1905

Many thanks for the Proceedings[1] . . . How mortuary that same Historical Society is; and how profoundly indigenous, after all! I contemplate directing that a complete set of the Proceedings be buried with me, when that melancholy occasion arises. This pamphlet has confirmed my opinion that, on the whole, they are my favorite reading. . . .

Here all goes pleasantly, swiftly, well. My audiences hold out incredibly. . . . Otherwise than at the lectures — and at these, too — things here grow so busily habitual that I have no more time or disposition, for the kind of thing Paris has meant to me before — museums, theatres, shops, other eloquence than my own — than I have for such matter at home. Which is mostly why I have not more eagerly offered to serve

[1] Of the Massachusetts Historical Society.

the Athenæum. But if I can, I shall be glad to — reëlected next month, or not. . . .

## To F. J. Stimson

PARIS, 30 *January*, 1905

. . . As usual, visions of penury haunt me; and I begin to wonder whether I can make my frock coat do for a second ten years. It has borne its first with more credit than I should have feared. One of the papers described my first appearance in it at the Sorbonne as embodying the type of a gentleman — as distinguished, I suppose, from a man of learning. Incidentally, the fact that I brush my hair, instead of running my fingers through it, induced in the same reporter's mind the conviction that I wear "les cheveux très pommadés." Can't you sniff the aroma of his Parisian fancy? . . .

We continue to see a lot of French people. Yesterday we lunched with a Legitimist lady, who has assumed charge of what, until Combes' time, was a convent school; and she had, to meet us, a marquis who would do at the Français, and a Secretary of Embassy fresh from Russia, where he reports the incidents less exaggerated than I had supposed. Only, it was a question of putting down a revolutionary movement compared to which — in war time — our draft riots were child's play. And, with all their errors, they have done it; which I am personally disposed to admire. We took tea with a Yankee transcendentalist, who had some radical professors to meet us. We took tea again with an incredibly clever Jew, who is among the best living authorities on the Fine Arts. We dined with a man in the Finance Ministry, and I was chummy with the prefect of police, who looks exactly like a country grocer up Medfield way, of a hustling turn of mind. . . .

## To the same

PARIS, 17 *February*, 1905

. . . A most estimable professor, the other night, gravely congratulated me on the fact that America, in spite of every temptation, has not yet produced a drama. "Le théâtre n'existe que dans la décadence."

Here it exists in a new form, oddly like the vagaries which make modern music sound to me like impure noise. The curtain goes up. A lot of people, admirably made up, talk. Nothing happens. The curtain goes down. This is repeated four times. You remark that every part is admirably performed, and that some of the phrases are very happy. Nothing has happened; but then nothing does. "La vie n'a pas de dénouements; pourquoi la scène en aura-t-elle?"

Always affectionately yours,<br>BARRETT WENDELL

Oh, I forgot. It is usual, in the third act, for all the characters to attain a pitch of emotion which compels them to blow their noses, in various harmonic keys.

## To M. A. DeW. Howe

PARIS, 17 fevrier, 1905

MONSIEUR, — Comme je le trouve de plus en plus difficile à m'exprimer dans votre langue barbare, je vous prie de me permettre de vous remercier en bon vieux français pour votre lettre si aimable. En même temps je vous offre mes félicitations les plus sincères sur l'arrivée heureuse de mademoiselle votre fille, à laquelle je vous prie de vouloir bien présenter mes hommages, aussi que celles de ma femme et de ma fille cadette. Mon fils cadet, qui suit ses études à Genève, s'y joindrait volontiers s'il aurait pu prendre connaissance de cette nouvelle si édifiante. Ma fille ainée en ferait autant; mais, craignant les désastres d'une surprise trop forte, je me suis abstenu de la communiquer à elle par moyen télégraphique. Elle se porte merveilleusement à Shanghai, où elle parait dîner en ville dix fois par semaine.

Ce que vous m'écrivez de mon histoire abrégée de notre littérature me remplit de fierté. L'approbation des maitres porte quelque chose comme une couronne magistrale.

Je resterai ici trois semaines de plus. Alors, après un court séjour à Genève, je commencerai mon tour de province, qui durera jusqu'à la fin de juin. Je compte revenir en Amèrique au milieu de septembre.

Veuillez présenter mes hommages à Madame M. A. De W. Howe, et croire à mes sentiments les plus respectueusement dévoués.

BARRETT WENDELL

*To C. K. Bolton*

PARIS, 26 February, 1905

. . . This Paris life continues full of interest. Three or four things have turned up this week. One was Brunetière's lecture — he was dropped as professor when they reorganized the École Normale, and has offered a public course in a small hall, crowded by people who oppose the Government. Another was the "reception" of Gebhardt at the Académie Française — queerly like a Signet initiation before a fashionable audience. Hervieu, the presiding officer, "roughed" him for an hour, after the manner of Kittredge. That was the whole ceremony — after his own eulogy on his predecessor. A third thing was the last meeting of the Hull Commission[1] yesterday, which was quietly impressive. Old Sir Edward Fry, in very English French, ended by quoting "Peace hath her victories," and asserting that here England had gained one by which the world might well take pattern. The last ceremony I have attended was the annual meeting of the Sorbonne, where the Rector read what was virtually a President's Report, in a magnificent hall, blazing with gold and mural painting. Whence we all passed into a second, and drank acid champagne. It was unlike a gathering of the Harvard Academic Council. Incidentally, what impressed me was the age of University professors here. To all appearances I was among the younger quarter of the company; and I am fifty next summer.

Remember me to all the Committee, and believe me,

Sincerely yours,<br>BARRETT WENDELL

*To Sir Robert White-Thomson*

PARIS, 8 March, 1905

. . . Our Parisian winter is really at an end. On Saturday I gave my last lecture at the Sorbonne; and this afternoon my

---

[1] The Paris North Sea Inquiry Commission, which settled the controversy over the "Dogger Bank Affair" in the Russo-Japanese War.

final appearance there took place, in a most unexpected way. I was officially invited to be one of the public examiners of a candidate for the degree of Doctor of Letters. My duties consisted of an impromptu criticism of his thesis, with occasional questions, before a public assembly, for half an hour; and all this had to be done in French —such French, I fear, as must have made the head of Richelieu, in the church near by, ache afresh.

The lectures, I think, have done good in really promoting international friendship. Hospitality has been incessant, too; and we have seen people of the most widely various kinds in the most friendly way. I may write some articles about France when I get home. This will not be before September. . . .

*To F. J. Stimson*

GENEVA, 15 *March*, 1905

Your last letter from Santa Barbara has just come to me here. I wish it were a shade more buoyant. In fact, I begin to think, you will perhaps feel your old self the more when you attack regular work without feeling quite up to it. What I have in mind is that, throughout this most arduous of my years, I have not had what you might fairly call a well day. It takes me in the form of internal pain and such overpowering fatigue that, half the time, I don't feel up to walking a block. But I manage to do what is to be done somehow; and at last I begin to understand that, even though many wheels of the machine are getting worn, the old thing will run somehow for a while longer. If I stopped to ease myself, I should be done for. You had to, of course; but I don't feel sure that stopping much longer won't prove worse in the end than going ahead, whatever the doctors say.

As to writing, that seems to me more and more a matter of chance — of chance whether the spirit moves, and whether the public cares to hear its utterances. Quaker meetings had their deep human sense. Those often went to bed happiest who went unmoved by the spirit and unheard by the company. At worst, they had n't made fools of themselves, or excited envy, hatred, malice, and all uncharitableness. If you never put pen to paper again, you would have done enough to be remembered by those whose thought is worth while. As to the rest, may the Lord deal with them according to His pleasure.

My Paris lectures ended on the 4th: a distinct success throughout; more so, in all seriousness, than the *Transcript* man — who was honestly afraid of slopping over — might lead you to think. The actual result of them, I believe, has been to impress a lot of intelligent French people with the fact that we Americans have our own ancestral traditions, of a noble kind. We swerve from them, of course, being human; but we do not renounce them. The more I study our country, the more deeply true this seems.

We came here on the 10th to be near William for a week. To my surprise, my Paris reputation had preceded me. The American Minister gave us a big dinner; the Société des Arts gave me a formal reception, with a lot of set speeches, which seemed to me remarkably good, for they concerned themselves mostly with matters of American history, admirably summarized; the University has formally presented me with a huge, morocco-bound copy of its official history; and I have felt bound to accept an invitation to acknowledge all this courtesy by delivering, to-morrow night, before Calvin's own academic successors, an impromptu address concerning the "Effects of Calvinism on American Nationality"! All of which implies how pleasantly restful this week of vacation has been. We have dined out every night since we got here. . . .

*To the same*

LILLE, 25 *March*, 1905

. . . To my mind, one of your most admirable qualities has been material good sense. That has to underlie the other thing in men as well as in society. The heyday of Yankee idealism was precisely that of Yankee commerce. A soul without a body is less pleasant to me than a body without a soul. Temperamentally I prefer the fusion of the two, which makes humanity human. And, though I may be mistaken, I grow more confident with the years that something of that fusion is stronger in America than elsewhere. At this distance, occupied in trying to expound our national character, the idealism of it — even to-day — seems its most noteworthy feature. The essential vigor of that idealism lies in its material basis. Money and power for their own sake are base things, if you like. Valued, as our better sort temperamentally value them, for the chances they give for individual freedom of conduct, they seem to me admirable means to an essentially ideal end. . . .

My lectures here have caught on. Paris success, I suppose, involved provincial. But the Catholics will none of me, and decline to put any mention of me in the newspapers here affected by the better sort. Inasmuch as my personal sympathy is on the whole with them at this moment, — though I keep it quite to myself, — the situation has its humours. I did not hesitate in my Paris lectures to opine that the religious history of America pointed to the conclusion that religion cannot usefully exist without due submission to not too aggressive authority. I shall amuse myself by reiterating this opinion here on Tuesday, the 28th, if God spare me so long. At this moment, His hand is laid with unusual tenderness on my physical organism. . . .

*To the same*

ARLES, 20 *April*, 1905

. . . As to my eminence, to which you pleasantly refer, I have just had a novel evidence in the smoking-room. To me, over my coffee, entered four English youths, unpretentiously of the intelligent middle-class. They were disputing as to who B. W. might be; and pouncing on a copy of *Who's Who*, they informed themselves audibly in my presence. I should have deemed this the acme of greatness if it had not transpired that the landlord had boasted of my presence in the house — assuming the whole world to know who I was. He somehow had caught on to my Sorbonne lectures — which the intelligent English youth were disposed to ignore, as "rot" or some such matter.

But it was certainly funny — funnier still in view of the esteem in which I am commonly held at home. . . .

*To his aunt, Miss Sarah Barrett*
[*On the death of her sister, Elizabeth Barrett*]

LYONS, 6 *June*, 1905

. . . Poignant as the bereavement must be to you, it is you who had the more strength to bear it. I cannot imagine how dear Aunt Lizzie could have confronted life alone; and when the worst of your illness last winter came, I was filled with dread for her. What I mean is that, with the years, she has seemed to me, unconsciously to herself I think, and I dare say unperceived by you, to have grown in nature more and more reliant; while you have seemed more to retain the strength which has always made you the one on whom we have all tended to rely.

I don't know that such thoughts can bring much comfort, if any. But I can't help feeling that there must be endless, constant comfort in the memory of your wonderfully unbroken and devoted lives together — lives which have had, I think, a singular beauty, in their quiet maintenance of all that is best, and simplest, and sweetest in the old traditions of New England; keenly alive to its higher and sincerest pleasures, serenely disdaining what is trivial and bare. I have often felt, as the years pass, that you and Aunt Lizzie, in your own gentle way, lived on the whole, the happiest lives I have ever known well. It will always be a happiness to think of you as you were together. . . .

*To Sir Robert White-Thomson*

BOUQUERON, NEAR GRENOBLE, 30 *June*, 1905

. . . My lectures really ended on Wednesday. They have been a wonderful pleasure to me; and I hope that I may be able to make a book of French reminiscences and impressions. At present, though, in this stifling heat, I feel as if I should never have energy enough to think them into articulate form. We go hence tomorrow, to pass Sunday at Moutiers, where we are to lunch with the Bishop of Tarentaire. Then we hope to find some pleasant spot somewhere in the Mt. Blanc neighborhood. You shall hear again when we are settled. . . .

*To F. J. Stimson*

CHAMONIX, 6 *July*, 1905

. . . After all, I am rather glad that we came; for the mass of Mont Blanc is really so grand as to make one forget that it is a commonplace. In life as in literature, I think, my elder taste delights more and more in the big, simple things, less and less in the recondite. Only I want a glimpse of the edge of Italy before I come home. Not a journey into the heart of it: I should be afraid of new disillusionment. But just to cross the Alps, to feel the streams running madly toward the unseen beyond, which still kindles the embers of my old boyish imagination, to get one glimpse of the half-tropical verdure, to dream of Rome really at the end of the roads, — the Rome of old fancy, I mean, not Pius X's with all its modernity, — is what I yearn for now. I rather think we shall take donkeys round the edge of Mont Blanc to Courmayeur — and shall drive to Aosta, and so northward again by the Grand St. Bernard, where the monks still breed their huge mongrels. The suppressed convents of France make me sentimentally Catholic. The Chartreuse, crammed with Sunday sightseers, almost converted me. So did the nuns at Moutiers on Sunday. European human nature can never find another religion so much to its needs. We Protestants are nobly wrong, like some drastic medicine which should do a body good by vexing his bowels. As for aggressive free-thinkers, they are socially poisonous. Unaggressive ones — like me — are just normal excretions, not worth the trouble of a prayer from the devout. . . .

## LETTERS
### 1905–1907

*To the Master of Trinity*

BOSTON, 18 *October*, 1905

MY DEAR MASTER, — Professor Palmer, who has been of us at Harvard all his life, — he took his degree in '64, — has just published, after years of quiet work, an edition of George Herbert which seems to me worthy of a place in your Trinity Library. I have ventured, accordingly, to send a copy to the Library; and, as I thought the book might interest you, I have sent it to you for a glance in passage. Palmer, who was named for George Herbert, has had a peculiar affection for his work. He has frankly set it forth in a somewhat individual manner — of arrangement, and the like. I am sure, however, that no other editor of Herbert is either so learned, or half so devoted, as this; and I am sure, too, that you will be glad to see this tribute from across seas to one of those memories which make Trinity the wonderful fact it is. When you have looked the books over, may I ask you to send them to the library, with the little card enclosed with them? . . .

*To Sir Robert White-Thomson*[1]

BOSTON, 24 *November*, 1905

DEAR SIR ROBERT,— It seems incredible that so many weeks have passed since we got home. No time has ever gone with me more swiftly, or much less productively. Two years out of three is far too great a proportion of life to spare for absence from regular duties, if these same duties are to be comprehensible. I feel, more than ever, that kind of bewildered distaste for my academic work, of which I wrote you a little in England. If I yielded to impulse I think I should give it up. On the other hand, one is unwise at fifty to relinquish at once occupation and a tolerable proportion of one's income. So I fancy that I shall end by subjecting impulse to wisdom, or such substitute for wisdom as I happen to be possessed of.

---

[1] A visit paid by the Wendells to Sir Robert and his family at Broomford Manor, as the travellers were returning home via England, was a happy episode of the year abroad.

Apart from this merely professional discontent of mine, which vexes Edith most reasonably, all has gone delightfully with us. It is pleasant to be at home — and pleasanter still to be welcomed most heartily. We have hardly dined at home — alone — in a month. It is all very informal, at this time of year, or rather it was till last night, when we dined with friends who are about to bring out a pretty daughter, and who gave her first dinner on a scale which excited my envy — happily untinged by hatred or malice. But I think nothing in life more constantly pleasant than quiet meeting with friends, few enough at a time to make the talk general. And this Boston seems even pleasanter in fact than in fancy. . . .

### To Frederic Schenck

[*This letter, written after the freshman year of a favorite pupil of Wendell's, who later became his assistant, is one of many illustrating his readiness to help the promising student.*]

NAHANT, 18 *July*, 1906

DEAR MR. SCHENCK, — . . . Now for Dante. I am delighted that you have got so much out of the reading in this first — and hardest — month. If by chance you have at hand *Johnson's Encyclopædia* — very probably it is in the Lenox Public Library — you will find Arthur Marsh's article on Dante extraordinarily good: at once compact and illuminating. The *Divine Comedy* is to me inexhaustible. I read it first in Lowell's classroom — J. R. L.'s, I mean, the most human instructor ever vouchsafed Harvard youth — in '76. What impressed me then, as well as the colossal system,

> *Vuolsi così colà, dove si puote*
> *Ciò che si vuole,*

was the supreme finality of the style, and the immensely stimulating imaginative power of a thousand phrases and passages which linger still in my mind. Dante is the only poet whom I find myself constantly quoting. Perhaps Lowell's influence had something to do with this. You might glance at what I wrote about it in a little reminiscent article at the end of my book of essays called *Stelligeri*, and, far better, you might run through Lowell's essay on Dante. When one knew Lowell, his writing always seemed provokingly inadequate as an expression of his vitality; but, now he is only a memory, I find it more living than I used to.

Dante is too vast, too complex, too remote for any summary. After thirty years, I can only recognize, not understand, the immensity of him. But two or three facts begin to emerge — perhaps I might rather say impressions, though one hates that canting, rather decadent word. In the first place, he is actually the most central fact in all European literature: he strives to comprehend and to summarize every tradition which preceded him; he does so in essentially mediæval spirit, yet he stands on the threshold of modernity. He is at once cosmic and Italian in the sense in which men are Italian to-day. In the second place, his intense mediævalism, absolutely genuine, is nowhere else so evident as in the extraordinary, superhuman complexity of his poetic purpose in his quadruple *Divine Comedy*. He meant it himself, throughout, to be at once literal, allegoric, ethical, and something else, which I never try to remember. It is the spirit of this, combined with the colossal power of his mastery, which makes him so consummate an exponent of the Middle Ages. In the third place, allowing one's self modern fantasy, it is hard to resist belief that, from the first record of Beatrice in the *Vita Nuova* to the final scene in Paradise where she once more takes her place in glory, the work of Dante expresses the growth of a supremely ideal personal passion. Do you know his consummate little sonnet: —

> *Guido, vorrei che tu e Lapo ed io*
> *Fossimo presi per incantamento?*

Put this beside the vision of Cavalcante in the *Inferno;* put all together; and you will begin to find how inexhaustible the supreme poet is. This first attack of yours must be toilsome. I can't believe that it will stay so.

In the *Purgatorio* and the *Paradiso* you will find many abstruse passages. Skip, if you like; but not so much as to lose the vast unity of the whole.

You ask if he is to be taken literally, concerning Hell, for example. No more, I think, than Milton concerning Eden.

It is enough for any poet, if he produce for the moment "that willing suspension of disbelief which constitutes poetic faith." But that he made an imaginative cosmic system is why his comedy is divine. Think how we wonder at Balzac or Zola, who made only imaginary Paris; and this man made a universe, so truly that we can fall to wondering whether he believed it actual.

As to Gibbon, Bury's edition is by far the best; but I am not sure that one can get it in America. Milman is doctored with Anglican medicament. In both the text is immortal. The true wonder of Gibbon is double. He expresses consummately the temper of the full eighteenth century; and, given his point of view, he grasps historic material with a firmness and decision unparalleled on anything like such a scale.

If Froissart bore you, drop him. Try Joinville, though; whose work, particularly the first part, is essential, I think, to the mood which would understand sympathetically the great architecture of France.

And, incidentally, if you find the things you are at repellently tedious, don't hesitate to browse elsewhere. You know the *Romance of the Rose*, I believe; and something, I suppose, of the rhymed chronicles such as Wace. *Roland* is worth reading as poetry — not as language, to my mind, for which opinion my colleagues would send me to Coventry.

Another quite different region worth exploring is the Assisi of St. Francis. Sabatier's *Life of Francis of Assisi* and his editions of the documents of the period are as well worth reading as the *Fioretti* themselves. They throw light on that wonderful canto of the *Paradiso*, just as that throws it on them.

The real thing, you see, is to prowl wherever you can and will in the regions you choose for your field. I don't know whether this rambling letter will help you. If not, ask me questions more precise. If, on the other hand, this be of any use, write again, as you did before; and you shall have the same kind of answer. . . .

*To the same*

NAHANT, 17 *August*, 1906

. . . Your kind words about *Stelligeri* are most welcome. Rather a surprise, too. That little book was, in its own way, the most genuine piece of work I have ever done. It grew, I mean, spontaneously. The different essays were written occasionally, at different times, with no thought that they belonged together. Then I flashed them together with the opening one, which gives the book its name. And hardly anybody ever read them. I can find in them now, however, the germ of almost everything which I have thought since.

The book ought to have had an epilogue, which I wrote too late—my impressions of Chicago in 1893. It is buried in the files of the *Harvard Monthly* — the October number for that year, if I remember right. If you have a spare half-hour in the college library some time, I wish you would look it up, and tell me whether you do not agree with me that it belongs with the others, and that they would be the clearer and the stronger for it.

As to the meaning of tradition, I grow more and more to believe that the commonplaces are true and that the commonplace reasons for them are so mistaken as to disguise their truth. It is like the principles of the Common Law — the courts decided right, as a rule, and were quite wrong in the justifications on which they were apt to base their decisions. One recoils from bad reasoning; one resents, accordingly, vitally sound conclusions. That is the matter with radical temper in general. The most useful work which any thinker can do is to illuminate the commonplace.

And, anyhow, the commonplaces of culture, as of society, have their value, even though hard to illuminate. They help us sympathetically to understand whence we are come; they teach us the language in which those who have recorded the past were apt to think.

> *Veut-on savoir d'où nous venons,*
> *La chose est très facile;*
> *Mais pour savoir où nous irons,*
> *Il faudrait être habile.*

Which adroitness, I conceive, is best prepared for by studying whence we came. Take your classics and your Bible, for example. Men have thought in the terms of them until modern folks who don't are like coolies trying to comprehend abstractions in pigeon-English. Which does n't mean either that dogmatic theology is so, or that it makes any difference whether you can tell subjunctives from optatives by name. The thing is to feel, so far as one can, what one's forbears have felt. The impulses of heresy are noble; so is the truth of creeds. Sometimes I grow to feel that the use of heresy is to vitalize creed. After five-and-twenty years of English, I reverence the classics more and more.

All of which is a good way from Dante. In your place, I think, I should read now in a somewhat more desultory way — skimming in the translation over the passages which are abstruse and baffling; lingering over those which seem more significant; and trying only in these instances to catch the music, the inevitable idiom, of the true text. This almost musical phase of the poem always seems to me not its least marvel. As the movement of its meaning carries one away from the depths, the movement and the sound of its phrase grows ethereal, until at last one is beyond and above this world, in a region of mystical ecstasy, such as those who feel music find hovering about the notes of some wonderful orchestra — merely sound-making, to less sensitive ears.

As to the Italian, why don't you try a few days with the *Vita Nuova?* You won't care for it, in any such sense as that in which you may come to care for the *Divine Comedy;* but it will help you, in more ways than mere language, to understand the masterpiece. I don't feel sure, by the way, that some skimming of the *Decameron* might not help, too. Except in Italian, Boccaccio seems to me unwinsome. In his own language, he takes you into the full sunshine of the early Renaissance — near enough to mediæval things to throw backward glances of light on them. . . .

*To the same*

NAHANT, 28 *August,* 1906

. . . This is n't a real letter, as the weight will have told you. It is only a line to say that the question is not of being orthodox, but of understanding orthodoxy. You touch on modern poets; you are quite right in doing so. But every one of those poets had orthodoxy behind him, to break from. And the greatest of them — Shakespere — was remarkable in his own time for strict adherence to the best fashion of experience — in all respects — then prevalent. Technically he is almost unique for lack of petty "originality." What makes him immortal is that he did best of all what all were doing.

The great moments seem to me those when energy, which has been confined by tradition, breaks the outworn bonds of it. This was the case in New England, when New England was memorable. Nothing but conscious knowledge of orthodoxy could have made Emerson what he was. Those who begin with him have as yet got nowhere.

But it is all too much to write about now. I am very glad you feel the urge of Dante, as he rises above earth. There is more of it still — along with all the theology — in his *Paradiso*.

You are right about the heretics to a great degree; but they have not proved the enduring masters of such discipline as makes individual heresy potent.

*To Senator Lodge*

[*In conclusion of a letter of thanks for a copy of Mr. Lodge's newly published volume*, A Frontier Town, and Other Essays]

NAHANT, 3 *October*, 1906

. . . May I slip into diplomatic jargon and take this occasion once more to tell you of how deeply, as the years pass, I am growing to feel the immeasurable usefulness and public service of the life you have led through all these years when I have been trying to help boys to make themselves into better men than most of them turn out. I don't mean, of course, that I agree with everything, or can pretend to understand no end of things which folks less wise even than I suppose themselves expert in. What I do mean is that, as one grows toward the end of maturity, in surroundings where more and more one feels the fatuous weakness of personal irresponsibility, — the distorting moral result of a life no one of whose words or actions can more than accidentally affect the course of events or of affairs, — there comes a constantly deeper sense of what, in fullest scope,

the lives and the careers of those few men mean who have had
the power and the chance to live their best years in regions
where their conduct makes directly for the welfare and the
future of our country. The more deeply this sentiment has
rooted itself in me, the more confidently glad I have felt that
Massachusetts, and New England, and the country, have had
you as their servant — doing, better than we praters would
ever have done and with a courage one grows more and
more to understand, the kind of public work which, beyond
all things else, stirs one's admiration, and, years ago, when
one was still young, would have kindled ambition of the true,
right sort.

## To the same

NAHANT, 8 *October*, 1906

Edith tells me that I began with the wrong paper. I don't
regret this; for it touches the chords which vibrated, perhaps
too loud, in my note of this afternoon. But I am glad that I
was steered straight to the "History" next.

It does not stir me like the others; but it sets me to thinking
more. In one point, if I understand it, I don't agree with you;
this is the question of impartiality. If impartiality in histo-
rians means inhuman lifelessness, you are right. If, on the
other hand, it means sympathy with all phases of earnest
emotion, — each in itself too intense to understand the other,
in the heat of conflict, — I think you are mistaken. Neither
Puritans nor Cavaliers were all in the right; nor Calvinists or
Unitarians in our own New England; nor patriots or Tories
in the Revolution; nor Unionists or Secessionists in the Civil
War. At least I can't feel them wholly so; nor can I arouse
myself to imaginative fervor over any great contest until I
can impartially feel it noble on both sides, in devoted sincerity
of ideals essentially incompatible and incomplete. The difference between you and me I take to be that between a man who
has known the stress of life, and thus has to be partisan in conviction, and one who has only admired it, and thus can thrill
conscientiously with pretty various impulse. It is the difference,
I fear, between real experience and quasi-histrionic admiration

thereof. But, if history be literature, it is not; and so is the poor little story which I hate, but have — like anyone who makes what living he can by spouting — unhappy community of spirit with. Your true artist, I think, must sympathetically understand much which repels his past; and therefore must be impartial. "Gossip" is the life-stuff of which history is made; documents are the mere formal expression of what gossip informally shows us. Statistics, with all the ologies they may include, are only data by which we may test our philosophers. Where you are all right is in the distinction between evolution and development; and the wonderful precision with which you remind us that we are, unawares, in a new ethnologic epoch — or is the right term anthropologic? Meanwhile, men stay men; and though they cannot generalize from older times, and probably never can, yet they can do so most nearly, not when they have classified data, like Alexandria's grammarians, but when they can feel that the race which enters remains on its new stage, — higher or lower, I don't know, — it is the same human thing which has been wise and foolish through the little flash of light which we call historic time.

### To his Mother

NAHANT, 7 *October*, 1906

. . . On Thursday evening, I expect to go to Washington with Archy Coolidge — to lunch on Friday with the President, and talk about the Sorbonne lectures. . . .

### To the same

BOSTON, 15 *October*, 1906

DEAR MAMMA, — I had a pleasant six hours in Washington, and a night at Gordon's, and another at Oyster Bay; and got home to sleep last night. A cold I caught in the sleeper is pretty well over.

Roosevelt was most cordial, full of fun, far quieter in manner than of old, and the picture of health — his skin is as clear as a child's, and his tendency to corpulence diminished. I liked his wife. . . .

My new book[1] is out, and pretty to look at; but rather unsatisfying in style. I think I shall wait to send you a copy until you get home. . . .

## To Senator Lodge

BOSTON, 31 *October*, 1906

Are you by any chance free for the evening of Friday, November 9th? If so would you be willing to come here, to meet a few students, whom we are trying to get and to keep interested in a newly established degree with distinction in history and literature? The plan is Lawrence Lowell's, during whose absence abroad the management of the affair is in my hands. About forty undergraduates — mostly of the more agreeable type — have been attracted by our blandishments. And, by way of humanizing the situation, I have asked them and the committee . . . to come here for the evening in question. I want it to be as informal and friendly as possible; no speeches, or anything of the kind; just talk and a little supper. And I am sure that nothing could help the occasion, and the effort to get students of the right sort more alertly interested in intelligent work, than the presence of a man like you, whom they all would be more than glad to meet, and who exemplifies better than anyone else I know just the ideal of scholarship which we want them to care for. . . .

## To James Ford Rhodes

BOSTON, 18 *November*, 1906

DEAR JAMES, — There is so much to write that I shall probably end by writing nothing. To begin with, your welcome letter from Nice came a day or two ago; and just after it your final volumes. They are a worthy conclusion of a work for which great is not too big an adjective. I have dipped into them half at random — the Credit Mobilier, the Tweed Ring, Blaine, Sheridan at New Orleans, and so on. And it happens that I have lately been likewise running through passages in Thucydides and in Tacitus. In all seriousness, your grasp and

[1] Liberty, Union, Democracy.

your poise as a narrator do not shrink beside a comparison like that. And the adequate compactness of your style is really masterly. Lord, how thin it makes Rhetoric!

Your preface, too, impressed me deeply. It shows me for the first time just how — and how rightly — you are now attracted to the French Revolution. Haskins and I — by the way, his father died of apoplexy ten days ago — were talking of this yesterday. Neither had previously phrased to ourselves what your brief words made clear to us; namely, that from the moment the negro question subsided, the actual question of American history became no longer merely national, but in fact those of the social revolution begun in France and still active throughout the European world. America is, in every sense, pre-revolutionary still. The question is becoming whether it can remain so. If it can, democracy is justified. If not, revolution with us would mean the mortal wound of world-democracy. With such a field before you, of course you need to reflect on nineteenth-century Europe. But don't let it absorb you. *Reculez pour mieux sauter; mais sautez toujours....*

My Lowell lectures on France have attracted unexpected interest; and I am to repeat them of afternoons — to the benefit of my self-esteem and of my purse....

*To Mrs. John V. L. Pruyn*

BOSTON, 15 *March*, 1907

MY DEAR MRS. PRUYN, — The print of the old Harmanus Wendell house which you so kindly sent me brings me more pleasure than I can quite find words to express. It is not only a fresh assurance of the friendship, and the sense of old kinship which is so welcome. But it adds to my own scanty records of my Wendell ancestry a very vivid image. Of the emigrant, Evert, I now have one admirable souvenir, a photograph of the window he placed in the old Dutch church of Albany. This Harmanus, I believe, was his grandson, and a cousin of Abraham, my ancestor in that generation. A portrait of the first Jacob Wendell, Abraham's younger brother, is our earliest family picture. Of that I have an excellent photograph, and when I was last in Holland, two years ago, I found the country churchyard where the emigrant's mother was buried in 1657. Behind her, all is misty. The family seem to have been ruined Protestant exiles either from the Southern Netherlands or else from some Catholic province of Germany. It was clear that she did not really belong in the quaint little village where she died; and there was a faint record that she came there widowed. . . .

## To Horace M. Kallen

[*Mr. Kallen, professor in the new School for Social Research, and, until recently, editor of the* Advance, *the official organ of the Amalgamated Clothing Workers of America, had graduated at Harvard in 1903, was studying at Oxford in 1907, took his Ph.D. at Harvard in 1908, and for three years thereafter was an assistant and lecturer in the Harvard Department of Philosophy. The sympathetic relation between Wendell and so pronounced a liberal has a notable significance.*]

BOSTON, 4 *December,* 1907

DEAR MR. KALLEN, — The photographs of me here procurable I dislike. The French one I can't get, this side of Paris, if I can then. So I send you a funny little print of it, lately made by Scribner's, to show what the author of the *France of To-day* looks like. It is more to my taste than any other. How good it is, the Lord knows. I have a notion that I should detest my own personal appearance and find my own voice and manner irritating. . . . And the methods of speech practised by my younger brother — who is said to talk just like me — have invariably appeared to me like perverse affectations. I am rather glad not to have phonographic records of my vocal enormities. . . .

As I look back on our friendship, nothing marks it more than your growth out of personal limitation of view into that broadening sympathy with other kinds of men which is essential to true scope, and which, to keep vital, must persist. The problem, at this moment, grows pretty clear. It is at once to preserve your own individuality and not to let this shut out understanding of different ones, a toleration of them. As I write, it seems to me that you could not do better, now and then, than to run over Franklin's *Autobiography* and the letters with which John Bigelow cleverly supplemented it. His self-management was the shrewdest I have ever met between the covers of books. . . .

# VII

## A DECADE OF TEACHING, TRAVEL, AND FRIENDSHIP

### 1908–1917

Towards the end of his life Barrett Wendell was fond of telling the story of a little colloquy between himself and his younger friend, Professor Merriman of Harvard. Thus it ran: "In all the twenty-five years you have known me, Roger, have you ever heard me utter one liberal sentiment?" To which came the reply, "Not one, sir," followed by Wendell's devout ejaculation: "Thank God!"

Over against this tale — presented in Wendell's own version of it — must be set the dedication of a recent volume, *Culture and Democracy in the United States*, by Mr. Horace M. Kallen, the exponent of advanced liberal thought to whom a letter of Wendell's was quoted at the end of the preceding chapter. Reverently he has inscribed his book: "To the memory of Barrett Wendell, poet, teacher, man of letters, deep-seeing interpreter of America and the American mind, in whose teaching I received my first vision of their trends and meanings." The letters to Mr. Kallen still to be given reveal one side of Wendell's sympathies, as those to Senator Lodge reveal another. To either of these friends he might have written, as he wrote in memorable phrase one day to Mr. Kallen, less than a year before his death: "After all, the difference between a reactionary and a radical, at heart, is only that the one longs to retain whatever is good and the other to destroy whatever is evil. Neither can be quite right or all wrong." Rebuked at an earlier day by Senator Lodge for too lenient an attitude towards one whom neither admired, Wendell detected and acknowledged in himself the workings of "our insidious Harvard tendency to resist what we call prejudice." The signs of such resistance were by no means always clear to others.

Indeed, the man that Wendell — in President Lowell's phrase quoted at the very beginning of this book, "thought himself to be" — was more and more pronounced a conservative, reactionary, "last of the Tories" — call it what you will. In his talk, as in his letters, there was an habitual assumption of this rôle. It was assumed without effort, for it represented a prevailing temper of thought and feeling. At the same time he was writing letters that betrayed unexpected sympathies; and more than one of his friends, with ways of thinking less completely conservative than those for which he so often spoke, must remember well that through a period when conversations between holders of divergent political opinions were hard to conduct without strain, there was never a time when Wendell and a reasonable companion could not talk freely and profitably on topics however burning. Those who did not always agree with him could therefore believe that when he assumed a rôle he sometimes overacted. In the realities of sympathetic personal intercourse this did not happen.

What frequently did happen was the indulgence of the humors which were so essential a part of him, and contributed so much to his own amusement. "Perhaps one of his greatest charms," his daughter Edith — Mrs. Osborne — has written in some "Recollections" of her father, "was the diversity of his moods. They ranged from humor to irony, from sarcasm to pathos, from sunshine to storm, in such quick succession that one never knew what to expect; his mind grasped ideas wholesale and leapt forward with such rapidity that his bewildered audience was left far behind. And one could never be sure of just how much he really meant. He would assume a quizzical expression and make some outrageous statement, arguing, for the sake of argument, with as much fire and energy as if it were a vital issue to him. In so doing, he often found himself in hot water, for he would forget, from one week to the next, the particular tangent he had digressed upon, and as flatly contradict himself, much to the indignation of some virtuous old lady who had previously hung breathless upon his words."

Many instances of the effects, sometimes embarrassing, of so volatile a temper are recalled. Here, for example is an anecdote of Mrs. Osborne's about a messenger-boy who had greatly irritated her father one evening, first by his impatient ringing of the doorbell, and then by standing in the hall, "his hat cocked over one eye, dividing his energies between whistling loudly, and chewing gum. It was the crowning touch to set Papa's nerves ablaze. He told him sharply to be quiet and to take off his hat. The boy paid absolutely no attention. Papa repeated his request, without further result; and then, leaping to his feet, strode into the hall so fiercely that the boy was quelled to silence, but still obstinately retained his hat upon his head. His rebellion was of extremely short duration, for without more ado Papa removed the cap, and to his consternation disclosed a discolored and rather gory bandage. All his anger vanished in sympathy; he gently asked how the boy had been injured and why he had not explained that he was keeping his hat on to conceal the fact. The misunderstanding was completely dispelled, and clutching a crisp new dollar bill, all his bravado gone, the boy departed, wreathed in smiles, and profuse of thanks."

Then there are two stories of football games, told, respectively, by Wendell's older and younger daughter. In the first, they were returning from Cambridge, —

Wendell, his wife, and his daughter Mary, — and as they were boarding an electric car a man in the crowd thrust Mrs. Wendell aside, and was pushing through the door when Wendell managed to arrest his progress by hooking the man's umbrella with the crook of his own walking-stick: "Be careful, sir," came the protest, "you are breaking my umbrella." "On the contrary," said Wendell, "I am mending your manners."

The second anecdote may be quoted from Mrs. Osborne's "Recollections": "I remember going to a Brown-Harvard football game, shortly after the Harvard Stadium was completed. Papa, ever impatient, was extremely annoyed by an over-zealous enthusiast who kept standing up in front of us, thereby entirely cutting off our view. He repeatedly asked him to sit down, without any result, and finally, his temper getting the better of him, he took his cane — without which he never walked abroad — and mashed the man's hat in. I was terrified; the surrounding spectators highly entertained. The man looked around angrily, shouting, 'Who did that?' Papa, equally angrily, replied, 'I did. Come out, and I will buy you a new hat.' They exchanged visiting cards, and were gone from the game long enough to effect the necessary purchase."

There was no such offer to make amends when Wendell vented his rage against a newspaper photographer by rushing out of his house and kicking over the camera set up near his doorstep to "snap" his younger daughter, as she left the house on her way to her wedding. The privacy of his household was not to be invaded: indeed there were many domestic antics, generally of the "fooling" variety, not intended for the public eye, — barking like a dog at unseen visitors; symbolizing his own physical weariness, sometimes only too real, by crawling upstairs to bed on his hands and knees; and conducting himself

Xmas greetings from the port
of Portsmouth, in which we
have long drunk to Uncle Blunt's
memory, and shall drink while
it lasts. Then he will sadden
our small dining-room there

PW

"Uncle Blunt," with Autograph Christmas Greetings

otherwise like anything but the dignified figure known to the outer world. Unseen these harmless pranks proceeded, as unheard were his performances on the piano, when, dressed for a dinner party earlier than his wife, he would seat himself at the piano, his fur coat thrown back, and run habitually through the brief operatic repertory known as "Papa's going-out-to-dinner tunes." The occasions for these were astonishingly frequent, since dining out, both in the society of men and women and in masculine company only, at his smaller and larger clubs, was a pleasure which he relished keenly, and obviously the more because his own agile and distinctive wit made him the most welcome of guests.

An element of the ceremonial entered into much of Wendell's private life. At Portsmouth a plumber, with whom he had many dealings and a most friendly relation, saw in this something of cause and effect. "Yes," he said to a summer neighbor, "Professor Wendell's a nervous man, a very nervous man — and it's no wonder: he puts on his dress suit every night for dinner." But ceremony in general was more refreshing to Wendell than this observer realized. At the Jacob Wendell House in Portsmouth, acquired by Wendell for happy restoration in 1910, one little rite, observed daily, had a flavor entirely characteristic. It is described in Mrs. Osborne's "Recollections": —

"Over his dining-room mantelpiece hung by faded yellow ribbon a charming pastel of our 'Uncle Blunt.' Who he was, except a seafaring merchant, I have only a vague notion, but it is certain that he left some lovely English silver and the aforesaid portrait behind him. Papa liked to think that 'Uncle Blunt' had taken on a happier expression and looked with secret approval on the reëstablishment of order. And he whimsically began a habit, which soon came to be a recognized custom (and will be remembered as chief among the traditions of his Portsmouth) of pledging 'Uncle Blunt' in a glass of port after dinner. No matter what the provocation, or who the company, he never neglected this rite. Failing health — and prohibition — made no difference; night after night he bowed gravely over his raised glass to the quaint old face upon the wall."

The Jacob Wendell House, in which this scene was regularly enacted, came into the possession of Wendell's grandfather in 1815. It was then forty or fifty years old. For many years before Wendell acquired it in 1910, it had been occupied by a bachelor cousin, whose care for its more ancient contents — the accretions of nearly a century — had consisted in letting them alone. The result was the survival of much excellent furniture, however neglected, from an earlier day, of great quantities of family papers, and of the "makings" of a little formal garden, entirely in keeping with the house itself. The garden, with its geometric beds, modeled after the pieces of a mother-of-pearl Chinese puzzle, and bordered with white wooden boards, was there when Wendell's grandfather bought the house — all "less changed, I like to think," as Wendell himself wrote of it when it became his, "than almost any other New England homestead where a family has lingered on for a hundred years."

To the restoration of all these elements of an old New England dwelling, Wendell, with the invaluable coöperation of his wife, devoted himself assiduously. The happy result was that an ideal setting for one possessing precisely the inheritances which he valued so highly emerged from the comparative chaos. With the daily toast to "Uncle Blunt," Wendell's own performances of ballad-tunes on the musical glasses inherited from his Barrett aunts, chimed in perfect harmony. His antiquarian zeal expressed itself not only in bringing the appearance of the house, within and without, to its former state, but also in arranging and studying the mass of old letters, journals, and other family memorials with which the attic was found to overflow. Altogether the Jacob Wendell House contributed to the final decade of its restorer's life a happiness which nothing else could have provided.

In the decade with which this chapter deals there were many other occasions for happiness in Wendell's domestic life. His daughter Mary had been married in the preceding decade,[1] and her son, Thomas Gordon Wheelock, — early taught, in deference to grandpaternal feelings, to address his grandfather as "Mr. Wendell," — afforded the first outlet for a devotion to the infant children of his own blood, which illuminated his later years. The marriage of his three other children fell between 1910 and 1914: that of his elder son, Barrett, to Barbara Higginson a daughter of Mr. Francis Lee Higginson, of Boston, on June 18, 1910; of his daughter Edith to Charles Devens Osborne, a son of Mr. Thomas Mott Osborne, of Auburn, New York, on January 18, 1913; of his son William to Ruth Appleton, a daughter of Mr. Francis R. Appleton, of New York, on October 7, 1914. Into the welfare of the new families thus formed Wendell threw himself heart and soul, paying daily visits to the nurseries of the grandchildren within reach, devising all manner of pleasures for them, and thereby vastly enhancing his own.

The period was marked no less sharply by its sorrows — the deaths of his mother, in December, 1912, of his aunt Sarah Barrett, in May, 1913, of all his three brothers, Gordon, January 31, 1910, Jacob ("Jac"), April 22, 1911, and Evert, August 27, 1917. To these contractions of a deeply cherished family circle, — broken, through many preceding years, only by the death of Wendell's father, —

---

[1] See *ante* p 134. In the spring of 1919, following a divorce, she became Mrs. Reinier Gerrit Anton van der Woude. Geoffrey M. Wheelock died in June, 1920.

there are poignant references in the letters that are to follow. In this period also there were grave questions of health — especially an operation for mastoid in March, 1914,[1] and a motor accident in the spring of 1915, more serious in its consequences than in its immediate effects. A general abridgment of physical energy, due to these and other causes, led him, at the beginning of 1917, to lay down his teaching at Harvard, and to welcome his appointment as Professor Emeritus.

Though the decade was less fruitful in the field of Wendell's productive scholarship than that which preceded it, there were two notable additions to the list of his published books: *The Privileged Classes* (1908) and *The Mystery of Education, and Other Academic Performances* (1909). The paper which gave the title to the first of these volumes was based on Wendell's contention that the "privileged classes" were best represented, at the time of his writing, by the laboring man who sprawled over two seats in a street-car, forcing such a citizen as himself to stand, in spite of having paid the same fare as the man with the dinner-pail. In a later paper contained in this volume Wendell declared that it had "often been my temperamental misfortune to express myself in a manner that has appeared frivolous." Inevitably *The Privileged Classes* was so regarded in many quarters. In reality, its obvious total purpose was to defend what Wendell called in this very book "our old national belief that men in this world should be free to win not their aspirations but their deserts." It was not to be expected that Wendell's presentation of such a belief would be popular. The acme of dissent was attained in a letter from Chicago, where *The Privileged Classes* was delivered as an address

[1] It was characteristic of Wendell's quickness and firmness of decision on important matters that when this possibly fatal operation became suddenly imminent, he made instant financial arrangements for his household, attended calmly to all preliminary details, and joked of this and that until he went under ether.

and printed, partially, in the local press. This letter was addressed, "Mr. Barrett Wendell, professor on the Harvard University, Harvard." The Chicago post office supplied the "Cambridge, Mass." The letter read: —

"Dear Sir! — You goat! That's all!

"My proposition:

"Come on to Chicago and take charge on the stock-yard's hogs, and live alone the science. You will do more success for the whole nation. Yours trouly,
                                        "PAT O'MALLEY"

The letter is endorsed as having been acknowledged by Wendell within a few days of its receipt. If he dealt with this correspondent as with others who objected to the newspaper reports of his address, he asked him to read it in its entirety and forwarded a copy for the purpose.

*The Privileged Classes* contains, besides a paper on "The American Revolution," two essays on educational topics, which link the volume closely with *The Mystery of Education*, made up wholly of such papers. It was quite characteristic of Wendell to begin the essay which gives this book its title with a tracing of the word "mystery" through the mazes of Liddell and Scott, back to the Greek verb signifying "to wink." "As one puts aside the exhausted volume," he declares, "one can hardly help reflecting that if we keep our lips closed and solemnly wink at one another, nobody else need ever know that we do not know all about it."

As a matter of fact, he did know a great deal about the inadequacies of American education, especially with respect to the teaching of English and of the classics. In many pages of these and other writings, as in many spoken words, he deplored, as his work in teaching drew to an end, the apparent futility of much of it. In the final paper, "Of Education," in *The Privileged Classes*, there is, however, a passage which may surely be taken to represent his serious view of the matter: —

All which anybody can as yet assert is that, in the opinion of occasional observers, no teachers and no methods have as yet justified, by irrefutable results, the still general faith that if you honestly try to teach youths how to write English, they will learn to write it with idiomatic freedom. The task is worth trying a good deal longer. If the end can be achieved, every disheartening experiment will have been justified by the ultimate result. And even if the end be never achieved, not a bit of the experiment need be regretted. For it will have proved at last that the only way to write English is to make sure of what you mean and then to express it as well as you can, in the terms and the rhythms which unconfined English usage has made wildly idiomatic. One can always comment, in passing, on this turn of phrase or on that. There was never a page written which might not have been written better. But English style, like happiness, may finally turn out to be most nearly attainable only by those who never directly seek it.

The delivery of the academic addresses contained in these volumes took Wendell to Chicago, Haverford College, Johns Hopkins, the College of Charleston (South Carolina), and the University of Virginia. In 1909 he read at the Harvard Phi Beta Kappa the poem, "*De Præsede Magnifico*," in which he analyzed, with characteristic candor, the qualities of President Eliot, then retiring from office, and left no doubt in his hearers' minds either of the divergences of view between himself and his subject or of his deep appreciation of one, who, for all these differences, "remained incarnate magnanimity." Still another academic occasion took him in the spring of 1916 to Texas, where he made an address at the State University in Austin, visited other places, and renewed his personal relations with Professor John A. Lomax,

a former graduate student at Harvard, for whose
*Cowboy Songs* (1910) Wendell had written a warmly
sympathetic introduction.

Of all the excursions of this time, the journey round
the world which Wendell made with his wife and daughter
Edith in 1910–11 crowned his lifelong devotion to the
pleasures of travel. Equipped with all-availing letters of
introduction from President Taft and others, he made the
most of his opportunities to see not only the countries of
India, China, and Japan, but also their rulers. His
letters will tell the story, as also of that shorter journey
to England in the summer of 1914, when, having declined
an offer to serve as the Harvard Exchange Professor at
Berlin in the ensuing winter, he learned in mid-ocean,
on his way back to America, that war had broken out
in Europe.

The letters written during these years are of a bewildering abundance. When other men would have had recourse
to physical exercise or games for relaxation, Wendell
habitually took to his pen. To a high degree his letters
represent his current moods. In the years immediately
before and after 1914, these were frequently based upon
deep dissatisfaction with the conduct and drift of affairs
in his own country and throughout the world. To "explain him on his own terms," it is only fair to present
typical expressions of his sentiments, embodied perhaps
most clearly in his comments upon such historic figures
as Theodore Roosevelt and Woodrow Wilson.

## LETTERS
### 1908–1910

*To H. M. Kallen*

BOSTON, 10 *February*, 1908

. . . The book on France has gone better than I expected —
more than three thousand copies having been sold before
New Year's. Precise accounts have not yet come in. My only
indiscretion since has been a speech in Chicago on the "Privileged Classes," which was distorted by reporters and has
brought me diverting correspondence. The *Transcript* printed
it at full, innocent length last week. I shall send you a
copy. . . .

*To Sir Robert White-Thomson*

BOSTON, 30 *March*, 1908

. . . And now comes your welcome appreciation of my
Chicago speech. Hastily written, this has attracted so much
attention that I now expect to put it in a volume of essays,
to be ready in the autumn. I shall revise it, of course; and may
write a kind of sequel to it. Far as we have begun to go in this
country toward socialism, it seems to me that we are still in
less danger than any part of Europe. To raise the voice does
little good, I fear, beyond the fact of the wail, but I am tempted
to do so — as the most useful thing I can see now to do. . . .

*To the same*

BOSTON, 6 *May*, 1908

. . . My wife is gone for a week to Washington, to attend a
general meeting of "Colonial Dames" — the rather comical
name by which a society of women is described who occupy
themselves pleasantly and not uselessly in preserving the older
traditions of America. In several instances, for example, they
have rescued and restored old houses, keeping them as museums
of our colonial history. A year ago, they rebuilt and restored
to its pristine condition the ruined church of Jamestown —
the first English place of worship in America, and an interesting
structure architecturally as well as historically; for, in rough

brick, it attempted to preserve the then still prevalent forms of perpendicular Gothic, and the stubborn material combined with imperfect artistic skill to produce a singularly vital and picturesque effect. The "Dames" meet annually in Washington. Edith is president of the Massachusetts Society. . . .

*To the same*

BOSTON, 22 *November*, 1908

It is at once a pleasure and a somewhat saddening thought that you find *The Privileged Classes* applicable to England as well as to America. Modifying the terms of what you write me, the general truth you state exists, I rather think, not only here too, but all over the world. The elder time, with all its faults, inevitable to human nature and instantly evident on its surface, tended everywhere to emphasize and I think to develop the ideal of the gentleman — of a class, not necessarily so protected or so inaccessible as is sometimes believed or pretended, in honour bound by the conditions of its existence, to perform the higher public and social duties. It varied superficially. In England, it was land-holding; here, at least in the North, it was mercantile and professional — somewhat as was the case in Renaissance Italy; on the Continent, it was on the whole military. But the heart of it — and the virtue and the faults of it — stayed the same everywhere.

Everywhere now the time and spirit is against it. Inferiority, in the widest sense, is now presented as a more instant claim to popular esteem than superiority. The passage in the Litany, praying that we be delivered from envy, hatred, and malice, and from all uncharitableness is the least answered of them all. I do not mean that the rulers of the moment are abominable. Their virtues, however, like their failings, are rarer. What I mean is incarnate in the contemptible hero of Mrs. Humphry Ward's *Diana Mallory*, pretending to lead when in truth he only follows like a slave, as contrasted with the old Liberal whose heart he breaks. And meanwhile things are not only done more carelessly than of old, for all the honest effort of the baser sort, but they cost so much everywhere that all the old ideals are being turned out of existence. We have lived, I think, in times which the future will see to be more like those of Antonian Rome than like any other before us. The new, incalculable factor is our incredible control of natural forces — steam, electricity, and applied mechanics. Really, we are passed into an ethnologic era as new as that of fire, of the wheel, of metal. Not inconceivably, the trouble men of your time feel, and of mine, is only that we must confront the new era with the ideals of the old. But it needs strong faith to feel buoyant. . . .

*To the same*

BOSTON, 13 *December*, 1908

. . . We are still in supreme suspense concerning the presidency of Harvard. After forty years of service, President Eliot has resigned — his resignation to take effect in May. His successor must be elected by the Fellows — six in number — and their choice confirmed by a Board of Overseers, who keep such questions under consideration for a full month. At present, no one knows whether any choice has been made — still less on whom it may have fallen. Our own hope, and that of almost all our friends, is that the new president may be Lawrence Lowell, one of our dearest friends, whose book on the Government of England, published last summer, has given him wide and delightfully recognized reputation as an authority on constitutional history. He comes from the family which during the past century has been perhaps the most distinguished in this part of the country for character, power, and unobtrusive public service. And he has what I personally believe essential to the full usefulness of a Harvard president, a considerable personal fortune. . . .

*To R. W. Curtis*

BOSTON, 17 *March*, 1909

DEAR RALPH, — . . . The only event in our funny local life has been Ned Wheelwright's classical dinner to Lawrence Lowell. He conceived the plan of serving nothing except what he could find warranted by Latin authority. He took me into his confidence, and we delved in all sorts of musty books — Horace, Juvenal, Apicius, Macrobius, and whatever else. The result was a wonderful Latin bill of fare, which no one pretended to understand; a series of surprising dishes, surprisingly good; a greeting to Lawrence in unintelligible but agreeable Latin verse by Teddy Williams; supreme content on the part of Lawrence; and marvelous freedom from indigestion. It had never occurred to me before that the ancients empirically practised the principles of Brillat-Savarin. . . .

I have had a real chance to read Henry Adams's *Education* at last. It took a good while; for I found that one missed the meaning if one read fast. In final effect, it seems to me a marvelous presentation of individual reminiscences in the historical environment of the nineteenth century. This feature of the work to my mind makes all the detail secondary. I admire it immensely. . . .

*To Sir Robert White-Thomson*

BOSTON, 29 *May*, 1909

It was a pleasure to hear from you again; though your mention of that appalling measure of Lloyd-George saddened everything. To me it seems utterly bewildering; it deliberately denies all that has hitherto seemed essential to civilization and substitutes untested, and to my mind ignoble, ideals. It carries to extreme the principle that submergence is in itself a proof of merit — that excellence is a splendid vice. One finds the roots of it, no doubt, in all the dreams and the utterances of the Revolution — not least in the sentimental philanthropy of Wordsworth. But sympathy with suffering humanity is one thing; artificially imposed suffering is another. Here, by a queer historic chance, we are somewhat protected by our written Constitution, framed to protect possessions from unbridled aggression. How long it will do so, one cannot tell. . . .

*To E. S. Martin*

NAHANT, 20 *June*, 1909

DEAR DAN, — Inasmuch as you can't write without good sense, good feeling, and a touch all your own, I could n't help finding in your comments on scholarship a good deal of both wit and wisdom. It seems to me, though, that you have missed Lawrence's point. All three of us would agree as to the general ends and aims — praiseworthy or deplorable — of modern youth. The real question gets down to that of how they may best be attained. If scholarship and that kind of thing tend only towards scholarship in perpetuity, then you are right. Of course, few able youths nowadays wish to be professional scholars. If scholarship, on the other hand, has such gymnastic value that a good classical man, for example, has a positive advantage in legal or political argument, or in practical conduct of affairs, over a man of equal natural ability who has less training, then you are a bit off. Personally, I think you are; and for the reason that, unawares, you have accepted the orthodox doctrine of Eliot — that education is a specialized training for a specific end.

Experience abroad has tended to prove, during the nineteenth century, that men who do hard work at universities manage thereby to get a winning pace in the race of life. There is a good deal of evidence to the same effect in this country — Choate, for example, and Carter; down to W. K. Richardson, and Gardiner Lane, and Beekman Winthrop, and Theodore Roosevelt — all Phi Beta Kappa men. So a state of general feeling which makes able men loaf seems to me unfavorable to the best development of their general power. . . .

*To James Ford Rhodes*

NAHANT, 3 *July*, 1909

DEAR JAMES, — *Le Roi* — for which amusement no end of thanks — found me in the throes of my Phi Beta Kappa poem. This wretched job had proved one too many for my slight working-power. In the middle of June I had to go to Charleston to give a Commencement address at the College there. Ned Wheelwright went with me, by sea, taking along his small boy Jack. . . . I liked Charleston — its people — and they said they liked my speech, which seemed to me more impressive than lucid. It concerned the Study of Expression. The upshot of it all, though, was that with this task, joining on the end of college work . . . I found myself, on Class Day morning, when the thermometer jumped about anywhere over ninety, without a line written of the poem to be delivered six days later.

Somehow or other I got it done by Sunday night. Monday and Tuesday I polished the two hundred lines or so, as well as I could; but the polishing went on till the last moment, and did n't look lustrous then. I made four new lines in the car between Lynn and Boston, on my way to the platform. So the fact that it went off tolerably was a surprising relief, from the reaction of which I am not yet risen to the point of work.

Woodrow Wilson made the oration, on the Spirit of Learning. He pointed out the error of Eliot's ways without mention of him; and greatly 'commended himself to such as love the prospect at Harvard above the retrospect. Then I came with my hundred heroic couplets, rougher than Donne, here and there, and not a bit ingenious, in which, God help me, I did my best to say what I think about Eliot, in a manner at once true and — to one who does n't look too deep — laudatory. The gist of it is that he may be called the Edwards of Channing.

> As Edwards, holding Calvin's precepts true,
> Came to his succor, made them live anew,
> So Eliot now arrests our happier state,
> Edwards of Channing — each securely great.

I gave his ideals and independence honest praise; but permitted myself a little satire.

> He loved statistics — never seemed to care,
> So we got freshmen, who the freshmen were.

And so on: —

> He never showed resentment; rather, he
> Remained incarnate magnanimity;
> But even so, took languid interest
> In that poor thing — though dear to you — your best.

There you have some naked bits of it, — better than the whole, — listened to after an hour's oration by the most excellent of hatchet-faced beings, in a theatre cooler than usual but still hot enough to threaten one's collar.

Commencement, the day before, was pleasanter. Lawrence has quite captured the public heart. If his manner lacked Eliot's stateliness, it had a human simplicity winning enough to even things. His formulas were excellent — as well phrased, I think, as Eliot's ever were . . . Lawrence's speech in Memorial was clear, firm, convincing — emphasizing his hope that he can make college opinion do something for scholarship. . . .

*To Sir Robert White-Thomson*

BOSTON, 9 *November*, 1909

It is no wonder that the lines on Eliot perplex you. The circumstances were unusual. I was called on to give the Phi Beta Kappa poem — a long-established annual matter at Harvard — by Lowell, his successor, and one of my dearest friends, at a moment when no such poem could possibly treat of anything but Eliot's remarkable career. The challenge I could not refuse. My personal relations with Eliot had been by no means cordial. Yet he had really commanded my respect, as a man. I attempted, in this unusual form, to state the case for him at its best, leaving to be implied my own constant dissent from his principles.

Among those principles none was less welcome to me than the honest bigotry of his Yankee Unitarianism. This was not with him a matter of theology, to any just degree; it was rather one of philosophy. His whole conception of life seemed to me based on dogmatic assumption of human perfectibility, as set forth classically hereabouts in the works of Channing. Accepting this, he deliberately seemed to shut his eyes to everything inconsistent with it. If facts did not agree with what logic would deduce from Channing's major premises, so much the worse for facts. Eliot was never dishonest. He was only almost damnably perverse.

Yet, in his real magnanimity, there was something admirable. To attack him, or condemn him, then and there, would have been not only indecent, but heartless.

So I trusted to that summary of ancestral New England philosophy, thinking of it, for the moment, almost without reference to its theological aspect and expression. The basis of Calvinism is Calvin's assumption that human nature is totally depraved. From this dogma, Edwards reasoned logically to a point where he got fatally away from life. Honest man of genius that he was, he carried Calvinism to an impossible reductio ad absurdum. Yet he believed it all; and had the secure greatness of honest logic. Just so, I think, Eliot carried to complete absurdity the contrary philosophic dogmas of Channing — that human nature is in itself perfectible. The influence of Edwards is now extinct, except as a matter of history. So, I believe, will that of Eliot, the "Edwards of Channing," be in two or three generations. His office, the "need he has fulfilled," is really, I think, to set forth, with logical perfection, the error of a system which, untested thus, might do more mischief than — thus tested — it will. His beautiful, self-neglectful honesty makes his work — like that of Edwards — at once great, and almost final.

Yet, to grasp what I meant, one had both to know our local philosophy, till one almost forgot its theologic methods of expression, and to read between lines of which the satire had to be implicit. Even here, I think, the full meaning has been hardly remarked. Elsewhere, it must have been obscure.

Always affectionately yours,<br>BARRETT WENDELL

*To Senator Lodge*

BOSTON, 9 *January*, 1910

The Speeches have proved even more welcome than I knew at first. Without studious care, I take them up, again and again, finding them always doubly meaning. For they are not only so expressive of yourself that one hears your voice echoing in memory; but every line of them justifies, to my thinking, your gladness that the lines were spoken.

So the mood, which grows about them, at least with me, is not quite so critical, in any sense, as I should have thought it would be; it is rather sympathetic effort to guess what life must be when life, in its full vigor, is at once a matter of tremendous controversy on all sides, and a game, to be played by rules more technical than they seem. The parliamentary phase of it, you see, chances to affect me most profoundly. In America, I should think, we have never reached that extraordinary development of public life, as the occupation of a distinct class, which makes the private friendship of English public men a puzzling fact to us. They have such an instinctive, hereditary sense of the great party-game, that again and again they seem — what they really are n't — neglectful of principle to a degree which would make one feel them little better than colossal gamblers. Here, as there, though, one cannot avoid both turns of the problem: the need to win, and the need in winning of adherence to policies as constructive as conditions will ever let them be.

There may be men who have reconciled these ends as steadily and as admirably as you have, and do, and surely will do. No man could do so better. If I had any comment to make in connection, the while, it would take, I think, the form of a question. Though I cannot from memory specify given instances of what raises the question, I feel pretty sure what the question is: Do you always quite avoid the human impulse of setting up a straw man on the other side, and then unstuffing him? Do you rely quite enough on the great strength of your own positive facts and powers? I am not a bit confident here. I feel disposed to believe, though, that, with such strength and such equipment as yours, you would never err in relying on the power of direct assertion, made with the calm certainty of intellectual authority; and that there are few more pregnant lines, when temptation to needless controversy assails one, than that of Dante: *"Non ragioniam di lor, ma guarda e passa."*

Always sincerely yours,

BARRETT WENDELL

*To the same*

BOSTON, 7 *February*, 1910

When I wrote you this morning my instant word of how much your sympathy means to me, I did not add the brief account of my brother's fatal illness, which I venture to send you now. If you think the circumstances warrant you in sending this letter on to the President, I should in no wise object. Still

I do not urge it. The facts, however, seem bearing on a petition for pardon, said by the newspapers to be either before him or on the way to him.

My brother Gordon was an experienced man of business in New York. He was called last year to serve on the jury which tried the case of Morse, now serving a sentence at Atlanta. When called, Gordon was so far from well that his physician was prepared to give him a certificate of inability to serve. This he declined to ask for, believing his public duty more important than his personal comfort. He had, of course, no idea either of the hardship he should be exposed to, nor of the fact that this would prove ultimately mortal. In the course of the trial, the conditions of imprisonment to which the jury was subjected by order of the court, produced — by reason of bad air, lack of exercise, and thick tobacco smoke in close quarters — an attack of what I may call heart-failure. The trial was suspended; and Gordon was taken home, under guard. He might have then withdrawn, with his physician's authority. His sense of public duty, his knowledge of the fact that to stop proceedings at that moment, just because he was ill, would delay the course of justice, impelled him to insist on serving. When the trial ended, he was utterly broken in health. The intervening year has been one of slowly certain decline.

In speaking privately of this jury to me, he has always been cheerful and deeply patriotic. Every man of them, he said, seemed animated throughout only by earnest desire to do his duty at any cost. Gordon came out of that six weeks' ordeal with a fresh sense of the simple honesty of true American citizenship.

In his own way, it seems to me, he gave his life for his country. I know that he was glad to. The public service the country demanded of him was not of a kind to touch popular imagination. To me, this does not make it less heroic.

All this would be a matter of private feeling, not one for you, and far less for the President, if Gordon's last days had not been in some degree troubled by effort on the part of Morse and his counsel to excite belief that his illness was drunkenness; and to urge that on this ground the judgment of the court should be set aside by Executive pardon. I have every reason to fear that those who spread this falsehood knew its falsity.

*To the same*

BOSTON, 1 *May*, 1910

DEAR LODGE: — You were never better, to my mind, than in the characterization of Calhoun. What appeals to me most, I think, is that you set him forth in full historical perspective. So, it seems to me, one must ultimately look on all anywhere who have been foci — or is it better focuses — of political force. The final test of them all is their honesty — their devotion to the ideals they stood for. Your honest enemy is a nobler fact, for us all, than your pliable friend. Thus I have grown to feel, at five and fifty, about the men who took the other side in '61, when you were a big boy and I was a little one. The America to come must be the country of us both; just as the France to come must be the France of Old Régime, Revolution, and Empire, fused. Here, I rather think, I should now go far beyond you. To commemorate the Confederate dead in Memorial Hall now would evidently be injudicious — injudicious because the very suggestion blows up embers that had best die. Sometime or other though, I for one should be glad to see their names placed there, finally asserting that the grand heroism of the war was utter devotion to the ideals that seemed true, whether these ideals were ours or those with which ours had to fight to the death for life.

The *Herald* article came this morning. . . .[1] I hope that you will find what I have written welcome. Be sure that I have never written anything with more unreserved eagerness. There is not a word of it which I have not felt for a good many years. If setting the words down can be of any manner of use, it will be a very deep pleasure; for generally what I have been able to do in this world has seemed a very thin frill on the edge of reality.

[1] A biographical paper, "Henry Cabot Lodge, Statesman," written in support of his reëlection to the U. S. Senate.

*To Sir Robert White-Thomson*

BOSTON, 2 *June*, 1910

. . . My old cousin Stanwood, who had a life interest in our old Portsmouth house, has died; and the question of what to do with the house — which you perhaps remember — has worried me. At last, I have decided to buy it for myself, and to pass it on to B in turn. It is by no means imposing, of course; but it has been ours for nearly a century; and if I let it go, one link with the past would be fatally broken. B likes it, too; and so does Barbara. We shall go there hereafter, I hope, for a month or two in spring and autumn. . . .

*To the same*

PORTSMOUTH, 16 *October*, 1910

. . . I write from that old Portsmouth house of my grand-fathers, which you perhaps remember, eighteen years ago. It finally became mine in August, with all the old furniture: in pretty bad order, to be sure, but intact. We have had a busy two months in cleaning it of rubbish and restoring it to life. Now Edith and I feel queerly content here. She is fixed here, at least for this month. I must be in town three or four days of the week, but come back here for the rest of the time. There is more of our old times left than I dared hope: furniture anywhere from 1750 to 1825 — hardly any later; papers, of one and another kind, by the hundred — the oldest I have yet found was 1709, in the writing of the son of the staid old Dutch lady whose photograph I sent you;[1] a good deal of old glass, a little old china, and so on. In New England the old order passes so swiftly that I know hardly any other place so wholly of the olden time. In the room where I write I have pictures — mostly, alas, photographs — of six generations before me: not quite successive, but all directly ancestral. You can understand how glad I am to have saved the old place, which I shall pass on, I hope intact, to B and Barbara.

---

[1] Elizabeth Staats, who married first John Wendell, ancestor of Barrett Wendell, and then John Schuyler, grandfather of General Philip Schuyler, of the American Army in the War of Independence.

We mean to come here in spring and autumn; and hereafter to travel in summer instead of taking houses.

More real travel will begin for us soon. I have leave of absence from January 1st — which means, in view of the Christmas holidays, from December 20th. We mean to start about Christmas time, to go as quickly as we can to India, and after a month or so there perhaps to go to Java before proceeding to Shanghai, for our visit to Mary. President Taft, of whom we saw a little this summer, took my breath away by offering me personal letters to the official people in Asia. This will give us a rather unusual chance, I think, to see the regions we go to. Our plan is to go to Bombay, by the first steamer we can get from Marseilles; across India to Calcutta, thence to Singapore, making perhaps one excursion to Java, which President Taft eagerly advises; and so on to Shanghai. We had hoped to come home in June by way of Siberia, in which event one of the things we looked forward to was a glimpse of you in July or August. As things look now, however, the danger of quarantine may scare us home across the Pacific.

It all seems rather too bright a prospect to be realized. I need travel, though, so much that I shall have to go somewhere. . . .

*To the same*

Boston, 5 *November*, 1910

. . . Among the innumerable and disordered family papers at Portsmouth — some as old as 1690 — I have come across the copy of an old commission, of George II's time, appointing a remote grand-uncle of mine to His Majesty's Council for the Province of New Hampshire. Among the signatures is one of a Brudenell, the first time I have come across the name here. He was of some official board, of which the head seems to have been the Duke of Newcastle. Of course he had no idea what commission he was signing. It makes, though, a faint link between your people and mine some century-and-a-half before we met each other.

The family papers are far more numerous than I supposed, and in utter confusion. I shall not attempt to sort them until

I get home. They are mostly either private letters or accounts. Here and there, however, I have already lighted on interesting matter. My father's grandfather, born in 1731, was in correspondence with many of the Revolutionary worthies — notably Hamilton and Hancock, who was his kinsman, and John Paul Jones. I have found no Washington letters; but there may be some. Offhand, I should think the number of papers — in stray trunks and boxes — at least ten thousand. The Portsmouth furniture proves remarkable for America. Sorted and restored, it has admirable examples of American Chippendale, of Hepplewhite, and of Sheraton. And some of the glass and china, of the 18th century, is very good. The oldest thing I have found is a stoneware ale-jug of James I's time. . . .

*To H. M. Kallen*

[*One of the birthday presents habitually sent to Wendell by Mr. Kallen was a gold pen with which the giver hoped a novel would be written*]

BOSTON, 15 *December*, 1910

DEAR KALLEN: — . . . Personally I am more used up in nerve than I quite realized until night before last, when I had a kind of momentary faint after dinner, pronounced by my doctor a matter of nothing more than fatigue; but unpleasant to the friends with whom I chanced to be dining. The sum of it all is that I really need the change of scene so near at hand — and probably, as well, the servant my wife insists on taking along, to the utter depletion of my slender pocket-book. My only reassurance in this case is the chance — almost the certainty — that if I don't spend what little I have, it will be grabbed by the mob who have less right to it than I. Your sympathy should be with me — a way-down. What your forefathers suffered through the centuries before I had any recorded, we are beginning to catch now. It's eternal justice, I dare say; only it was n't Louis XVI's head they were really after — in the sight of God.

Your pen has had an unexpected history. I am not writing with it; and the novel, I fear, will never be written. It waited for the novel, though, virgin of ink, until I came into the old house at Portsmouth — the most significant spot just to me on the planet. Then, I somehow turned to it; every line I wrote there, of any kind, was written with nothing else. I have left it there, to write with whenever I write thence, with a deep feeling that the instrument, like the place it is come to dwell in, has a spark of that vitality inherent in things material when they come charged with messages of things ideal — of the spirit. The charm of it all is strange, but happy. I have growing in mind a queerly personal book, which may never be written, or if written never see print: a plain record of how New England, American tradition, has appealed to me, and sunk into me, all my life. If I ever write the same, — not a novel, but a bit of human truth, — your pen will do the work.

*To Senator Lodge*

BOSTON, 18 *December*, 1910

This is only a word of good-bye, just before we start round the world, to be back again, I suppose, in August or September. I send it on purpose too late to be answered. You have more than enough to do without bothering about mere greetings of friendship.

I can't go, though, without sending this renewed assurance of how much your kindness has meant to me during the past years, and how much more deeply than ever I have felt, during these past weeks, the immense usefulness of your public career. What is more, I feel constantly more sure that among the sort hereabouts whose opinion is serious that usefulness is beginning to gleam with a clearness which could never have been quite so certain without the mists of the past and the injustices of the present.

Had it been anywise in my power to help you in this coming contest, you know how eagerly I would have done so, not only for your own sake but for that of the state and of the country. The only help I can conceivably give is in one word of advice, — if I may call it so, — which has been hovering in my mind ever since I heard that you are to speak here in January.

Both when I have heard you speak and when I have read your speeches, it has seemed to me that in controversial passages you are less sympathetic than in passages directly, simply assertive. At this moment, furthermore, it seems to me that public speech has generally taken a monotonously negative, vituperative turn; and therefore that a clear, direct, impersonal utterance would be apt to have double effect — that inherent in its own strength, and that which would come from refreshing, not quite expected contrast. If I am right, the less you touch on opponents or their views, and the more you assert, with simple conviction, the principles which have made you what you are and which we believe should prevail, the more efficient your speech will be.

You were never better, if I may trust the published summaries, than in your last speech in the Senate, on the Tariff. I wish I had heard it. . . .

As I read this over I am rather appalled at my cheek. You will give me, though, I feel sure, not a bit more consideration than an impractical, academic creature of friendly disposition may deserve.

## LETTERS: 1911

*[Wendell, his wife, his daughter Edith, and a courier, Robblee, previously their chauffeur, made their way to the East by way of Cherbourg, Paris, Genoa, and the Suez Canal, arriving in Colombo, Ceylon, January 21, 1911. Journal letters to his son William describe their experiences in detail. From these and from letters to other correspondents the selections must be confined to a few characteristic or informing passages. Early in 1912 Wendell made the beginnings of a book, unhappily never completed, on his observations in the East.]*

*To H. M. Kallen*

THE GALLE FACE HOTEL, COLOMBO, CEYLON,

*31 January,* 1911

DEAR KALLEN:— Your word of introduction to Mr. Ramanathan has given us very great pleasure. I called on him immediately after our arrival. He received me delightfully, making eager inquiries about you; and then, we hardly knew how, plunging into his own philosophy, which was what I most wished to hear. He introduced one of his sons — a barrister, who has studied at Cambridge (Christ's), and sent the son with a motor car to show us a Buddhist temple in the afternoon. He also lent me two or three summary books on Ceylon. These I returned next day, when we had another lesson in philosophy, interrupted by the arrival of a stout, turbaned friend of his, with extremely off-hand English manners. So I took my leave. A little later, he called on us with Mrs. Ramanathan; and invited us all to dine there last evening on our return from a four days' motor trip "up country."

Nothing could have been pleasanter than the dinner — one of his sons and a son-in-law were the company. After dinner he showed us jewels, Benares stuffs, musical instruments, how to roll turbans, and so on; touching little on realities, as distinguished from the illusion of the moment. And he sent us home in his very comfortable carriage. Throughout, his whole manner of greeting has been completely European. So was the dinner, in service, and almost in cookery.

But the whole range of thought is as far from Europe as if Europe had never boiled up out of the chaos into which it seems beginning to subside. I am still too dull of wit — too unskilled, anyway — to discuss it. In certain books at which I have glanced, particularly in André Chevrillon's *Sanctuaires d'Asie*, it seems to me pretty well set forth. To meet it incarnate, however, amid the physical surroundings which have developed and maintained it, gives it an utterly new character. It does not appeal to me: nothing does, I find. Truth seems to me a phantom which occasional other people believe themselves to have materialized. The working blunder of the moment is enough for me — a position which I take to be tolerably pragmatical. Had I dwelt — and my forbears before me — in this quivering evanescence of the tropics, unspeakably more splendid, more swift, more repetitory, more generalized than anything we know familiarly, this utterly strange mysticism, touching experience with the subtle skill of a musician sweeping strings, would have been deep planted, I can feel. . . .

## To his son William

Colombo, 31 *January*, 1911 — A little before two came a card that a student from the Oriental College was waiting to take me there. He was a brown, barefoot boy of seventeen, in white, bare-headed; but his collar was fastened, I observed, with native uncut-diamond studs. He turned out to be the son °of a Calcutta Brahmin, himself indisposed to Hindu orthodoxy, and therefore sent here to study Pali and Buddhism, as the next most respectable thing. Incidentally, he told me that at the end of his studies he expects to go for a while as a teacher to Chicago, under the auspices of a newspaper called *The Open Court*. Near the hotel he picked up a country bullock-cart, in which we jogged along, past a native primary school, discharging dozens of brown Singhalese children, the girls in cheap European dresses. The whole country might have been in the interior. At the end of a half mile or so, we turned up a narrow lane between orchards of cocoanut. Five minutes brought us to the college, or monastery — low buildings, among them a small temple, all white-plastered;

and a cloistered court within, where the rooms of the monks —
yellow-draped barefoots, of youthful and benignant aspect—
were oddly like the old ones in the University of Virginia.

Sumangala, the chief priest, received me most cordially in
his room. A handsome, gentle man of thirty-two, speaking
good English; he has been quite ill, partly from grief at the
loss of his old preceptor, a few weeks ago, and he lay on his
couch, in his yellow robe, talking of Buddhism, Henry Warren,
and Lanman, who once asked him to come for a while to
Harvard. An old scribe showed how they write Pali on palm
leaves — incising the letters and rubbing in India ink, which
bites permanently. Then they took me out into the cloister,
and gave me a little feast of orange, pineapple and the milk of
a young cocoanut — cool, almost effervescent, smooth as the
wine of Orvieto. Finally, the student drove me back, in a
fine big bullock-cart, and we got comfortably home, a bit after
four; and no one had stolen my cigarette-case, which I had
left on my dressing-table.

1 *February*, 1911. — At half past four or so . . . Edith and I
drove to make a dinner call on the Ramanathans. We found
her at home, entertaining a Scotch Anglican divine, who told
me that in Scotland no one may bear arms without personally
"matriculating"; and that they allow only three sons in each
generation to do so. Then he rode off on a bicycle; and Mrs.
Ramanathan ordered a young cocoanut to be brought in,
so that Edith might taste the milk. We were about to go when
Rogindra turned up with his wife — a slight, barefooted girl,
with a Brahmin mark on her forehead, a nose ornament, and
a wondrous diamond and ruby necklace. It seems that their
little girl, of three or so, has been down with fever, but is
better. So we sat under the cocoanut palms for a bit longer;
when Mr. Ramanathan turned up in his motor, from inspecting
a temple he is building as a family duty. He talked of this,
showed us photographs of it, and offered to take us there to-
morrow morning. Then, in answer to Edith's question, he
made a discourse on the four stages of Brahminism: good conduct; ritual; spiritual communion; and knowledge of God. By

this time it was sunset — we drove home in the dusk, past a lake, which almost reflected the new moon. In this latitude the crescent is almost parallel with the horizon, — horns up, — and beneath it, half-way down, blazed the evening star. At night the belt of Orion, just after dinner, is in the zenith.

Ramanathan's religious discourses impress me as the utterance of one to whom his faith is immemorially ancestral; while to all Europe religion is an exotic — derived from Asia. The difference is subtle, but palpable. . . .

2 *February*, 1911. — This morning Ramanathan called at 8.30 — an hour later than he had proposed, by reason of some motor trouble — and drove us in a wagonette, exactly like the old one at New Castle, to a Hindu temple, in process of alteration — mostly at his expense — from brick to granite. Thus temporarily desecrated, it is accessible. The masons were at work with the tools and the methods of fifty centuries ago, vigorously and skilfully. The architect wore a breech-clout, earrings, and a gold necklace; and can draw faultless plans. The priests, stripped to the waist, were smeared with ashes and painted with religious marks — three horizontal lines. The musicians, summoned for us, squatted in a corridor, and played wildly, loudly, barbarically, passionately. I smashed my sun-helmet against a scaffold, and did n't swear. One priest was as fat as Phillips Brooks, similar in fleshliness of countenance, and nude to the hips. He is said to be very spiritual — as was the late Bishop. In the corners of the court-yard are little painted chapels of Vishnu. . . . In one corner, under a corrugated iron roof, stood the great car of Siva, with its grotesque carvings, and its solid wooden wheels. And Ramanathan, taking us about just as an English gentleman might, who was restoring a country church, discoursed on theology, architecture, and the like, in the full terms of Europe.

He wore a turban and a single-breasted frock coat of light silk, with trousers and shoes like anyone else's. I gathered that he has risen to a height of Brahmin purification which renders him immune from defilement, and therefore at liberty to conduct himself with Europeans in a completely European manner. The whole experience of knowing him has been illuminating — never more so than this morning, in the midst of a work in which he is doing his best to replace in imperishable granite a monument of his antique faith set up in brick by his father about 1855 — "some seventy years ago," he added, with serene Oriental disregard of chronology. Every line of the structure, old and new, every broken brick wall, and every freshly carven granite stone, was made in the form and by the actual methods of immemorial antiquity. To rear a granite wall, for example, they disdain cranes; they pile sea-sand against the lower tiers, covering the sculpture, and haul up big blocks, on cocoanut rollers, by dozens of hands — "all masons, none coolies" — pulling on big twisted ropes of cocoanut fibre. Their hammers and chisels they forge on the spot, to work with. Their carvings, astonishingly true, they make almost without marks, by the eye. There is something about it which seems as normal, as instinctive, as the nest-building of birds. And there is something just as antique, just as immemorial, in the singularly pure mystic philosophy, swathed in endless, cumulative veils of grotesque visual or mental symbols, which Ramanathan, half in exposition, half in something verging toward prophetic ecstasy, incessantly set forth. The wild music of the immemorial instruments — a silver pipe the chief for the religious hymns — has the same immemorial diuturnity. Alexander might have happened on just such a scene of building; Herodotus; whoever strayed hereabouts in the days of Agamemnon, Moses, Rameses.

In one way or another, one feels assured, it will all survive this passing physical dominance of our own race as serenely as it has survived the rest. The Dutch are dead as Methuselah already. The normality of it all; its candid recognition of the evanescent fluidity of material life; its consequent indifference to what we call history, science, and physical or earthly truth. Veracity is impossible — a pastime, not a virtue — until you come into ecstatic perception of mystic divinity, essentially ineffable, and manifesting itself in grotesque semi-divine forms

— elephant-headed; four-armed; whatever else. All lead straight to absorption in divinity. Amazing, incredible as it seems, it has the inevitableness of a creed in which nothing is exotic. . . .

*To Miss Sarah Barrett*

CALCUTTA, 12 *March*, 1911

DEAR AUNT SARAH: — . . . I sent you a post-card from Mount Abu. Before that, I forget when I wrote. We had a pleasant three weeks' globe-trot to Benares, Lucknow, Cawnpore, Agra, Delhi, Jaipur, Mount Abu, Ahmadabad, and Bombay — the regular Indian tour, taken backwards. It has been rather uncomfortable and a bit fatiguing. We shall remember it, though, as picturesque and in various aspects novel and interesting. From Bombay we came straight back here, in forty hours — fourteen hundred miles. The journey proved easier than we expected, and less tiresome.

The Viceroy, Lord Hardinge, has been very cordial. We lunched with him yesterday, and went on to see him preside as Chancellor at the Convocation of Calcutta University — equivalent to our Harvard Commencement. It was not unlike it in general character, though somewhat less elaborate. The odd thing was to see most of the dignitaries, and all the students, with features like ours, black as Virginian darkies. It was queerly grotesque — as was a fine old Maharaja on the platform, with a cloth-of-gold turban and an aigrette of exquisite pearls and emeralds. He looked very like Dr. Weir Mitchell, a model of dignity; but finding his shirt uncomfortable in the middle of the proceedings, took his clothes to pieces and adjusted the matter, as coolly as if in a bath-room. His clothes, I hasten to add, were of the draped, Indian variety.

Both Ediths are well and happy. To-day we are to lunch with Harcourt Butler, the Minister of Education — a nephew of our old friend, the Master of Trinity, at Cambridge. Late in the afternoon we shall start for Darjeeling, where we shall stay until Wednesday, — this is Sunday, — in hopes of a glimpse of the somewhat capricious Himalayas. If the weather is clear, the view is said to be the most impressive in Asia.

Three quarters of the time, though, it is hidden by clouds or haze. We return here on Thursday, the 16th, to dine with Harcourt Butler. On Friday, the 17th, we sail, early in the morning, for Rangoon and Singapore; thence, on the 31st, for Shanghai, where we should arrive, if all goes well, about April 10th. . . .

*To Robert Grant*

SINGAPORE, 29 *March*, 1911

DEAR BOB: — The rather empty letter I sent Amy a week or two ago will have told you already why you have not heard from me long ago. I was utterly tired out — far more so than I understood; and the tropics, though deeply recuperative in power, are n't exhilarating at the moment. Also, I will confess, prudence in strange climate has persuaded me to drink a great deal less stimulant than I am used to at home; and it is awful to find out how one misses the same. On Sunday last, quite fagged by a tremendously torrid and very interesting day ashore in Penang, where there is a wondrous Chinese temple, I treated myself to champagne at dinner. I absorbed it as a panting fish might suck in sea-water; and have felt better ever since. If good on earth, I am now persuaded, I may live again as a golden carp in some ever-flowing fountain of sound French vintage, not too dry — if so may be in a climate where human beings, not given to the final dissipation of physical exercise, should not be compelled to bathe and change three times a day. And Lord! how I hate whisky and soda!

All of which nonsense shows me, I hope, better — more nearly in my habitually unright mind. As I began to scribble the first draft of a new stimulant has been vouchsafed me — the first real shower of rain we have had since New Year's. The air was pantingly hot, and soaked with humidity. This is now precipitating in rich fat drops, dragging down with them some trace of the fresh, dry coolness of upper air.

Singapore, though, has been maligned. It combines the beauties of the Maine coast — a gently varied outline of hills and islands, happily wooded — with the brilliancy and the luxuriance of the equatorial tropics, if there be such a region in physical geography. And the Governor, who looks like Cabot Lodge, is most friendly; and so is the Bishop, who is excessively Anglican but a good sort, very like his grandfather[1] the first English gentleman, of the old type, in whose house I ever stayed, seven and thirty years ago. . . .

## To A. Lawrence Lowell

[*On the death of his cousin and brother-in-law, Francis Cabot Lowell. Wendell had arrived in Shanghai the night before and was at the house of his daughter Mary, Mrs. Wheelock.*]

SHANGHAI, 10 *April*, 1911

DEAR LAWRENCE: — The letters awaiting us here have brought the grievous news of Frank's death. We had had no word about him at all before — few letters of any kind, during our swift, remote travel. Neither of us was a bit prepared for the end.

It comes benumbingly — with less instant surge of emotion than if we had been near, with even deeper sense of irremediable change. For, far beyond most of us, I think, he was a constant fact, of unequaled simplicity, sympathy, kindness, strength, in the lives of all who had the happiness to know him near them. What I feel now, most profoundly, is a wondering sense that, in the full completeness of his great purity, he takes his place already and forever among the characters, gathering in our tradition from eldest New England time, who beautifully justify our national fervor. There have been other phases of human nature elsewhere, wondrous and admirable for others perhaps beyond anything of ours. There has never been anything else comparable for me with the simple greatness of heart and spirit which makes me feel more and more with the fleeting years that New England was not all wrong in its faith that time should show it chosen of the Lord.

Until these very days, though, that greatness of soul had seemed to me rather of elder time than of ours. The happy familiarity of daily life, the unthinking equality of loving fellowship, has kept — has always kept, I suppose — together

[1] Sir Henry Ferguson-Davie, father of Lady White-Thomson.

those who have been altogether coeval. It is only now that I feel, as never before, how close beside us, beside me through almost forty years, there has been just such simplicity and beauty of life and spirit as has made me think the past heroic. So the deepest feeling is rather of reverent gratitude for his unfailing presence in the years now gently come to an end than of overwhelming grief that the end is come. There is no more wondrous certainty than that of the memories which make sacred the regions of the earth where for awhile they lingered. . . .

You will know, without my telling you, how my heart goes out to you in this deepest of bereavements. Let it bring us, who are left together, even closer than ever.

Always affectionately yours,<br>
BARRETT WENDELL

*To his son William*

SHANGHAI, 24 *April*, 1911. — After luncheon Mary gave me the telegrams of Jac's death, received yesterday. Geoffrey had come to meet me with them this morning, but the boat was too late to wait for, and the servant to whom he gave them for Mary misunderstood his orders. So she did not know of them till Geoffrey came home for luncheon; and then thought best to keep them till the meal was over. The fact is bewildering, unusual at this distance, and in my present convalescent condition. B telegraphs that nothing now requires my return. The immediate question was what to do here. With what consideration I could give it, I decided that we shall do best to make no formal mourning; for the reasons that if the case had been reversed this is what I myself should prefer, that mourning would distinctly inconvenience friends who have been and are kind to us here, and that this was the course which, for the same reasons, we took a few weeks ago when Lizzie Greenough died. I sent, through B, an answering telegram of condolence, and inquiry as to whether I had not best shorten my journey. But the code is unsatisfactory. I can write him in full, and get telegraphic answer by the time we get back from Peking. On the whole, I am glad that chance put me so far away at the sad moment; for I could have done nothing, so far as I can see, which cannot be as well done by the others, and I shall be better able to advise and to help in time to come for the strength which this journey is slowly bringing. . . .

30 *April*, 1911. — . . . To call on Kinnear, who was out; so home, having left Edith and the youths at a Municipal Concert. Tommy was alone. I sat with him above an hour. He grows older, talking of battles and the like gravely, and getting a map to see where Nelson fought at the Nile and at Trafalgar. He also brought out his mother's photograph books, wherein are snapshots and the like of the family through thirty years. It touched me deeply, thus to look with the little man at images of what had gone before him. We just turned the pages, naming the faces we recognized, which generally meant little to him. I preserved austere, ancestral dignity, affably talking of odds and ends. But these were the records of the dead days and of the dead — no very sad story involved, nor any not commonplace. Only I did n't know, when they were alive, how much I might have cared for them, and enjoyed their presence; and I don't know now how much what I have done or left undone has distorted the children from what they might have been. I ended very sentimental — but had to dress for a pleasant dinner at Leveson's, where we went late by reason of delayed carriage. . . .

1 *May*, 1911. — . . . Poor old Jac is with me all the time, not unkindly or troublously, but tenderly. He was really, simply affectionate, I think — a boy at heart to the end. . . . I am coming now to feel nearer to him than I have felt since he was really a boy in years as well as in nature. I shall remember him, I can begin to see, as if he had never grown up at all; but had come to a laughing end while he was still in college. A happy memory this will be. I rather think it will be the memory generally persistent with those who knew him and who cared for him: many of whom, in later years, I found far from congenial to myself. But this was as if they had been friends of boyhood, not of real maturity. One does n't delight,

in middle life, in college nonsense and the like; the irresponsibility of Bohemia is after all a good deal like that of boyhood. As for the children . . . they are dear little things; and in need enough of encouragement and help to command it unstintingly from many . . . .

PEKING, 15 *May*, 1911. — . . . At eight to the Legation,[1] where the Princes Hsun and Tao came with their wives to meet us at dinner: de Cartier, Cazenave, Morrison, Everts, — Secretary of the Belgian Legation, — and his sister, who know the Frank Lowells, and the de Menocals, the Eustises, Straight, the Fairchilds, the Tenneys, and two or three more. Prince Hsun and his wife are very fat; Prince Tao and his, slight and delicate. The men are brothers of the late emperor, I believe, and certainly of the present regent — uncles of the baby emperor. Hsun is the head of the navy; Tao of the army. Princess Hsun, very chubby, highly painted, and glittering with diamond rings, took a great fancy to Edith, whom she insisted on leading to dinner in person — thus avoiding, pretty easily, inconvenient taking of arms, etc. The Princes sat on each side of Mrs. Calhoun, the Princesses, in the Manchu head-dresses, on either side of the Minister; next each of the four sat some one who speaks Chinese — Tenney next Princess Hsun, a somewhat rippling missionary, Miss Corbett, between me and Prince Tao. She interpreted well; but the talk was neither profound nor animated: on his part, royally, though diffidently, interrogative and constatory; on mine civil and, at Miss Corbett's suggestion, as metaphorical as occasion allowed. He is a delicate-looking man of thirty or so, exquisite in refinement, gentle in manner, thought to be sincerely progressive; Prince Hsun is softly fat, with the general aspect associated conventionally with all the vices of Oriental despotism. He was very cordial in manner, though, and I dare say that his looks bely him as much as was the case with the late Bishop of Massachusetts. The Princes have asked us to dine with them on Thursday, when Prince Tao says that he will have the imperial band, of eighty pieces, to play.

[1] The Hon. William James Calhoun was then U. S. Minister in China.

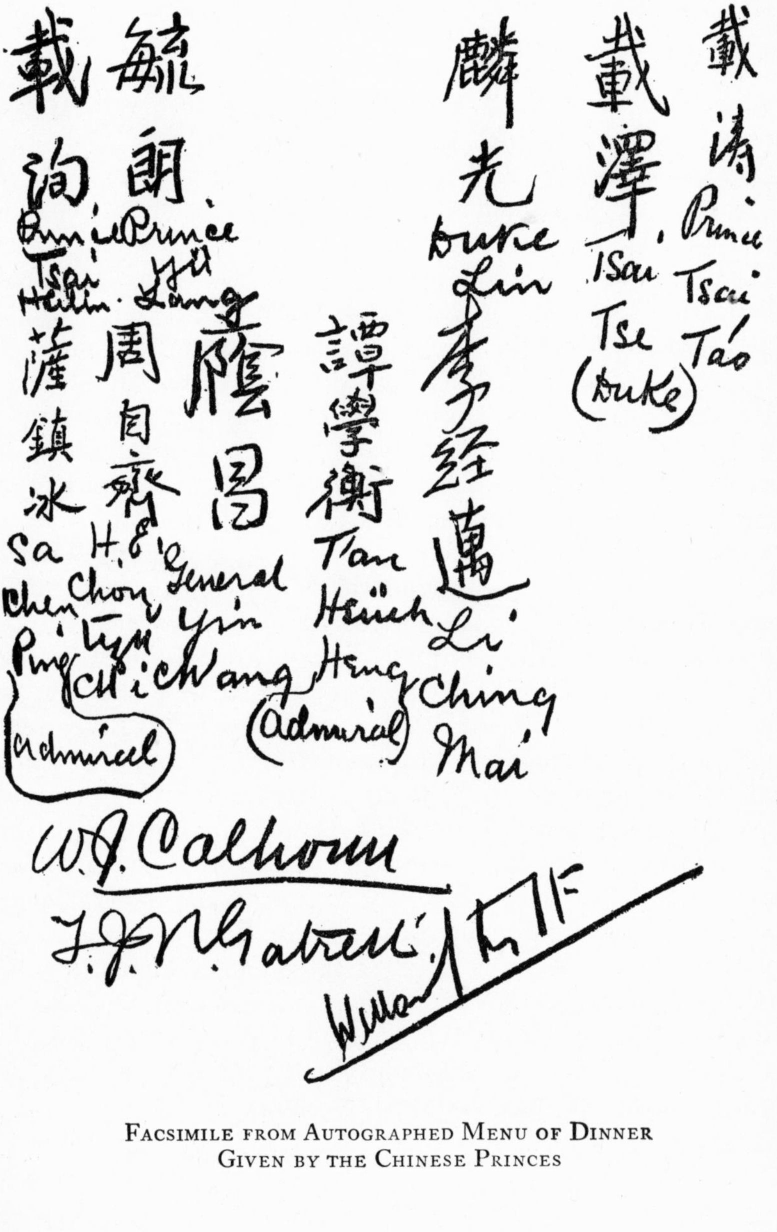
載濤
Prince Tsai Tao
載澤
Tsai Tse (Duke)
麟光
Duke Lin
李經邁
Li Ching Mai
譚學衡
T'an Hsüeh Heng (Admiral)
蔭昌
General Yin Ch'ang
周自齊
H.E. Chou Tzu Ch'i
薩鎮冰
Sa Chen Ping (Admiral)
毓朗
Prince Yü Lang
載洵
Prince Tsai Hsün
W. J. Calhoun
Willard Straight

FACSIMILE FROM AUTOGRAPHED MENU OF DINNER
GIVEN BY THE CHINESE PRINCES

18 *May*, 1911. — . . . At seven we started to dine with the Princes Tsai Hsun and Tsai Tao; stopping at the Legation to be picked up and guided by the Calhouns. The drive was through a thoroughly Chinese quarter which I had not seen before — some narrow dusty streets leading to a new, broad one, with much finer shops and restaurants, elaborately gilt signs, and so on. A turn up a side street brought us to a gate of the Princes' house, which is surrounded by a high wall of grey brick. It is Prince Hsun's house, where the brothers combined in entertaining us. Like the other Chinese houses we have seen, — Straight's, Morrison's, the de Menocals', — it is a series of courtyards, with one-story buildings, admirable in proportion; this, however, is much larger in all respects, and exquisitely clean — perhaps freshly dusted for the occasion. Servants, in peaked conical caps, red-tasseled, around. As we walked in, the Minister and I were half run-down by a carriage with evident right of entry. It proved to contain a delicate little lady in Manchu costume, highly painted and scarred with smallpox. As she got out she greeted Calhoun, who presented me to her — the sister of the present Empress Dowager. So I gravely bent over her pretty little hand. She knows no more English than the rest. We left our wraps in a pretty room, electric-lighted, with European furniture; and a Chinese gentleman with the double-dragon order — director of education, I believe — led us through a very large courtyard, in which a huge red stage for the band had been put up, as if a theatre, to the veranda where the Princes and Princesses were awaiting us. They received us with cordial informality.

Apart from the Calhouns and Straight, who came late, and Miss Corbett and another interpreter, — Dr. Gatrell, I think, — the company were Chinese, of the highest rank: several imperial princes and dukes, two admirals, the commanding general of the army, in a German-looking uniform, Lord Li — surviving son of Li Hung Chang — and a few more; those of higher rank with their wives. At table the Princes sat together, their wives opposite. On their right, in each case, the Calhouns; on their left, Edith and I. Miss Corbett was next me; beyond her a highly rouged elderly duchess, of some-

what inquiring disposition. Next Edith was Dr. Gatrell —
if I have his name right. The dinner itself was completely
European: cooked and served, it seems, from this hôtel des
wagons-lits, whence came all the tableware too, and happily
the wine. The manager was observable in the background;
the waiters he had brought along. It was well done.

Meanwhile, in the courtyard, the imperial band played —
far enough away to be agreeable — a good deal of European
music and some Chinese. This carried off the evening; for
the talk could not be very animated, particularly as the delicate
little Princess Tao, next whom I sat, said nothing whatever
from beginning to end, though civilly and briefly responsive
when I ventured to address her through Miss Corbett's inter-
vention. Mary got along better, with some gentlemen who
spoke English; little Edith sat pretty mum beside an elderly
pig-tailed duke, in spectacles, with a cold in his head, and the
facial aspect of a member of the Great Elector's Tobacco
Parliament. A forced affair, socially; but almost unique, they
say. Chinese ladies of rank have rarely dined with men anywhere; the men, rarely with ladies. Nothing 'could have
exceeded their quiet good breeding — a matter, in most cases,
of affable silence. The dinner was pretty long.

Afterwards we passed into the room where we had been
received; and looked at the vases and so on. There was a
wondrous white vase of the Han dynasty, some two thousand
years old, with exquisite metallic gleams said to come from
silver ore in the paste; and a very large vase of dull red lacquer,
curiously carved over every inch. When we took our leave,
we cordially shook hands with everybody. As the Minister
came to the steps of the veranda, the band played the Star
Spangled Banner very well. So an end.

Straight[1] came back with us and sat for half an hour talking
it over. The manager and the servants, returning with the
tableware, were unprecedentedly respectful. On the whole, it
seems to me, these very noble Chinese regard us much as we
regard them — in most cases completely confusing social

[1] Willard D. Straight was then acting as representative of the "American Group"
of bankers in China.

classes, and considering the fact that another race is alien equivalent to demonstration of its inferiority. They are at once too well-bred, however, and too prudent to make this sentiment obtrusive; and their courtesy, thousands of years in the making, is as noteworthy for ease as for grace. It has the grace of instinctive finish. All the same, as I said to de Menocal at the Legation, when the Princes were there, I could n't help feeling that in meeting us at dinner they felt as we should feel in sitting down to table with Booker Washington. The sentiment might be of disgust, it might be of resignation, it might be of philanthropic, advanced, patronizing self-approval; the one certain fact is that it could not be unconscious, nor unaffectedly genial. . . .

[*On his return to his daughter Mary's house at Shanghai*]

28 *May*, 1911. — . . . At the house I found B's long letter telling of poor Jac's end; and a number of sympathetic words — from Fred S., Wadsworth L., Briggs, Castle, James Rhodes, Woodward Emery, and Alice. It is sadly happy to know how much his friends cared for him, and how eagerly his good work in his new profession[1] was appreciated by all. What B writes makes me freshly glad that I was not at home. I could have done nothing whatever which he — dear old chap — did not do more tactfully and more firmly than I could. . . .

2 *June*, 1911. — . . . At 5.30 I spoke before the Royal Asiatic Society — mostly female and to the eye unlearned — on "Traveling Impressions of India and China." Bourne presided, rather heavily. *Succès d'estime*. My thesis was that India embodies the extreme Guelph ideal and China the extreme Ghibelline of the Holy Roman Empire. Edith says she could n't follow me, and I don't much wonder. Florence Ayscough looked in later, to say good-bye. And I carried Tommy upstairs to bed — I suppose for the last time.

DAMPFER "PRINZ EITEL FRIEDRICH," *Saturday, 3 June,* 1911. — Up at daylight to pack; and Mary, disheveled, turned up in a green dressing-gown to look on and help. A warm,

---

[1] That of an actor.

sticky day, it turned out, but sunny.  Rather a conscious breakfast, diverted by the report of yesterday's speech, which I
enclose.  This says nothing I did n't say, but does not follow
what I meant to be my thread; and breaks off nowhere.  It
impresses me though, as good enough in substance to warrant
my plan of making a book about this journey, or rather about
the impressions it has made on me.  The ideas in the report,
taken from what I said off-hand, without notes, seem to me
capable of development.

Our luggage got off in wheelbarrows at half past eight.  An
hour later I followed, in the victoria, with Tommy.  T. had
possessed himself of five Mexican dollars, which he desired to
spend in my company, on condition that I should not interfere.
We stopped at a large shop called Weeks's, where he bought
for two dollars a huge knife, with a chain, for himself; and for
two more a silver pencil case for grandma.  I dissuaded him
from disposing of the other dollar in gifts; and we went on to
the jetty.  There we were soon followed by the Ediths and
Mary, in the motor-car, the richer for three delightful Chinese
dolls. . . .  At the jetty Robblee was waiting; and the luggage
already aboard one of Geoffrey's tenders.  Mrs. McNeill —
who leaves for Dalny and England to-night — came to see us
off; so did the Ayscoughs, and Leveson in a white suit.  We
went aboard at about half past ten, fouling a junk and carrying away part of her rotten starboard bulwarks on the way.
Geoffrey and Tommy sent back in a small tender as soon as
we were aboard — T. keeping a remarkably brave face, but
looking somehow as if he did n't want us to go, and never see
him again as a little child.  Mary stayed aboard till the regular
tender brought on the herd-like and deeply uninteresting passengers.  Then she went back, in the Vulcan, which had brought
us out — our last glimpse of her a pongee figure, with a big
shade hat; waving its hand, and then sitting down, looking
the other way.  Our visit to her has been altogether happy. . . .

Tokio, *Sunday*, 11 *June*, 1911. — . . . After luncheon I
went with Charles Osborne and Robblee in rickshaws, through
half an hour of liquid mud on macadamized pavements, to an

exhibition of wrestling. Tokio streets are as wide and as comparatively colorless as those of Peking — in better general order, though, particularly in the matter of the buildings which line them. Japanese costume is more general than I expected: in the rain they carry oiled-paper umbrellas and wear tall clogs, which keep them an inch or two above the mire.

The wrestling was in a large circular building, where most of the seats were straw-matted platforms, for the Japanese; but round the walls was a row of large boxes with chairs. The wrestlers performed on a raised platform in the centre, covered by a wooden roof ultimately lighted by electricity. Until this was turned on, one could hardly see anything. Skillful, the wrestling; and much to the taste of the audience; the wrestlers, mostly fat, nude except for breech-clouts, and agile. The umpire, in old Japanese dress, with a gleaming lacquer fan, was splendid. The bouts began very slowly; and all but one, after a dozen false starts, were over in a few seconds. We were too far off, and my eyes too little skilled, to observe the finer points; it was as little amusing as cricket to one who does not know the game.

Presently came into the box a Japanese guide, with an Englishman and his wife, whom I had seen at the hotel. The seats bore no numbers; but, after some discussion behind me, the guide came up and said that I had taken places reserved for him. To all appearances, it was simply because I had no guide to protect me. Somewhat vexed, I gave up my seat and Robblee's — Charles was already bored away — and asked for the guide's name, to report him. Thereupon the monocular British major, I believe, exploded, and called me rude. Mad all through, I replied quietly that his expression of opinion had the value of proceeding from one who appeared to be among the highest living authorities on the quality in question.

He sputtered like a leaky valve; I left him sputtering, and — much upset myself — sat down in the outside corridor and gave an interview on literature in general to a polite Japanese journalist who had followed me from the hotel. . . .

BARRETT WENDELL AND HIS FIRST GRANDCHILD

12 *June*, 1911. — Fair day, sunny and not warm. To call on O'Brien,[1] our Ambassador, a tall, grey-bearded man, charming in quiet manner. Back by half past eleven to find Sakai, of the Foreign Office — who proves a Harvard man, short, plump, spectacled — already waiting to take us to lunch at Marquis Matsukata's. Had to get into frock coat — a process slightly delayed by missing trousers, which the boy had taken to press. Still we got off by noon. Half an hour in rickshaws, partly through a lovely park of tall, shady pines, with green grass under them. Matsukata's house, in good European style, is in a fine large garden with a little pond in front of it, beyond which rises a low hill covered with old trees: dense, rich foliage. A miniature stone pagoda at one side, marking the spot where one of the Forty-Seven Ronins killed himself.

At the door two `Japanese butlers, in European dress-clothes. The Marquis, a fine, white-haired old fellow, moustached, looks thoroughly French in his frock coat and white waistcoat. He speaks only Japanese; but his two sons, a friend, — a Baron, who took the Harvard LL.B. in '74, — and Sakai translated so easily that one hardly felt the barrier. The Marchioness, a stout old lady slightly marked with smallpox, wore her Japanese dress; so did her daughter-in-law, who spoke English. All the men in frock coats. An excellent luncheon; but the talk did not go deep. Afterwards we sat in the open Japanese house — a part of the house — and looked at the garden — as exquisite a bit of old artificial landscape as I ever saw. . . .

Tokio, *Sunday*, 18 *June*, 1911. — A fair day, with occasional sunshine and no wind. In the morning the Ediths and Charles Osborne went to church; Robblee and I to the Shiba temples. Very like those at Nikko, though not quite so beautiful in scale, in proportion, in detail, or still more in setting. Still, in the sunny quiet of this summer morning, one could linger over their gorgeous delicacy in a way which took one more than ever into the spirit of this remote, exquisite art. Barbaric it

[1] The Honorable Thomas James O'Brien, U. S. Ambassador to Japan, 1897-1911.

seems in some aspects, just as European art, I suppose, must seem barbaric to eyes trained in the tradition of art like this: the true difference being that each has emerged in its own distinct way from the gropings of experiment and aspiration to the mastery of achievement. And which is the higher or the better there is no certainty at all. Each has mastery, calm and complete: ours of structural form, theirs of decoration and color. Ours is the more enduring; theirs the more glowing. But they are too far apart for happy fusion.

To lunch with the Ambassador, O'Brien, who sent his carriage for us, with men in red Japanese hats and with the stars and stripes in moonlike circles on their liveries. Mrs. Shipley — one of Admiral Carpenter's daughters from Portsmouth — was there with her daughter: a charming woman, and a pretty girl. Shipley is naval attaché here and at Peking. The Ambassador advises us to accept Murai's house at Kyoto; and tells me that Murai made his money by buying up tobacco shops just before the Government confiscated them and established monopoly. Mendenhall has since added that Murai's attention was called to tobacco by missionary tracts against it, setting forth the immense and growing Japanese demand for cigarettes.

In the afternoon, we all left cards at Komura's and at Matsukata's; and then kept on, in rickshaws, to the pretty grove where the Forty-Seven Ronins are buried. The story of these, perhaps the most touching story of Japanese chivalry, I read in '73, in Mitford's *Tales of Old Japan*, on the Colima, when I thought I was coming here, ten years short of half my present age. So I could understand something of the quiet worship still going on. You turn aside from a main street and instantly find yourself in a short road leading to the wooded graveyard on a little hill. On each side are purely native shops, full of prints and figures and other mementos of the Ronins. Hundreds, I should think, of Japanese — mostly of the lower class, but sometimes officers and so on — come thither of a holiday; and linger among the grey gravestones, lighting little sticks of incense on the tiny altars before each. So in the tall shady grove the sweet smoke rises forever. I have hardly ever seen so deeply natural a shrine; never one so pervasively human — so instinct with religious, devotional feeling, yet so free from formality, austerity, gloom, terror. Hardly sublime, but serenely beautiful — and quietly proving how the old spirit of Japan is alive in the people. . . .

TOKIO, *Wednesday*, 21 *June*, 1911. — Clear and warm, until evening when a cool breeze set in. At a little before ten we went to the Embassy — the Ediths in train dresses, with hats, I in dress clothes with white gloves. At ten the Ambassador started with us for the palace — Edith going with him in his victoria; little Edith and I following in the landau, my dress clothes decently dissembled under my old summer ulster. The palace is a large, quiet building, so little salient that I already forget its features, in a fine large park, within the walls of the old castle. At the door were several servants in gold-laced liveries, cocked hats, and so on. A large, cool entrance-hall, whence a chamberlain led us through long, carpeted corridors, with windows on one side and the closed, lacquered doors of large rooms on the other, to a pleasant sitting-room looking out on the park. The furniture here was of comfortable, commonplace European type — chairs and sofas covered with some light greyish silk material. The whole place was perfumed with some unusual incense, smelling like benzoin, and strongest in the sitting-room — probably to affect invading clothes. Here we were joined by the master of ceremonies, and by a pleasant, bearded man called Nagasaki, who was to interpret: all in court dress. Later came the fat little smooth-faced chamberlain of the Empress, and one or two more. Presently the Ambassador and I were led along another corridor where a lacquered folding door opposite a window was open, with a gentleman in court dress on each side. Just short of the door we stopped, until in a minute or two the quick sound of boots on the wooden floor within indicated that the Emperor was at hand.

Then, at a signal from the master of ceremonies, the Ambassador stepped forward to the centre of the door, bowed and entered — I following some six feet behind.

The Emperor was in uniform, and on either side behind him, in the small room, an official in court dress stood at attention, motionless. He is about my height, stout, large-featured, with a thin moustache and beard, small eyes, and heavy expression. Not very grey, but looking old. He spoke in a low, rather mumbling voice, first a few civilities to the Ambassador. Then the Ambassador stepped a little to the right, and I stepped forward. The Emperor shook hands, in his military glove; my right hand was bare for the honor. He asked how long I had been in Japan, whether I had visited the University, and so on; then wished me a pleasant journey, and shook hands again. I then backed out of the little room, followed, in a minute or so by the Ambassador. Nothing, in a way, could have been less impressive than such a passing formality. Yet I find the memory of it vivid and deep. This man, who has no special distinction of feature or presence, no formal manner different from that of any other Japanese gentleman, except that he did not smile, somehow seemed like one tired beyond compare with the burden of life. Indefinitely old, he looked; he might have been the dynasty incarnate. Not alert; a bit perplexed with life; but brave, sturdy, proud, determined, and not ungentle. The history of him has marked his person.

Meanwhile, the fat little chamberlain had presented the Ediths to the Empress; and as we approached her reception room close by, we saw them smilingly pass the end of the corridor. With her the etiquette was precisely like that of the Emperor. A Japanese lady in a high-necked dress with a short train interpreted; another stood, with hands clasped in front, behind her. The Empress is a tiny lady, looking so much like the Italian Mrs. George Lee that, except for the Empress's age, you could hardly tell them apart. Her manner and her questions resembled the Emperor's. Like him, she did not smile. In a minute or so we backed out, in the same order as before.

A chamberlain kindly showed us the State rooms: throne-room, dining-room, and so on, which are well described in *Murray*. What most caught my eye were some large Japanese tapestries, copying old paintings of hunts, one near Fuji.

The other works of art, and so on, were admirable in quality but of more familiar type. The rooms are masterpieces of modern Japanese workmanship, European in outline, Japanese in detail. . . .

Tokio, *Thursday*, 22 *June*, 1911. — Coronation Day — so the city was much decorated with Japanese and English flags; and there was general holiday.

At ten Sakai came with a professor of the Imperial University to take us there. We all went in rickshaws — nearly an hour through holiday streets. The University is in the large grounds of an old Daimyo's place, with a fine old red lacquer gate, and near the buildings a ripe old garden. We were received by the President, who speaks a little English, and a number of professors, all Japanese, in frock coats. This dress of ceremony is here tyrannical; only they allow themselves straw hats. After a while they took us to the library, which proved so interesting that we stayed there till lunch. Four hundred thousand volumes — well catalogued and shelved: among them all Max Müller's library. A glance at the shelves showed European history and literature well kept up. Their treasures — old Japanese MSS. and so on — were brought out for us. The department where they are copying and publishing the historical records of old Japan is admirable. At one, a big luncheon, with almost all the faculty of literature, and several of science and medicine. I sat between the President and Mrs. Terry, whose husband — a Yale man — has long been professor of law.

Soon after lunch Yokoyama called and took me away, after some debate with Sakai, to see Count Okuma, at Waseda University. . . . A picturesque rickshaw-ride. The University is in beautiful grounds — or perhaps they were the private grounds of Okuma, a shaven old gentleman with a grand air, who talked affably about dramatic literature, through an interpreting professor. . . .

Kyoto, *Friday*, 23 *June*, 1911. — Left Tokio at 8.30 — Sakai coming to see us off, and also Nakayama, young Matsukata, and Baron Kamada, of Keiokejuku University — the last in frock coat and top hat. The Japanese cars are uncomfortable for long journeys, generally having only long, sidewise seats, like an American electric car; but Sakai managed to engage for us the one compartment on the train, to the vast envy of staring fellow passengers. . . .

At Kyoto we were received not only by Hattori, Mr. Murai's secretary, but to my surprise by Tagasaki, the Secretary of the Governor, and by Inagaki, the Governor's interpreter. The Governor had sent his carriage for us too — a fine landau, with two footmen. So we drove in state to Mr. Murai's villa, where we found a splendid European house, in a lovely park, all ready for us; and dined; and slept to perfection.

KOBE, 30 *June*, 1911. — As this paper shows, I write at about half past six, looking out on a crowded, smoky harbor — our dream of splendor is at an end. . . .[1]

At ten we all started in rickshaws with Hattori, and went to Iida's big and alluring shop, where we bought some odds and ends, and I did them the honor to sign my eminent name in their book of distinguished autographs. A little man named Nagato, a pupil of Miss Denton's, did the honors. I bought rather pretty leather pocket-books, as parting gifts for Hattori and Inagaki. Then Charles Osborne and small Edith went off by themselves, and a man from Iida's took us to a small native shop, where Edith was duly fitted out in a diaphanous ecclesiastical vestment and stole, thought suitable for a tea-gown — to the vast delight of observing men, women, and children. To a fan shop where I bought a few rather pretty fans. Then home, to finish packing, and to lunch. After luncheon, Fuller called to say good-bye. At three the Governor's carriage appeared for the last time, and we drove off in state. Incidentally the pretty little maid had showed us how she tied her big sash, or obi; and the smiling butler had served sauterne and champagne for luncheon.

At the station we were met by a long-moustached ecclesiastic with a pot hat, who had been sent by Count Otarsi, Abbot of the Hongwanji temples, with farewell messages; by the Secre-

---

[1] The Wendells had just spent a week as guests at the villa of Mr. Murai at Kyoto.

tary of the University; by Tagasaki; by Tanada, President of the Doshisha, with three girls therefrom, bearing bright nosegays; and by one or two more. With Hattori and Inagaki, it made a most impressive farewell. By and by the train rumbled in from Tokio; and we got into the only first-class carriage, rather cramped and dusty; and I bowed my farewell from the platform; and so we subsided into private life. The carriage filled — with Eurasians, I think — till we were packed in as in the Boston Elevated railway. The journey of two hours, by way of Osaka, was dull. Getting out at Kobe station, I was pushed this way and that by some rather elderly women of the operative class. And at the hotel we were sent up in a rather dingy lift, like a herd of cattle. *Sic transivit gloria mundi.*

At that moment, the glory of this sunset world revived itself, in the person of one Fujieda, a moustached and dapper young man, who has been in America, learned less English than he supposes, and become a journalist. He has been interviewing me for a good half-hour, with a view to a column in some Japanese newspaper. I confined myself to admiring commonplace, which he gave every symptom of politely misunderstanding in every detail; to all appearances, however, he gathered that my sentiments are amicable. . . .

*To Sir Robert White-Thomson*
MUJANOSHITA, 16 *July*, 1911.

As my post-card will have told you, your letter of May 24th was more than welcome. The post-card hardly implied how dazzlingly busy we were when the letter came. Letters from President Taft to the authorities here have made us almost guests of the nation. Certainly no ambassador could have been received more hospitably or with much more attention. The Foreign Office deputed one of its chief secretaries to meet our steamer, and to care for us during our stay at Tokio. We were presented to the Emperor and the Empress; entertained by Cabinet Ministers and Elder Statesmen, as well as by university people and men of affairs; given, at Kyoto, the use of a wonderful villa, on a royal scale, together with that of the governor's carriage, with running footmen; and generally received at temples, museums, and the like by the chief authorities thereof, in semi-state. We had a marvelous week-end, on the shore of the Inland Sea, with the descendant of the Daimyos who were locally sovereign there for seven hundred years. Their castle is burnt; but their shrines, their personal estates, and their heirlooms remain. And when our friend comes, three or four times a year, to his pretty country house on his ancestral property, the whole country turns out to receive him, just as you might imagine some loyal little mediatized duchy behaving, in the heart of a German forest.

It was all wondrous, but pretty tiresome to the body; and dear Edith almost went to bed from sheer fatigue, after three weeks of it. So, after a quieter week at Nara, with its wondrous thousand-year-old temples and trees and works of art; and after an exhausting, but immensely interesting, excursion with Mary — who has joined us, and who left Tommy with her mother for the interval — to the sacred mountain, Fujisan, we have all retired to this pretty hill-region, to rest for our last two weeks this side of the Pacific. We sail from Yoko-hama on the 27th. We expect to get home, after a little travel in the west, about September 1st. I wish we could have returned by way of Europe; for various reasons, however, this has proved impracticable. . . .

## To W. R. Castle

S. S. Mongolia, 8 *August*, 1911

DEAR CASTLE: — At last we are on our home stretch at sea, after a day in Honolulu which will linger in memory among the pleasantest of all. A day or two before we got there, came a wireless message of welcome from your father saying that he would meet us at the pier. So he did, with your sister, inconveniently early for them I fear, on Sunday morning, day before yesterday. From then till we sailed, twenty-six hours later, your people kept us in a happy whirl. They had a motor with them. We went first to the house, where your mother welcomed us with wondrous fruits. Then your sister took Edith off for surf-bathing; and your father drove my wife and me to Kaliula — altogether, I think, the most enchanting spot I know.

What carried me off my feet is that, for all the complete strangeness and novelty of the landscape, its extraordinarily definite beauty is exactly what I have always supposed the South Sea Islands to look like, ever since I dreamed about them after reading boys' stories of adventure and ship-wreck.

Then we drove down in time to motor to the Pali pass before luncheon. What might have been the shadowless monotony of noon-day light was relieved by scurrying clouds, with here and there a spit of a shower. That view is one of the supreme; only, I should think, a shade too perfect in composition to live with. Day in, day out, I should rather stay at Kaliula. . . .

In the afternoon we motored again — to the Aquarium, near which an open-air concert was going on, whence came, above the band, the sweet notes of a woman's voice, singing a Hawaiian song; then we called on my old Portsmouth friend, Frank Hatch, deep in mourning for his wife; and then went round Diamond Head, and got back in time to meet no end of people, mostly Harvard men, who had been telephoned to-gether for tea. A few I knew — Dillingham, Brigham, Ballou, Horne, and one or two more. All were as friendly as if I had known them well. We had to go a bit after six, having engaged ourselves to dine with some English friends at the Sea Side Hotel. So the Sunday ended, in a cloud of mosquitos, and with imperfect service and cooking, looking out from that exquisite open dining-room on the moonlit surf — not too high — and at the black outline of Diamond Head, sharp against the luminous blue of tropical night.

Yesterday morning . . . your father came for me a little before eight, and took me to the Museum, which Brigham had opened for me. It is among the most interesting anywhere — the amazing Hawaiian collection perfectly installed, and exquisitely defined by the rich collection from Polynesia. Back to the ship at half-past nine . . . where your sister, and Frank Hatch with his pretty daughter, and our English friends from the Sea Side, and Dillingham, and more, collared us with wreaths of flowers: altogether the prettiest farewell custom I ever saw. We were off at last about half past ten, backing through the green water, sprinkled with flowers, where glowing brown boys were bobbing about, diving for bits of silver. . . .

Honolulu surprised and delighted me. It is among the loveliest places I ever saw; and as a first glimpse of America, after seven months of sea and Asia, it is immensely reassuring. It has, I think, much of our national simplicity and more than much of our national vigor, with surprisingly little of our new national vulgarity. . . .

*To H. M. Kallen*

PORTSMOUTH, 15 *October*, 1911

Forgive me that I have not written sooner, in answer to your letter, and in thanks, too, for the pamphlet on comedy. Well done, that; and full of stimulating power. Forgive me, too, if I have n't yet sent letters. I have been at Cambridge little, so far; and here have not accessible a Wisconsin catalogue; so I still do not know whom I know there, if anybody. In any event, I will send the letters to you, to use or not as you will. There can be no question, I think, that what friends I have there are so far from intimate by this time, that I should hesitate to write them directly from a clear sky.

What you write of the atmosphere there makes me more sure than ever that you are fortunate to breathe it. There is no need to say how little it is to my taste — or to my deepest convictions, for that matter. La Follette I know only from the public prints, wherein he seems to me named by God to mark him for what he shows himself — a distorted fool-fire, a begrimed Will-o'-the-Wisp. Fantastic, to me, man and name alike; mistily, freakishly untrue to the vagrant nature of the soul of him, if in the murk of his flickering dashes he could so much as suspect that they who would build on earth must toilsomely tread the solid earth first, humbly confessing that men cannot be gods or even imps; and that work must be done with evil stuff if it is to be done at all. To the flickering, the very fact of solidity seems evil — as indeed to them it is; for the very essence of their being is swampy miasma, incompatible with chains and pavements, and what else make the present the foundation for the future.

But there you are. In this country and this age the Will-o'-the-Wisp is as the Star of Bethlehem to Christian fancy. And the Lord alone knows, in his ironic wisdom, which flickers the more delusively to mortality.

Harvard stifles me, more than I expected. I have been there too long. The day is dawning, no doubt; I like the auroral gloom. But I feel infinitely old; and would be content to depart in peace if my Lord, the President, would suffer his servant to, with some manner of pension. Lowell I love. He is perhaps the dearest of all my friends. But I am too nearly tired out, I find, to be of much use in the new dispensation. My true function was to keep a thread of way open for it still in the Cimmerian midnight of the old. . . .

*To Chester Noyes Greenough*

18 GRAYS HALL, 20 *December*, 1911

DEAR GREENOUGH: — The pleasure the Catalogue[1] brings me, with its implicit assurance of constant affection, is even greater than I thought it could be. Even by itself, too, it would have had deeper interest than I had begun to imagine. It is ninety-five years old; yet I find in it not only the name of my great-uncle Samuel Barrett, whom I knew well, and of another kinsman, George Ingersoll, whom I vividly remember; but many whom I either knew or can see in memory as clearly as when their faces were familiar in life. Edward Everett was in the faculty; George Bancroft a senior; Sidney Bartlett a junior; Henry Upham a sophomore; Ezra S. Gannett a freshman; and so on. And when it comes to impressions of personality, they are almost as vivid as if I had known or seen the bearers of name after name — to my memory only names. I know where they came from, what they did, what became of them, whom they got. It is a great many years since the stars have twinkled for me so radiantly as at this moment when I write to you. The mood is that of *Stelligeri:* after all, I have never made record more sincere and constant than therein.

Always affectionately yours,

BARRETT WENDELL

[1] A copy of the Harvard Catalogue of 1816

*To H. M. Kallen*

BOSTON, 26 *December*, 1911

. . . In this epoch of ours we are all alien, unless we are too dense to feel the utter strangeness of the incessantly moving years. At my age, in my mood, the world seems madly bound nowhither. I can't help it; at best I can dimly see and stammeringly record what I fancy might have been tolerable resting-places on the journey. Even Asia is shaking itself out of its spiritual phase into one as crassly material — and so as essentially discontent — as that of Europe. The best we can do, I begin to feel, is to tell the story of it all, as smilingly as one may.

I am trying to put my impressions of Asia into some manner of form; but not as yet with much promise of result. . . .

*To his daughter Mary*
[*On Wendell's return from China he adopted the practice of sending a weekly journal-letter to his daughter, Mrs. Wheelock.*]

OYSTER BAY

26 *January*, 1912. — . . . To Oyster Bay by the 4.30. On the train was Roosevelt, with a big soft black felt hat, more obvious than usual. He was friendly. Arthur Hill, Hart, — my colleague at Harvard, — Norman Hapgood of *Collier's Weekly*, and a man named Sullivan, whom I don't quite place, were his party. I sat next them: Roosevelt talking incessantly, and constantly in the first person singular. On the whole the impression was disagreeable.

BOSTON

29 *January*, 1912. — To New York at 8.08. At present one changes at Jamaica to an electric car which runs under the East River to the Pennsylvania Station, on Seventh Avenue and Thirty-Second Street. In this car I observed near me a large moustached man, in a fur coat and cap, deep in a book; and did not recognize him as Roosevelt till he looked up and beckoned me to sit beside him. Then he talked incessantly and quietly about matters literary and academic. He finds debates, where sides are chosen by lot, objectionable for their insincerity; but would like to see college magazines or papers somehow in competition for a medal, or some such matter. At least that was what I took him to say. He is so exuberant of speech that he's not quite easy to follow. . . . He was far quieter, though, in look and manner as well as in speech, than on Friday. Overwrought, he seems, to a disturbing degree. My present guess is that the trouble between him and Taft will make in the Republican convention a split which would defeat in the election a party more popularly strong than that now is. One or the other will probably be nominated; and the election in November will go to the Democrats unless they split worse. Just now, it looks as though they might agree on Woodrow Wilson, a dangerously doctorian though honest and well-informed man. Should Roosevelt win the election, I

should expect him somehow to retain the presidency for life, unless his overwrought condition should lead to a disturbance of reason beyond dispute. Four years ago my classmate Moody, then a Justice of the Supreme Court, told me that he had earnestly advised Roosevelt, an intimate personal as well as political friend, to withdraw from office permanently; on the ground that the strain thereof, combining sovereignty with party leadership, was unendurably great, after eight years, for any human power. . . .

25 *February*, 1912. — . . . At nine or so I was called up by the *Herald*, for comment on Roosevelt's announcement, just given the press, that he will be a candidate for the Republican nomination. This does not necessarily mean for the presidency itself; for if the nominating convention does not choose him he will hardly start an independent campaign. I declined comment, on the ground that I have no special knowledge of politics. In fact, he seems to me dangerous, having steadily tended toward radical extreme; but then, no one seems safe. I feel as if social revolution were near, probably inevitable. Cæsar may therefore be preferable to Brutus — if Brutus were in sight anywhere. . . .

26 *February*, 1912. — . . . To dine with Jack Wheelwright. Jack was born February 26, 1856, and so, on his fifty-sixth birthday, had a little company of intimates: his brother George, Moorfield Storey, Bob Grant, Russell, a brother of poor Billy, one Tom Frothingham, Nathan Matthews, and me. It was humanly charming. Bob Grant sat next me. He sympathized with Roosevelt's radical opinions; but is an intimate friend of Taft's. Months ago he asked Roosevelt, an old friend, to stay with him sometime when he came to an Overseers' meeting; Roosevelt invited himself accordingly for last night; told Bob whom he wished to dine with, — literary folk, — W. Thayer, William Allen White, etc., and announced his candidacy from Bob's house; thereby committing Bob to opposition to Taft. And Bob was Taft's best personal friend here. I told Bob that his only possible course was to invite Taft to stay with him during an approaching visit to these parts. . . .

28 *February*, 1912. — Up at half past seven, of a bright cool morning. After a cup of coffee, to Sturgis Bigelow's, at exactly half past eight. Bigelow was already at his desk, scribbling letters, in a brown suit and looking remarkably alert, with his bald head and his bushy well-cut white beard. In a minute or two Roosevelt came down in a grey suit with cutaway coat. He was astonishingly quiet in manner and aspect. I could not decide whether it was because it was early in the day, or because the first announcement of his decision to run for the candidacy has pulled his nerves together — a little of both, I fancy. He touched on nothing political. . . .

Then Brooks Adams came in and we all went down to breakfast, where we were later joined by Kermit Roosevelt, a tall boy with a pleasant face and quiet manner, and a very small moustache; I do not remember ever having seen him before. He takes his degree at Harvard this year, having done four years' work in two years and a half, and proposes to engage in some phase of the rubber industry.

At table Roosevelt sat with his back to the window, and I directly opposite, so that his features were in shadow. His whole manner and talk remained perfectly quiet, and very friendly. He rather led, of course, but did not take the floor; and there were one or two intervals of easy silence. At first he touched on books, etc. . . . Then he strayed on to comment on the extraordinary inflexibility of the common people of America, who honestly believe themselves possessed of absolute truth, and can be neither understood nor influenced by one who does not sympathize with their point of view or assume it. They are honest at heart, and singularly simple in emotion; you can approach them only by honest appeal to this emotion, and can make no worse blunder than to touch lightly on anything which they hold serious. And so on, astute, but not profound. But when, apropos of the danger of inept pleasantry in American politics, I mentioned that T. W. Higginson was ineffective because of gentle misplaced humor, even before a Cambridge audience, both Roosevelt and Adams took me to mean that Cambridge audiences were intelligent, instead of that they were Higginson's nearest neighbors; and explained to me a truth already in my possession: viz., that Cambridge is probably the most densely local place — in point of ideas — this side Paradise, where the will of God unanimously prevails. . . .

We went up to the drawing-room with cigarettes; and there Roosevelt touched, with pretty firm references to constitutional history, on his views concerning the courts, in which Adams agrees with him. As I understood him, he believes in an appointed judiciary, rather than an elective; but is of opinion that, inasmuch as the courts ultimately derive their authority in this country from the people, the people should under certain conditions be allowed to revise judicial decision. He instanced the decision of the New York Court of Appeals that the Workmen's Compensation Act, virtually identical with the English, is unconstitutional in that state by reason of a clause guaranteeing the right of property. Here, he says, the court, representing the people, declares that the constitution, enacted by the representatives of the people, forbids the legislature, itself representative of the people, to do the people's will. To change the constitution by striking out the clause concerning property would be folly. To state special commandments, relieving the presence of the constitution in given acts, would be obviously wrong. He prefers that, after an interval of two or three years perhaps, the people be given the right to declare by vote whether their will as expressed in the constitution or their will as expressed in a legislative act shall prevail. I disagree, believing Cabot Lodge's Raleigh speech final on this point; but there was no use in arguing; so I only amiably listened. Presently reporters and the like became pressing; and Roosevelt went down to them; saying a pleasant word of good-bye. The only trace of excitement he had shown, or of the mental instability which I remarked at Oyster Bay last month, was towards the end of his legal talk, when his voice grew a bit loud and emphatic. I describe this interview in extreme detail, because it occurred at an historically important moment.

Until after the convention, what I have written should be held confidential; at least in no wise to be published. He seems to me honest in his self-confidence, in his belief that nothing but radical policies are sure to save the nation, and in holding himself the chosen man of the people. He is right in saying that the reactionary Republicans of to-day are really old-fashioned "Cotton Whigs." He is wrong, I think, in believing that the Republican party has really prospered for any other reason than that it was quietly captured, soon after its radical start, by this kind of leader. But he may be really right in his contention that the moment for a social and constitutional revolution, under forms of law, is come. I like him personally; and admire his energy and honesty of purpose. On the other hand, his self-confidence and his general recklessness of speech are such that I conceive him personally to be untrustworthy as a friend and unmanageable as an ally. He is Cæsar; and is not quite sure that he is not God.

Of course the regular party — the Taft men — are furious; and the newspapers in general are against him. What I now hope is that he will not get the nomination. If so, and Taft does, he now thinks that he shall support the candidate. I doubt, however, whether he can hold his followers together, in support of a candidate whom he has so led them to oppose. The best hope for Republican success in November seems to me a deadlock in the convention between Roosevelt and Taft; and the emergence, as a candidate, of a "dark horse" on whom both wings of the party are to be brought to agree. . . .

29 *February*, 1912. — . . . All the papers are full of Roosevelt; and so far as I can observe are already beginning editorially to hedge. . . . Whether this is for fear of an avalanche for him or because of skillful use of money by his managers I cannot guess; perhaps a little of both. All people of the better sort are against him, as revolutionary and tremendously threatening to security of property. This unanimity is disturbing; for it implies a huge popular possibility on the other side. I have hardly known a time when so much political excitement was in the air, though it is not yet grown to the point of high feeling.

There is no use in trying to prophesy. . . .

4 *March*, 1912. — A clear day with a flurry of snow at noon, and a slight snowfall at night. At one, Edith and I went to New Haven, where we were met at the station by a handsome boy, with lovely smile and teeth, named George van Santvoord. He took us to Hadley's, where we found Mrs. Hadley receiving friends at tea, in a blue gown. . . . At seven Hadley took me to the Phi Beta Kappa dinner, fortifying me beforehand, and incidentally himself, with an excellent cocktail, a bit more aromatic than I am used to in point of gin. And Mrs. Hadley had a woman's dinner for Edith, evidently original. The Φ B K dinner was in a large circular hall, in the second story of a comparatively new building, containing a big auditorium, etc. Some two hundred men were there. I had the place of honor, between Hadley and Governor Baldwin, thin, spectacled, sparsely bearded, nasal, sensible, Democratic, a gentleman, and a teetotaler. . . . The speeches were mostly light in vein, and not memorably, though pleasantly, humorous. . . . I came last, and spoke seriously, to the effect that what is called social injustice is believed in only because modern folks think in terms not of generations but of lifetimes. Whoever knows any family history, high or low, from 1800 to 1900 will be content with the way God runs the world. Hadley really liked it. He out-Tories me; and yet is the head of the most American of American universities. We tramped home through damp snow; had ale or whiskey, as we would, with one good wine; and were abed by midnight. Hadley's fears as to the dinner proved groundless. There was plenty of fairly fortified claret punch, disdained by his Excellency of Connecticut, who stuck to tepid Apollinaris.

5 *March*, 1912. — Sunny and not too cold. Breakfast at 8.30. From 9.00 to 11.00 I looked at the Yale books. One Cochran, a very rich man who graduated there in '96 or thereabouts, has made a wonderful collection of old English books, including all four folios of Shakespeare from the Huth library, and a lot more of Huth books. He does not stick at two thousand pounds sterling for a volume he wants. These he has given to the Elizabethan Club of Yale, in the pretty little

club house; but they are actually accessible — in case of serious desire — to any member, who can study and read them as he will. I never had such contact with real treasures before. They have made me an honorary member. The club library, of less precious sort, is all, or almost all, of first editions. In the college library is the best collection of first American editions I ever saw, down to seven books of my own, in which I wrote my name, and such notes of their origin as occurred to me. . . .

*To Sir Robert White-Thomson*

BOSTON, 7 *April*, 1912

. . . Our own political situation is puzzling. President Taft has done well; but lacks popularity. Roosevelt has personally quarrelled with him; and has been persuaded by what seem to me flatterers that the country demands him to restore the prestige of the party. Roosevelt is honest, I think, and honestly of opinion that his candidacy is for the good of the nation. To my mind, however, he has been misled by flattery. The end will probably be a Democratic president for the next four years. Meanwhile, though we lag behind England in radical policy, we are on the same road. Strikes have needed military control hereabouts for two or three months; and a coal strike in Pennsylvania is just declared. One can hardly resist the conviction that our civilization — all over the European world — is fatally ill. . . .

*To the same*

[*On receipt of a lecture on Samuel Johnson by this English friend*]

BOSTON, 17 *April*, 1912

. . . One's fancy strays. I have liked to picture him to-day, in some still rolling and be-wigged heaven of his own, welcoming this word which should show him as he was, and scolding Boswell for any little fault he might pertly have chosen to find with it. But, most of all, I have vividly recalled what happened to me, in this very room, more than twenty-five years ago. Little Mary, as she was then, was very ill — for no more than a few hours, as I remember. There were some evening hours, though, which were terribly — perhaps unnecessarily — anxious. Without knowing where my hand should stray, I took from the shelves a volume which chanced to be that in which Johnson's prayers were somewhere printed, and read them. And, as I read, there came an unspeakable sense that if my little child must go, and could go to a state of being where such a spirit as his could await her, there was nothing to fear. You could trust him to take care of a little child; he was truly a saint. Sentimental, if you will, this strange assurance, which was like a moment of communion, has lasted with me ever since. It was as if he had lurched into this very little room, in the New England he could never have abided, and in gruff, grave, sweet tones spoken the comfort which could never fail.

Always affectionately yours,<br>BARRETT WENDELL

### To W. R. Castle

BOSTON, 28 April, 1912

. . . Politics are depressing beyond words. Roosevelt has brought the campaign down to a level of personal recrimination lower than anything in my memory. It now looks to me as if his appeals to prejudice would win him the Chicago nomination; but this does not mean the election. The party is so disrupted as to make Democratic success easy, if they do not blunder more than usual. Their probable candidate now seems Wilson or Bryan. What makes it all harder to tolerate is my own belief that Roosevelt remains honest, and blind to the mischief he is working. Really drunk with self-esteem and flattery, he has, I feel sure, no idea that he is not a savior of society, spontaneously called to his task by the divine voice of the people. . . .

### To Robert Grant

PORTSMOUTH, 2 June, 1912

DEAR BOB: — Your book[1] impresses me just as happily as I was impressed, when I wrote you, by the first installments of it in Scribner's Magazine. In no end of details, I disagree with what you believe in. That makes no sort of difference in my feeling that, whatever side we take, no greater service can be

---

[1] The Convictions of a Grandfather, published in 1912.

done to the country and to the moment than is done by putting one's case quietly and with the pervading sweetness of mature humor. What I like in the book is not its principles, but its temper — its style, in the full, most pervasive sense of the word. One puts down each chapter, with a sense, not of irritation, however wide of one's own the views therein set forth, but rather of conciliated sympathy.

In fact, I make no doubt, we all wish the same general things: that the world shall grow not worse but better, that men may be as free as free may be to win their deserts, and to enjoy the fruit of their labors. To some of us, like me, the tendency of the moment seems against all this; to others, like you, this tendency seems on the whole to work for what we long for. . . .

What each of us most needs is secure certainty that the other is sound at core. There could be no more admirable proof of this than such a book as yours. I only wish that someone could put the other side in half so beautifully sound and human a generalized temper. . . .

### To H. M. Kallen

PORTSMOUTH, 5 *June*, 1912

. . . For the moment, I am more despairing than usual. The whole outlook, not only of this country but of all the world, seems to me more than threatening — almost wholly ominous of decay if not of crash to come. It may be the fact that I am fifty-nine in August, it may be that my race — as oppressed to-day as yours ever was — has not the vitality to survive the test, nor yet a record which shall assure the future of what we might have been. It may be just the fact that I am weaker in will and therefore in both purpose and accomplishment than I used to think. Anyhow, when the planet cools, we shall be at one — whatever side we take now.

### To Sir Robert White-Thomson

AUBURN, NEW YORK, 2 *July*, 1912

Your welcome letter of the 19th has followed us here, where the Ediths and I are passing a week at the Osbornes.[1] Charles's

---

[1] Wendell's younger daughter, Edith, had recently become engaged in marriage to Charles Devens Osborne, of Auburn, New York.

farm, two or three miles from the town, is close to a lake. He is doing over and enlarging the house — a mere farmhouse to begin with — and making it very pretty. The dining room is delightful — paneled with the old pine panels of a disused Quaker meeting-house, where they have been taking on their rich color for a quiet century. In tone they are now almost like mahogany. The farm came to him through a division of his grandmother's estate, who died last year; it promises fairly well, mostly as a dairy; anyhow, it is good, unencumbered property, for which he has already been offered nearly twice the money it has cost him. His father, a man eagerly interested in politics and reform, has just returned from the Baltimore convention, full of hope that they have throttled Tammany there — although the candidate is not yet nominated. In that event, he thinks that the Democrats will carry the country in November; and govern well. As a Republican, I cannot share his confidence; but, in view of Roosevelt's dogmatic conduct, I can see no much happier prospect. For my own part, I am for Taft, who has little prospect of election. Taft is extremely infelicitous in public utterance; in conduct and character I have thought him good; and he has certainly been treated by Roosevelt in a manner which excites one's sympathy. The anti-English statement of which you spoke was a careless phrase from a private and intimate letter, of which Roosevelt published so much, without leave, that Taft, perhaps imprudently, published the whole. It had no real political significance; but much momentary effect, and very unhappy international. . . .

*To H. M. Kallen*

THE JACOB WENDELL HOUSE[1]
PORTSMOUTH, NEW HAMPSHIRE

23 *August*, 1912

Your birthday greeting is very welcome. As I start to tell you so, with the pen you gave me four years ago, though, I feel rather undeserving. It is high time that I had done more to warrant confidence so constant as yours.

[1] All of Wendell's letters from Portsmouth were written under this superscription.

The little book you send happens to fit into the kind of mood where I have been hovering lately. Earlier in the summer I reviewed the Diary of Cotton Mather, which carried me back again into the mysticism of old New England. Later I have been trying — without success — to put down some impressions of India, where all the outward conditions of life seem to me at once to tend towards the mysticism of Indian thought — if thought be the word — and to express it in a guise which, until one begins to enter into it, seems monstrous and unmeaning. So this message of mysticism from old Italy — a message quite new to me, for I never heard of the Blessed Angela before — brings a strange kind of trivial assurance that the eternities wherein this rolling little planet swims and bobs surge all about humanity everywhere, once we break the shackles of time and space. Only when the Blessed Angela, or the Yankee Puritan, or Ramanathan tries to imprison a sense of them in words, the idol takes the place of the divinity. Only silence can express truth — a fact, by the way, implicitly present, I should think, in the mind of Roosevelt, to whom all utterance now seems to present itself as deliberately mendacious.

The summer is passing quickly and pleasantly. The old house is more comfortable than I expected; and has for me, as it has always had, a real charm — a touch, perhaps, of fascination. I foresee that I shall try to write about it, and in it, by and by. Perhaps the years of delay won't hurt the book, if it ever comes into being. It won't be quite history nor yet quite fiction — rather a record of what tradition makes old New England seem to have been. . . .

*To Sir Robert White-Thomson*

PORTSMOUTH, 17 *September*, 1912

. . . Roosevelt's conduct seems to me deplorable. Unless I am quite mistaken, he has come honestly to believe himself the only possible savior of the nation. Though some good men support him, his following in the main is fanatical and rather more unprincipled than any other in our history. He is capable, in the fervor of his self-confidence, of attempting to seize the government by force. I do not yet believe that he will do so; but it seems to me conceivable that he may, in the event of a disputed election. In that case, he could probably control not only the militia of certain Western states, but a certain part — quite beyond my calculation — of the national army and navy. Fanatical hero-worship has combined with lack of principle to render them, in my opinion, not quite trustworthy. What the chances of the election are, I am unable to conjecture. A few weeks ago Democratic success looked more than probable. Wilson, somehow, has not strengthened himself of late. He is a good speaker, but no politician. Taft is very unskillful in politics, and speaks badly. Roosevelt is the most skillful of all our politicians, and admirable as a popular speaker. None of the three write with much effect. Roosevelt and Taft are prolix; Wilson rather flat, in this respect.

All three I happen to know. All are gentlemen, all agreeable. Roosevelt is of the old New York "quality"; Wilson a Southerner; Taft of good Yankee country stock. . . .

*To the same*

PORTSMOUTH, 11 *October*, 1912

. . . As our national election approaches, it differs from any other I remember in surprising lack of general excitement. This is said to be due to the fact that public opinion happens strongly to condemn, for the moment, any excessive expense in political campaigns; and that the placards, processions, and the like which have generally been arrayed have been suppressed, on grounds of prudent economy. The result is pleasant. It seems as if people were going to vote with quiet intelligence; though I doubt whether the outcome will be satisfactory. I now expect Wilson to be elected; and hope that Taft will poll a good vote. Otherwise, the opposition will be far from solid and trustworthy. . . .

*To H. M. Kallen*

BOSTON, 24 *November*, 1912

. . . As to the election, I am content. The Republican party was so broken by Roosevelt's bolt that it could not have controlled things. Roosevelt's bolt was of a kind which I should have regretted to see in power. Wilson, with his complete Democratic majority, and the seriousness of responsibility thereby put on him, will be the most nearly conservative guardian of our institutions now possible. I voted for Taft, not expecting his election but desirous of doing what I could to keep together an opposition not committed to radical doctrine. My mood now is of eager willingness to recognize whatever the new government does well. . . .

## To the same

BOSTON, 27 *December*, 1912

. . . It is vexatious that you should have been so ill — or shall I rather say so nearly ill. What you confide to me of academic morals rejoices my Tory spirit. That this is a naughty world is beyond dispute. That some human beings are less naughty than others is a tenable proposition. That the least naughty are those who are least disposed to vaunt the virtues of humanity seems to me certain. Wherefore to find in the heart of democracy just the meannesses of which those who practise them believe their comparatively innocent betters to be guilty brings me ironic consolation. It was the vices of others which brought Marie Antoinette, whom they could not dream nobler than they, to her heroic test. In a vulgar way, it is such baseness in our people which makes them, translating themselves into terms above them, believe our strongest and best men corrupt. All of which is in *Coriolanus*. . . .

## To Charles F. Thwing

BOSTON, 29 *December*, 1912

DEAR CHARLES: — Your doubly sympathetic word comes to me today. By a strange chance it was the same with my mother and with dear old Ned.[1] Both had fallen into infirmity, from which there was no hope of recovery. With both there was fear that the mere bodily shell might long survive. Both ended very gently, just falling asleep — my mother in her own house, in the room which had been hers since I was ten years

---

[1] Wendell's mother had died about a week before; his lifelong friend, Edmund March Wheelwright on August 14, 1912.

old. So the grief already has in it more than a touch of relief from dread of what might have come.

My younger daughter is to be married in less than three weeks. At the very end, my mother's death was so sudden that, a few days before, we had sent out the cards — not very many anyway. I have not recalled them, feeling sure for myself that it is best never to let the past cloud the future. . . .

*To G. F. Cherry*

18 GRAYS HALL, 27 *May*, 1913

DEAR MR. CHERRY, — The definition you ask for was off-hand — never written down. In effect, I think, it is that no one can be called a true American who retains a particle of direct personal traditions not native to this country. Immigrants, however worthy, bring other than American traditions from their old countries. Something of these their children are apt to preserve; and sometimes their grandchildren. Only when these traditions have faded into dim knowledge of whence a family came — without any definite personal memories — can full American nationality declare itself. Generally this takes at least a hundred years.

Sincerely yours,

BARRETT WENDELL

Glance, if you like, at the introduction to my *Literary History of America*.

*To Sir Robert White-Thomson*

PORTSMOUTH, 29 *May*, 1913

Edith and I are here for a day or two before coming for the summer; and I find at hand only this old paper on which to send you word at last that my dear old Aunt Sarah Barrett has died. Her end came very gently, some two weeks ago. A slight cold became bronchitis, and finally pneumonia. She suffered hardly at all. Twelve hours before she died I saw her last; and we talked cheerfully about everyday matters, and details of her affairs which she wished me to attend to next day. Before I had time to do so, word came to me that she had seemed, in the early morning, rather better; that after her breakfast she had fallen into a half-conscious sleep—a sleep, I mean, which was half unconsciousness; and thus, with no sense of parting, and with no suffering, she had passed out of earthly life. A wondrously happy memory she leaves. In many respects her life had been far from prosperous; but nothing had ever dimmed the serenity of her spirit or the stoutness of her heart. She lacked the kind of wit which has lightness of touch; her literal precision of thought and expression sometimes made one laugh, and sometimes vexed a little. But I never knew a human being who, through eighty-seven years, more beautifully preserved, and the more beautifully the better you knew her, the traditions of what we of New England used to call "quality." We laid her beside my grandparents on the 13th. . . .

## To Mrs. William G. Nickerson

PORTSMOUTH, 12 *September*, 1913

DEAR BEATRICE: — . . . If in a few words I should try to state what seems to me most dangerous in "progressive" dogma, I think that I should emphasize its insistence on the absolute irresponsibility of the people. Morally, this is as mischievous as similar insistence on the irresponsibility of a personal sovereign. In either case, I suppose, the irresponsibility is genuine; but God keeps good books, and in due time presents his bill. And the bills of those — monarchs, lords, or people — who have insisted on having their own way, regardless of law, custom, and the universe, have been — in the past — whacking.

I grow vagrant, perhaps, and rhetorical. It is a good while since I read Lecky's *Democracy and Liberty*. I remember no detail of it; but the total effect of it has lasted. We are living in an age of less liberty and less; every extension of suffrage makes the individual less free. Such bonds diminish all sense of responsibility. It was evil that many were once slaves of few, if you will. It is worse evil that now we are bidden believe that all should be the slaves of majorities —whatever their whims. . . .

As to "progressives," I am sure of one thing. Though there are good and true men among them, I have yet to find a public character whose mind and whose principles I fail to respect, who has not more or less allied himself with their movement.

## *To Sir Robert White-Thomson*

BOSTON, 27 *January*, 1914

. . . After all, it is not the material phase of a civilization which makes it most worth while, but the spiritual. And, if I am not all mistaken, the most excellent spiritual fact of the days which are passing has been the true-hearted English gentleman. Just on the verge of the Civil War, I think, in Charles I's last peaceful year, Fuller published his *Holy and Profane State*, wherein, if I remember, is the famous character beginning: "A good yeoman is a gentleman in the ore." And then all his England was rent; and they had their war, and their Commonwealth, and their Protectorate, and their Restoration, and their glorious Revolution; and men like you and me must have felt heartbroken; but those times bred Sir Roger de Coverley as an ideal. And the barest times of the eighteenth century gave us Parson Adams and Goldsmith's "Vicar"; and the Regency had Colonel Newcome. The gentleman of the days to be, and the yeoman, will not be such as we have known. But such a spirit as Major Gambra Parry so beautifully implies can never quite die. I put the book down at last, more sure than usual of the times to come, for all their troubles.

Always affectionately yours,

BARRETT WENDELL

## *To Frederic Schenck*

GRAND HOTEL, LYNDHURST, NEW FOREST
12 *July*, 1914

DEAR FREDERIC: — Your welcome word that all went well was waiting me here when we arrived the other day. On the whole, all goes well with me; but it is vexatiously slow. Looking back, week by week, I can see that I get better. Introspectively, day by day, I feel like one sadly reaping the fruits of a vicious lifetime — a sentiment tolerable only when honestly earned, and my most poignant regrets have always been for the discretions of youth. . . .

England seems to me sad: the country depopulated, the towns simmering almost pestilentially, confidence gone, life so far as it quivers a matter rather of intoxication than of vitality. I am not yet strong enough in head or hand to phrase what I mean. Tobey[1] somehow managed, I fear, to eradicate what little faculty of expression I ever had. Yet somehow I am yearning to set forth an image of a paradise where the hanged Abbot of Glastonbury, and the rest, wag their stretched necks in pious content that those who made them pay their penalty are at last paying their own. . . .

*To Sir Robert White-Thomson*

LONDON, 25 *July*, 1914

. . . We sail for Quebec in the Calgarian — an Allan Liner — early Friday afternoon. Nothing could have been happier than these English weeks, during which I have quietly seen just those whom I yearned to see — among whom you are first of all. The only cloud has been consciousness of the grave public dangers not yet past; and the course of daily life seems everywhere so unmoved that one is tempted to wonder whether the dangers are so terrible as to earnest thought they still appear. Not knowing how they may pass, I still dare hope that they shall. . . .

[1] The surgeon, Dr. George L. Tobey, Jr., who operated on Wendell for mastoiditis.

LETTERS: 1914–1917

*To Sir Robert White-Thomson*

PORTSMOUTH, 10 *August*, 1914

These last days make life seem more certainly a dream than any before in my life. When I sent you that parting word of good-bye from the Calgarian, there was no more sense that war was at hand than I had in those wonderful days at Broomford. The voyage was a little delayed by fog, but otherwise as commonplace as possible: a comfortable cabin, a well-appointed ship, and the best cooking I remember at sea seemed matters of importance. The wireless brought us news in mid-ocean that war had broken out; but it all seemed unreal and distant. We got to Quebec on Friday, and made our way home on Saturday. All are well here; all is quiet. I can hardly make myself realize that Europe is ablaze.

The suddenness of the outbreak and its intensity are unthinkable. The great anxiety which must possess the whole Old World — and which is already here perplexing all manner of business — has not yet touched my personal life. But at least one phase of the whole tragic truth begins to seem plain. Europe, I think, and above the rest of Europe, England, had begun to show very troublous symptoms of that weird disease which I have come to think of as the cancer of peace — Socialism. Its true spirit is envious, hateful, malicious, uncharitable, disorderly. It is the *dismisura* of Dante, on a scale vaster than he could have fully dreamed of. To cure such malady, to restore the knowledge that national life and world-life demand organic order, there is no other means known to history than the fever of war. Its very delirium ends in sad recognition of facts, of values, of duties, of responsibilities. For all its horrors, it has bred beyond all forces else the sense of honor, and indeed the grace of humility. England needed some such terrible tonic, if England is to be in the future what England has meant in the past. Already I seem to read between the confused lines of daily news some implicit assurance that the empty country and the festering towns which troubled me during the otherwise delightful weeks are rising to a common enthusiasm of devotion to country and to duty. The price of national salvation — in human blood — must be terrible. The trouble and the suffering to come may be beyond belief. But nothing less than such priceless price could begin to command the new national strength and certainty which I dare hope to be what it shall prove to have purchased. . . .

## To H. M. Kallen

PORTSMOUTH, 25 *August*, 1914

If I were yet a bit myself you should have a better word of thanks than this for your most welcome birthday greeting. To the eye I am more than well again; but somehow I can hardly make a pen run. Whether I ever can again the Lord alone knows — if there be one, and He trouble his wisdom with such matter of detail.

My birthday passed in pleasant solemnity. For the first time in years all four of my children came to make merry with me; and B's wife, and Edith's husband, and the girl who is engaged to William — why have n't we some word more English than *fiancée* and more human than betrothed? — and Tommy Wheelock. And we were all duly and stiffly photographed under the lilac tree behind the little garden. This, to be sure, was a day ahead of time; for on Sunday William had to go West for a month or so.

Our two months in England were delightful. Nothing went wrong, even to the moment when we were taken to the pier at Liverpool by the same motor-car which met us there at the beginning of June. The voyage to Quebec, though icy and foggy, was quite without disturbance. The news of war arriving from America by wireless seemed unreal; and we never received a despatch from England ordering us back. So now, lotus-eating in my Portsmouth den, I can hardly realize that the Europe we left hardly three weeks ago is in death-throes. Nor can I see at all what is coming. Of only one thing I feel sure: no less tremendous tonic could have saved the departing national life of England. I hope, though I do not feel sure, that this has not come too late.

I am really touched by your verses. Just now, I can't duly say how much.

Sincerely and affectionately yours,

BARRETT WENDELL

*To Robert Herrick*

[*In a letter of thanks for his new novel*, Clerk's Field]

PORTSMOUTH, 26 *August*, 1914

. . . In the matter of philosophy, we differ *toto cœlo*. Your assumption, somewhere, that the "Sunday-school" assertion that property and prosperity are on the whole where they belong is obviously absurd, seems to me an obvious absurdity. There may be accidental riches here and there, by reason of conditions which enable you and me to provide for our children. I cannot recall much poverty or insignificance in this world which has not been fully and honestly earned. To you, I suppose, my generalities seem special pleadings; to me, yours seem so. We must agree to disagree concerning ethical and racial values.

We can agree, though, that lies can't last; that the best service any man of letters can do is to state what he believes the truth; that if this be the truth of nature, of history, of the flickering course through consciousness of what we deem the universe, it will stand; and that if it prove delusive and a lie its very passing will prove its falsity, without any manner of stain on the memory of him who uttered it honestly.

*To R. W. Curtis*

PORTSMOUTH, 28 *August*, 1914

DEAR RALPH, — . . . So far, you see, it is not quite actual here — at least in this sleepy old remnant of the Yankee eighteenth century. As for trustworthy news, very little comes. This morning's newspaper brings the first official account of the rupture between England and Germany at Berlin, on which my comment phrases itself in the only words that I can find to express my opinion of what has been done in Belgium — *encore un colossaleté allemand*. My gender may be wrong: I was never much of a grammarian. My sentiment is genuine, though: until these last weeks, I never dreamt how I abhor Prussians. What surprises me in myself is a candid recognition that the strength which they now seem to show, in contrast with the weakness of England and of France, comes in no small degree from a real superiority of national condition. Under the German system, as I conceive it, every one must do his best, in peace as in war, for the national welfare. Under unbridled democracy it takes warfare to compel much besides adulation of the mob who hold the votes. There was never such unblushing deference to a worthless class — in distinction to assertion of common rights and duties — as has been shown to the masses, for years, here and in England and in France. The irony of it all lies for me in the fact that these Aristotelian democracies are in control of the men and the things I care for — including my precious self; and that the expert organization for national welfare of the Germans concerns men and things to me abhorrent. It is as if one were called to fight, bleed, and die for an utterly worthless absolute sovereign. One would loyally do so, I hope; but with full knowledge of his abomination. . . .

*To the Master of Trinity*

PORTSMOUTH, 25 *September*, 1914

MY DEAR MASTER: — . . . My own feeling about Germany is not simple. To me, the German character, or at least the Prussian, has never been sympathetic. I saw Germany first in 1868, when I was about thirteen years old. At that time, the Prussian domination of other than old Prussian dominion was new; and the Prussians were as hotly hated in Nassau, in Bavaria, and elsewhere in what is now their country, as ever they were in France. I was in Germany again in 1871, when the troops were still returning from France. The change, as I remember it, was marvelous. A sense of German unity, under imperial leadership, was genuine everywhere. From then till now, this has seemed to increase; and, so far as it has been German, — in the deep national spirit, — it has seemed to me, sympathetic or not, noble. So far as it has been Prussian, it has been strong, and I think sincere, but repugnant. It may

be a matter of mere chance, and it may perhaps be true, that
so far as my experience — which is very limited — has gone,
the kind of Germans who accept the Prussian code of life are
unique in one hateful way: their men of rank, their gentlemen,
are supreme in insolence, in brutal self-assertion. For the
gentler phases of human feeling, you must turn to their vulgar
— like two kindly little haberdashers of Cologne whom I
met in Thuringia in '88. Among all other peoples whom I
have seen, men of rank are gentler than their inferiors.
Among the Germans of the empire, the reverse seems
the case.

Yet they have, of their own, a national ideal, which —
partly by reason of this graceless brutishness of superficial
conduct — cannot brook rivalry. They must actually dominate
others than themselves, or be crushed. They have, I am willing
to grant, something like the spirit of Virgilian empire: *"pacis-
que imponere morem."* To the rest of us, the while, they are
what Carthage was to older Rome. If we are to live, and for
all our errors we believe ourselves struggling truly towards the
light, they must nationally die.

Forgive these long utterances of opinion neither ripe nor
profound. What you tell of the soldier's account of Belgian
warfare is my first real proof of the atrocities which have been
rumored. There is only one reflection to make. These Germans
are in a country not only hostile but righteously incensed by
an invasion unparalleled in the record of modern national
cynicism, effrontery, crime. They are exposed to dangers —
even though these dangers be of their own making — from
which the Allies are free. They are at once enraged by irregular — though humanly accountable and even justifiable —
attacks, and compelled by the demands of momentary self-
preservation to take measures abominably extreme. And I
cannot but believe that they believe in themselves.

A day or two ago came a sad letter from an old pupil, of
full German blood, but now living in America, an American
citizen. He is a really good and honest man of five and thirty
or so. His brother is an officer in some regiment of German
Guards; one brother-in-law is in the same command, and

another an officer on one of the naval ships at Kiel or wherever. His father, who has an estate near Wiesbaden, is an old, kindly man, whom I have known. Not a line from him has been allowed to come to the son since the war broke out. The son writes gravely, sweetly. Yet he is sincerely convinced that the cause of England — as distinguished from that of France and of Russia — is callously self-seeking, materialistically insincere. At this moment, it were cruel to dispute with him. In answering, I have touched only on private matters. That such mood as his can now be genuine is to me the most sadly tragic fact of all: and a deep assurance of the true tragedy which we have lived to see. . . .

## To his daughter Mary

BOSTON

11 *November*, 1914. — . . . Speaking of T. R., one of those present [at the Wednesday Club] told me that in a letter before the elections which have submerged the Progressive party, T. R. wrote that he saw what was coming, but that he had so placed himself that there was nothing to do but go down with the ship. The contrast between this and his public utterances is a depressing example of how honest men, in politics nowadays, can't speak out with candor; and, bound to say what their position demands, use language in a sense too Pickwickian for approach to truth. . . .

25 *November*, 1914. — . . . At tea-time Helen Storrow came for a little while; and old Miss Crocker — most gently sympathetic; and finally Schofield. His year at Berlin has made him more anti-German than most of us, if so may be. He realizes their strength and devotion; but feels not only their dense arrogance but also their deliberate and conscious effort to revive old heathen Teutonic ideals, as opposed to the sympathy inculcated by Christianity. He told of dining with Harnack, who expressed to Mrs. Schofield opinion as to the divine right of strength, which she found surprising in a theologian. She observed that his views were not quite those of the Church, in any sense; to which he answered that Christianity is a venerable ruin. . . .

*To Edward Bowditch, Jr.*

CAMBRIDGE, 8 *December*, 1914

DEAR PETER: — Your letter of the 22nd got to Marlborough Street yesterday — welcome for itself as well as for the picture it gives of the England where we were together so lately. Lord Cromer, I hope, is right. If not — and if England be what it looked like last summer — it is just a glorious past. The difference is in the fact that you touch on, of the unweakened vigor shown, to my happy surprise, by its gentlefolk. They seemed, a few months ago, submerged in the sentimental vulgarities of base democracy — stifled or indifferent, powerless to show again the qualities which have made them, as a class, the highest type of humanity which has come to my knowledge. Of course they have had their follies, their weaknesses, their vices; their limits; but these fade — like the intrigues of Elizabethan politics — into nothing beside the big simple-hearted energy with which, as a matter of course, they have done the day's work. They are doing it, now; and every agony of their mourning is a rag more of their glory, not to be upheld by artifice. Theirs is a station which has been maintained only — on the whole — by desert; and which has always been open to the deserving. By such qualities as theirs, and not by those of a populace, the same everywhere throughout human record, I am apt to gauge the reverend virtues of nations.

So, if their power now win, it will restore them to the moral rights of late vilely and everywhere denied or questioned. And if they fail, it will be admirably — for want of virtue in those they lead to acknowledge leadership and strive not to envy but to merit it.

Enough of lucubration. In your place, I should hardly have patience to read so much of it. . . .

*To his daughter Mary*

4 *January*, 1915. — . . . I passed the day at Cambridge, getting off some harmless fireworks at a faculty meeting. A man had the impudence to interrupt a speech by asking me how I knew when my teaching was worth while or not. I

answered, with bland candor — he is notoriously dull—that for more than thirty years I had recognized the truth that if I could not hold the attention of a class, I was wasting their time and mine; and that whenever, after ten minutes of effort, I failed to keep attention I always dismissed the class, assuming the fault to be my own, except on the occasion of a Yale game, when it was God's. He made no reply. . . .

## To Edward Bowditch, Jr.

BOSTON, 10 *January*, 1915

. . . What you finally write of the English spirit agrees with all else I hear. German influence here is making the most of the dispute concerning seizure of ships; but not, I think, with much effect as yet. In this matter, the conduct of our government seems to me unexceptionable. Wilson's speech in Indiana — or wherever — the other day, seems to me, on the other hand, the acme of canting, demagogic self-righteousness. My general distrust of those in power here nowise weakens. I am comforted by knowledge that those who love me best have usually held me more opinionated than wise. . . .

## To his daughter Mary

11 *January*, 1915. — After posting you a week's letter this morning, I went to lunch at the Tavern, where I sat next Poultney Bigelow. He was full of memories of your kindness at Shanghai, and of messages for you — politely generalized. Frank Watson, who brought him there, had been breakfasting at Sturgis Bigelow's with Teddy Roosevelt. T. R. expresses himself as anti-German; but seems unusually well-disposed to Irish Catholics. Just what he is going to do next I have no idea. He will almost surely try for the Republican nomination next year. It looks as if his present purpose were to keep up anti-German feeling here, but to stir up anti-English; thus putting the country in a position of antagonistic, instead of conciliatory, neutrality. Some such situation might give us, when the time comes, a certain mediatory value. If we can't be equally loved, we can be equally hated — which practically amounts to the same thing. . . .

*To F. J. Stimson*

BOSTON, 15 *January*, 1915

. . . So far as public matters go, I know less than the most ignorant. T. R. has passed a day or two in these parts. I was not summoned to an audience. Frank Watson was; who says he said that that which could reduce a nation could not reduce him. The ruler that was and to be, he says, expressed himself as utterly opposed to Germany, and gently at one with the Irish Catholics. He — i.e., T. R. — lunched with Münsterberg, Archy Coolidge, Robinson, — the Professor of English, — and Francke, von Mach, and so on. When he arrived, Archy tells us, he thanked Münsterberg — doubtless bidden to bid him — for his kindness in welcoming him despite his known opinions. I expect, if I survive, to die his subject; the virtue of loyalty has been denied me by a fate which has hardly ever afforded me a sovereign to whom I could conscientiously be loyal. . . .

*To his daughter Mary*

20 *January*, 1915. — . . . Just after breakfast came word from Rhodes that Lichtenberger, with whom he had asked me to lunch at the club, had just received from France a totally unheralded telegram that his daughter, thirteen years old, died last night. I went at once to Cambridge, to ask the poor man whether he would not come here to stay for a while. I found him a little dazed by the shock: very calm, and making preparations already to sail for home on Saturday; decided meanwhile to go on with his few remaining lectures. So he would not come to us, every minute of the next few days being occupied. I took him to town in the car; with B's help, and that of the French consul, deeply sympathetic, he arranged for his passage; and he did one or two pieces of business. I stayed with him till after twelve; he seemed to find the companionship welcome. . . .

*To F. J. Stimson*

BOSTON, 29 *January*, 1915

. . . Having taken occasion to express imperfect admiration for the present government,[1] in the letters I have scribbled you

[1] From 1919 to 1921 Mr. Stimson held the post of U. S. Ambassador to Argentina

before, it is only fair that I should assure you of my complete admiration for the letter from Mr. Bryan to Senator Stone on the charge that we have favored the Allies, and on neutrality in general. I remember no State paper more unexceptionable in both matter and manner. It has, too, a compact firmness, and a fusion of incisiveness with dignity, which make it really distinguished. Pride in our own public expressions is so far from usual with me as to be a joy almost acute. . . .

## To his daughter Mary

20 *March*, 1915. — . . . The *Transcript* has word of the death in Washington of C. F. Adams. I saw him last at the Historical Society, where he presided ten days ago, seemingly as strong as ever. We had a friendly word about the copy of the Flynt portrait I am to have made for the old Quincy house. So ends a friendship begun about the time I was married, unbroken, and — despite the odd gruffness of his manner — marked throughout by such sympathetic kindness as from an older man makes a younger glad to try to do his best, sure of hearty recognition. I never knew a better man; nor one who, even at eighty, will be more missed. The Historical Society will be lost without him. Charles Eliot is eighty-one today, full of vigor. . . .

## To H. M. Kallen

PORTSMOUTH, 9 *May*, 1915

. . . Just now I am dizzy in the murky horror with which the Lusitania massacre has clouded this one corner of the world hitherto left foolishly serene. In itself it is no more monstrous than thousands of other acts done during these horrible months. It lacks, indeed, much of their hideous detail. Am I all wrong, though, in feeling that the cool deliberation of this colossal murder has the peculiar vileness of utter freedom from the devilish excitement of armed conflict?

Here was a case where the thing could be accomplished only by such complete self-mastery as means self-control. In battle, or invasion, there are elements which should carry passion to monstrous extremes. Even Cawnpore, I think, was more explicable in terms of true human nature.

What will come of it I cannot begin to guess. Hereabouts, I am sure, there is for the passing while a unanimity of horror such as I never felt before. What has been done elsewhere has never seemed, even to me, quite palpably real. It was all far away. The people — whatever the term may mean — never grasped the full actuality of the former atrocities, any more than one quite understands the full fact of vulgar murder, as one reads the stupefying blatancy of daily headlines. This massacre has struck home.

But what can we do? I wish I had some gleam of perception — or a ray of sympathetic faith in the men who for the while control our national life. That they are honest I will not deny. That they make us helplessly unable to do anything but think and — if we may — feel, seems sadly true. . . .

*To his daughter Mary*

14 *May*, 1915. — . . . Wilson's letter to Germany, signed by Bryan, published this morning, seems to me irreproachable; and expresses, I think, the unanimous sentiment of the country. It may conceivably avert war with Germany; though this now seems to me almost inevitable. What it will mean, if it really comes, I do not foresee. With characteristic buoyancy, I now expect that, after making peace with the Allies, the Germans will slip over here and treat our coasts as they have treated Belgium — unless we leave our cities and supplies, and vanish into the Mississippi valley. . . .

I have pretty nearly decided to resign at the end of this year, though it may be impossible for me to get myself to literary work, after all. I certainly can do nothing of the kind so long as I continue at all at college; and there I feel completely worn out. Though I lecture tolerably, I find trouble in reading or studying even for a few minutes at a time.

The simple fact is, I suppose, that for some time past I have been on the edge of "nervous prostration" — whatever that may be. This might easily make me a chronic imaginary invalid; but I think I know my case and temperament well enough to regain self-control sometime, and escape this not comfortless fate. . . .

*To Frederic Schenck*

PORTSMOUTH, 16 *June*, 1915

DEAR FREDERIC: — . . . The work you and I have done together seems to me even more useful than I thought it would be when we began it. Nothing at Harvard does more to help men who are willing to be helped towards such larger thinking as the Germanized scholarship of the past fifty years has done so much to check. Nothing potentially enriches their minds more. They are given the whole world of literature to draw on all their lives; if they neglect it, the fault is not ours. That we are not severe specialists is really our strength. . . .

Now, in my case, my books have done a good deal to remedy this trouble. No one knows much about them; but there they are — things to be recognized unopened. They turn the presumption against me the other way, shifting the burden of proof that I am irregular to those who chose to lift it by a task of reading which they have never undertaken. In your case, a really good thesis, of which you are abundantly capable, would begin the same process. That is what I meant in urging that you now attack this work vigorously.. . . .

*To the Master of Trinity*

AUBURN, NEW YORK, 18 *August*, 1915

. . . Lodge is at once a serious man of letters and to my mind the most admirable public man now in our national Senate. If we had a few more of such quality in control of our national affairs, our history just now would not be such a pitiful blank. But I am bound to admit that, much as I admire and respect him, and care for him too, Lodge shines more in opposition than when his party was in power. For the moment, historic force seems beyond all human control; wherefore magnanimous criticism seems now the limit of wisdom.

What you write of your eyes troubles me. I do my best to write more legibly than sometimes. Whether the use of typewriting machines has wrought in England such havoc with penmanship as it has wrought here, I do not know. A generation hence I shall expect most Americans to be capable of little else than scrawling signs-manual. On the other hand, they are learning to dictate with a firm conciseness in itself admirable. . . .

*To F. J. Stimson*

CAZENOVIA, NEW YORK, 27 *August*, 1915

. . . Roosevelt's speech at the Plattsburg Camp seems to have got Wood into trouble. It was, to my thinking, immensely inconsiderate. On the platform it would have done. Just then it was almost seditious; and precisely what, in Wilson's place, Theodore would most violently have resented. . . .

*To the same*

PORTSMOUTH, 11 *September*, 1915

. . . The news of the moment is the request for Dumba's recall. It was inevitable, and delayed just as long as possible. He almost rivaled Genet. But the incident, coming just at the time when the German authorities sustain the sinking of the Arabic, makes Wilson's diplomatic victory less impressive than it looked a few days ago. The Hesperian incident also dims it. As I have written you before, I am not altogether sorry. Little as I should wish a war with Germany, I should welcome one as an assurance of renewed understanding with England. And, as things have gone, I can see no hope of avoiding a war with Germany, when the actual European war is over, except such utter defeat of her as should for a while preclude it. If victorious, she will certainly attack us; if just brought to terms, she will almost inevitably attack us, in the hope of collecting from our seaboard enough ransom to help pay her indemnities. So, if a power in the State, I should reluctantly go to war with her now, when we should have a fighting chance of inclusion in the terms of a world peace. . . .

*To Paul Kaufman*

BOSTON, 12 *November*, 1915

DEAR KAUFMAN: — It was good of you to call yesterday. Beyond a general shake-up, and a few scratches and bruises, I am all right. Just how soon I shall be quite in working order, though, I can't be sure. In case I don't feel up to meeting the class on Wednesday, you will perhaps be so kind as to go there, collect their papers, and either dismiss them or talk to them as you prefer. Meanwhile, I should be grateful if you will bring in here the fifteen reports I should have found at Grays yesterday. By Wednesday, I shall certainly be able to have read and graded them, and the sooner you get them here the better I shall be pleased.

What actually happened was that, thrown upward and forward, my shoulders struck the wooden top of the windshield, carrying it away and with it all the glass. It was just flexible enough to prevent the blow from breaking bone, as distinguished from bruising muscle. Then, as I collapsed, in a slight "shock," fragments of broken glass in the lower frame of the windshield scratched my forehead and cut my lower lip. It was a rather narrow escape, no doubt; but except for the nervous shock, it was completely an escape.

## To Lady Alwyne Compton

PORTSMOUTH, *November,* 1915

. . . Nothing could be lovelier than Portsmouth to-day, in clear autumn air, flooded with sunshine. In our mite of a garden, a few things are still languidly in bloom; white phlox, snapdragons, autumn anemones, roses, and climbing nasturtiums. We have only simple old-fashioned country flowers.

The prim old photographs of my family pictures, hung about the room where I am writing, look glad to see me unexpectedly. By a chance, uncommon in this country, I have got together photographs, from widely scattered originals, of five generations before my grandfather, with photographs of him and my father and me, my son and his boy. I am surrounded by ten generations of my family — all looking mute welcome to the new baby which is the fifth in that part of the tenth generation which comes through me. In all five I find, fantastically perhaps, a touch of stimulus to hope, in these grievous times. To my Dutch ancestors, the English conquest of the Hudson seemed fatal; and good came of it. To go no further, there never was more poignant civil war than the American Revolution, unless perhaps that which, in my own memory, so nearly destroyed the American Union. At least three times during the six generations before my father, things looked more desperate than they look to-day; yet nothing broke the spirit — in spite of much private misfortune. In our own little way, we have stood the test; and in a wondrously grand way, England and France are so standing theirs to-day that we who love them can feel in our love a solemn pride beyond words.

Sincerely, affectionately yours,

BARRETT WENDELL

*To Sir Robert White-Thomson*

BOSTON, 25 *November*, 1915

. . . In this tragic year, I feel more deeply than ever the tragedy of the American Revolution. It seems to me much what might have happened here if the Secession of the South had prevailed: a weakening disunion of forces which need to work in common, if the ideals which are as much ours as yours are to hold their own. And now, I feel almost helplessly, the smug neutrality of our Government is such a neglect of duty as would have been, in those years, a neutral Southern Confederacy, sitting by to watch a German attack on a threatened North. . . .

*To H. M. Kallen*

BOSTON, 28 *February*, 1916

It is more than a month since your letter came to me, and many days since the *Meaning of Americanism* followed it. I am still submerged in fathomless languor, which I begin to feel a wondrous anodyne, given by one knows not what to prevent the suffering of conscious world-despair. There comes to-night a wonderful letter from Mrs. James, in London. I had written her a message for Henry, if he should care for it. Do you know that I find myself going to copy what she writes: "Henry will have his wish for 'no partial recovery.' He is not suffering. Even the consciousness of his helplessness and mental confusion has translated itself into happy wandering, and pleasant foreign places, and old friends. And so he lies all day on an invalid's lounge, whence he can look off over the river, and see the barges make their slow way back and forth, and watch the clouds and the sunsets. Three weeks ago the end seemed not far off, but he is better again. He was pleased to see Harry, but does not miss him when he goes. It is long since he has refused to have letters, messages or even names. And he has never once asked about the war. We sit with him, Peggy and I, but we do not talk. Everything seems trivial in the presence of this great serenity of spirit."

That is all — and enough, without a syllable to spare. Unless I am all astray, there was never deeper teaching of how, after full bravery of struggle, there can come, on the brink of what we call eternity, the vast consolation of acquiescence. None of us can be other than we can. Those who, like him, can rest from an activity which so long as its strength endured has never faltered in aspiration, have even, unawares, a great victory of the spirit. And as for this world, — consciousness and all, as far as we can see or wish, — it is illusory, passing, poignant yet nowise final. I stray beyond meaning, perhaps, but not beyond sense of what meaning might be.

Your *Americanism* stirs me. You have taken something from my book on our ideals, but interpreted it until, except for the mere terms, I should hardly know that any of it had ever been mine. You set me to thinking — to wondering. Liberty, as far as it can be individual, must imply for salvation a willing self-sacrifice; union must mean toleration of difference in pursuit of what shall in the end help one and all; democracy must suppress all consciousness of class, content to condemn envy as a spiritual sin no less ugly than pride. If not, like strong drink, these elixirs — abused — must be damning. For the while, they seem so. All I can be sure of is that we few, failing remnants of the first who came here have somehow persisted through our American generations — now for some three centuries — with no loss of the better things which were inherent in us when we came. Rather, I think, our own better sort are among the pure and the good things still persistent — not so strong as old Europe, I dare say, but simpler of heart. I like to believe that what in us is thus worth loving foretells what may come, in generations more, to the America that is to be — provided we be not partitioned between Germany and Japan. If not, I shan't live to know; and I shall be glad if I may some day pass half as serenely as Henry James is passing.

With the family all goes well. Time moves swiftly. This afternoon I sat for a little while with my new grandson — six weeks old; and watched his eyes beginning to see things, and gleams of smile breaking across his plump little features. There are few things lovelier than these first tokens of happy consciousness.

### To R. W. Curtis

BOSTON, 5 *March*, 1916

This notice of Henry James[1] is a poor return for the greetings which have come to me before and since your welcome letter of January 27th — the last was the *Journal de Genève* which turned up two or three days ago. The sad truth is that since my motor accident in November I have been rather beautiful to the eye, but have passed listlessly abed pretty much all the time when I have n't had to be up. Such laziness has its harmless joy; it makes even thought a bit of a burden.

So when the *Transcript* telephoned me a request to write this thing within a few hours, I consented only because I feared that if I declined they would hit on somebody instead who did not care for James personally. Rusty pens, like mine, run to rhetoric. My own style, in print, pleases me as little as my own voice did when for the first and only time I heard it from a phonographic record. After all, though, one can only do what one can. Two or three friends of James in these parts seem to have liked what I wrote; perhaps you may find it not all wrong. I never knew him well; but I have known hardly anyone whom I liked better as a human being. His work, for many years, has been beyond my indolent grasp. The man himself when I last saw him, two years ago last summer, was

---

[1] "Henry James, An Appreciation," published in the *Boston Evening Transcript* March 1, 1916.

changed only in that he was beginning to grow visibly old. The few words that I quote at the end are from Mrs. William James. The rest of her letter touched on the happy wanderings of his broken mind — to old friends, old places, old sunshine. The letter came only a few hours before the news of his death.

What has happened in Congress during the past week or two changes my opinion of Wilson somewhat. I neither like him nor feel his general course to have been what it might have been. But I had not before quite understood the disloyalty to national spirit — the profound Bryanism of his party; nor the degree to which, in other parts of America than this, the traditional dislike of England has prevented the vulgar from admitting to themselves the full monstrosity of Germany. In this last crisis, I think, Wilson has shown force and courage. The better sort, everywhere and of all parties, seem for the moment in sympathy with him. A little more inadvertence on the part of Germany, and the break may come. If not, I still fear that the probably irregular actions of England in the matter of mutual trade may lead to trouble more deplorable still. . . .

*To F. J. Stimson*

GALVESTON, TEXAS, 30 *April*, 1916

DEAR FRED: — For two weeks I have been starring: first lecturing on the late William Shakespere at Charley Thwing's university in Cleveland, and lunching with a local Harvard club; then at St. Louis, where there was another Harvard Club dinner, and various dining and wining — the place is not only hospitable but affable; then to Austin, where I lectured on Shakespere some more, and addressed a Folk Lore Society, and stayed with Lewis Hancock, who is hospitality itself, and has two of the prettiest daughters imaginable; then to San Antonio, where they had a "fiesta" such as I never dreamed of, ending with a battle of flowers — no end of pretty girls, in clothes of incredible splendor, pretending to be duchesses and the like, with very negligible dukes; finally here, where the Southern sea breaking under my window is just like Colombo.

We go on to Houston and to New Orleans, whence homeward on Saturday, the 6th. Harvard clubs everywhere, and hospitality — but not so much drink as I had faintly hoped for. Sobriety I find incompletely favorable to digestion.

Edith is with me, making speeches on national preparedness which outshine what I have to say about Shakespere and Harvard. She is very fit.

As to general feeling among one's own kind, I find it surprisingly like that at home. Only everybody says that there is a disquieting amount of German sympathy and plotting just round the corner or over the way. I can't quite decide whether this impression is a bugbear or is based on fact. Roosevelt seems pretty soundly rooted in the esteem of whoever does n't go in for Wilson. His nomination I think probable. On the election I would not now offer a bet. . . .

*To the same*

BOSTON, 14 *November*, 1916

. . . Last night came word from R. U. Johnson that they have elected me — I cannot understand why — to the American Academy of Arts and Letters. This seems to me a real honor — as great as any honorary degree could be. When the Institute and the Academy met here a year ago, I was laid up by an automobile accident. The one meeting I got to impressed me deeply. The men were really in earnest, and had, as a group, a robust simplicity of feeling which made me more than ever regret my own temperamental isolation. The compliment they have paid me therefore touches me the more. I am not conscious of deserving it at all; nor yet that which comes in your letter. To me, my whole life seems to have been a bewildered effort to get ready to begin. But as to luck, — except in the vulgar detail of large fortune, — I have had, as in this case, more than my share. . . .

The election rather surprised most in these parts; and, as you know, seems to me disturbing; I grow blind, I suppose. It is reassuring to know that you, who have twice my sense, don't agree that things are tending all wrong. . . .

*To the same*

BOSTON, 10 *December*, 1916

. . . As to the election, my consolation is that you and a few others don't find it hopeless. I am like a Federalist in Jefferson's time, a sound Whig in Jackson's, or an honest Southerner in Lincoln's. There is doubtless another side than I can see, but it is beyond my vision.

And the European news now seems about as upsetting. In both England and France something like political revolution seems at hand. Russia is nowhere — probably more revolutionary still. The war in the West is at best a deadlock; in the East the Germans are virtually victorious, and the Allies in a state of enchanted inaction. For the moment, they might as well be crumbling in such fires as made an earthly end of Adelais and Arnaud. As to the spirit, I don't know. The purpose of free institutions is noble; the practice of them, so far, has amounted to the denial of excellence. . . .

*To Sir Robert White-Thomson*

BOSTON, 30 *December*, 1916

. . . Though pronounced not seriously ill, I find my general nervous condition so far from strong that I have decided to resign my professorship at Harvard, at the close of the present academic year. I shall then have taught there for thirty-seven years — almost twice as long as I was old when we met in '74. My pension will be about $2500 for life; and by way of experiment I have been reserving this year what actual salary is in excess of that sum. So I have proved that the reduction of income will not be troublesome. I hope hereafter to take to writing again. I am not sure, though, that I can manage to do much.

One thing I hope for is that the leisure will give me chance, if the war ever end, to go abroad again; and to see again the friends I care for so much.

Of public matters I have not the heart to write. Wilson's peace note was not intended, I think, to express hostility to the Allies. His appalling self-complacency, however, can hardly have appeared abroad in any other light. . . .

*To his daughter Mary*

BOSTON, 7 *January*, 1917. — . . . My resignation goes before the Corporation tomorrow — at their first meeting since it was sent the President, on New Year's Day. I was never more satisfied of the wisdom of anything. Either, as is unlikely, I am really breaking down, — in which case I could not long keep on with college work, — or else, as is probably the case, I have before me some years in which, without the burden of college work, I may be able to take up writing again. After these seven or eight years of abstention from it, I can feel myself riper in thought than I used to be, and perhaps able still to produce something more nearly worth-while than most which I have produced so far. I have now a faint project of beginning something in the way of personal memoirs, to get my hand in. That limbering of the hand is what I first need. . . .

14 *January*, 1917. — . . . To me my resignation is a relief; the Corporation has voted me a pension, on the Carnegie terms, above $3000; and I am getting letters which, if preserved in family files, will make my great-grandchildren suppose me to have been an intellectual and spiritual power. If you could imagine Franklin, Webster, Channing, Hawthorne, Phillips Brooks, and Billy Sunday rolled into one, and endowed with the self-complacency of Woodrow Wilson, you might have some faint notion of what a human being should be to accept such compliments as deserved. Still, one likes to sit, and be stroked, and purr. I am in a heavenly state of mind nowadays. . . .

*To F. J. Stimson*

SOMERSET CLUB, 26 *January*, 1917

How long it is since I wrote you the Lord knows. I have been mostly a-bed, crawling up and out only when there is need. My doctor at last tells me what I had not understood before, though he thought I had. That motor accident of last year shook up and displaced the stomach, which is permanently dislocated — curable, if at all, only by doubtful and dangerous surgery, nowise recommended. More than half the time it has

behaved quietly. When any nervous strain or other disturbance occurs, there is apt to be functional disturbance, resulting
in acute pain. This has been the case for more than a month.
I passed Christmas Day in bed. Week by week, I can see, I
get slowly better; but, as this bit of pathology implies, — for
only invalids shamelessly open their insides, — I am still far
from strong. The doctor cheerfully opines that unless things
take some now unforseen turn I am good — or bad, if you will
— for twenty or thirty years. . . .

*To the same*

BOSTON, 4 *February*, 1917

. . . Wilson's speech to Congress, breaking with Germany,
seems to impress everyone as faultless. So far as I can make
out, the sentiment here, among one's own kind and I think far
beyond our range, is of content that, since the break must
come, it is not with the Allies. There is clearly an aspect,
which Lawrence has seen throughout, in which Wilson's whole
conduct may be regarded as intended to give him — and the
country — the strength which may come from honest effort,
before breaking with Germany, to prevent the break by every
means in his power. If one may judge from the summaries in
the Boston papers, this is now admitted by the German-
American press; every utterance of which appears to be loyal,
in expression, to American citizenship.

Unless I am all wrong, the sentiment of the country is now
stirred more unanimously and more deeply than ever before in
my memory. No one pretends to know what will happen.
More are prepared for whatever may than I should have dared
expect. For one, I hope that the South American states may
take sides with us, even though, as all should see, it be doubtful
whether we, or they, are ready — in case it comes to war —
to join the full Alliance, agreeing to make peace only when
peace is made by all. If not, of course, America as a continent
will perhaps be left at war with Germany when peace descends
on Europe. What this might involve, you can guess better
than I. . . .

*To S. E. Morison*

BOSTON, 17 *March*, 1917

DEAR SAM: — . . . After all, the best I can wish the boy is that he may live to see this world happier than he has found it, and help to make it so. My own fate, as I now feel, has been the reverse of this. You see things differently, no doubt. What we all want, though, is about the same thing — fair play, reward for what is constructive, penalty for what is not, and above all no privileged class, high or low. I am half tempted to send him, as my first greeting, the *Privileged Classes*. I won't. One should n't beguile a boy by tracts which call in question paternal orthodoxies — unless, as I suppose must always be the case, the virtue of all facts is sure to be repellent. . . .

*To F. J. Stimson*

SOMERSET CLUB, 23 *March*, 1917

. . . As to Wilson, I grow old and prejudiced. My feeling is that, at first, he was headstrong beyond precedent. His appointments, with few exceptions, were not and have not been such as to command public confidence, as distinguished from his own. His Mexican policy seemed sheer assertion of personal impulse. To this moment, it seems to me otherwise indefensible. His domestic policy has done more to influence class prejudice, on both sides, than anything else in my memory. His European policy has seemed to me, and still seems, spiritless. At moments when appeal to our nobler traditions might have been imaginable, he has not made it. Nor has he ever, to this moment, backed brave words with prudent deeds. We are now virtually at war with Germany. So far as I can ascertain, we are no more prepared for it than we were when he succeeded Taft. And there is not in his Cabinet a human being in whom the country can feel unquestioned faith. . . .

*To the same*

SOMERSET CLUB, 30 *March*, 1917

. . . It is a week, I think, since I last scribbled you, off-hand. In that scrawl, I fear, I was at once stupid and inconsiderate.

Your question about Wilson, which I answered, really concerned only his European policy. My answer rather neglected this, turning only on reasons why I can't bring myself to trust him. For the precise matters at hand, these were imperfectly relevant, if indeed pertinent at all. It is more than conceivable that your own view — of his effort so to manipulate a belly as to make of it a conscience — is internationally, and tragically, true. On the whole, though, I could wish that it had been made earlier — before the reëlection of him seemed on the whole to register national preference of belly to conscience. I can hardly be alone in a feeling of shame when I think of our national course during the past three years; nor of indignant despair when I think of how the past four years have influenced class prejudice here and shaken all confidence in the just impulses of the authorities to whom we must submit. My consolation is double: in the first place, I can't possibly live through as many miserable years to come as I have lived through prosperous years in the moderate past; in the second place, as you have gently but kindly made clear to me ever since '72, I have a genius — if I have a gleam of any such thing — for being honestly but profoundly in the wrong. . . .

*To Sir Robert White-Thomson*

BOSTON, 31 *March*, 1917

. . . Of Mary Antin, too. I knew her first, years ago, when she was a miraculously precocious child, and when the preliminary sketches for part of her book — of which you wrote — were far more extraordinary than the book in its final form. A Jewish student at Harvard, son of a prosperous business man here, asked me to his mother's house, to meet her at tea. She was a queer, thin little thing, of fifteen or so, overdressed for the occasion and with dreadfully frizzed hair; but with eyes as honest as the simple heart of her. I gave her a reader's ticket at the Athenæum, our chief private library, where anyone there admitted can go to the shelves and read and browse among books — of which we now have some two or three hundred thousand. She has told me since that this was to her among the greatest and most helpful pleasures of her life.

She married rather young, I think. Her husband is — or was — a professor at Columbia University, the chief university of New York. She has lived there for years. Occasionally, when she comes here, I have seen her. She is still little, now a bit wizened, and a good deal more conscious than she was as a child. She has developed an irritating habit of describing herself and her people as Americans, in distinction from such folks as Edith and me, who have been here for three hundred years. My use of "folks," by the way, is old Yankee English, to my delight sanctioned by many examples in the letters of Horace Walpole. In 1854, for example, my mother was married at Dorchester, a town now absorbed by the city of Boston. Within a year or so it became uninhabitable, and my grandfather moved to the little house in West Cedar Street where, in '92, you saw the Copley portraits, now mine. The Antins live in Dorchester now. When I mentioned to Mary that my mother's people once lived there, she was of opinion that their departure had proved them not "really American." Yet she stays honest, genuine, aspiring and, though no longer a prodigy, she is a woman not only of intelligence but of admirable personal quality. By this time, I should think, she must be some five and thirty years old. Whether she has children I don't know. If she has, their children may perhaps come to be American in the sense in which I feel myself so — for better or worse, belonging only here. And that is the kind of miracle which America, for all its faults and its vulgarities, has wrought. . . .

*To his daughter Mary*

5 *April*, 1917. — . . . Well, the war seems to be on, and the Lord knows what will come of it. I am deeply glad that we have escaped the danger I have dreaded, of war with the Allies. But, plaintively weak in nerve, I feel frightened at what war may mean. Hereabouts there is little enthusiasm, except that flags are displayed everywhere. Wilson's speech to Congress was admirable. The country has really swung away from Germany at last; nor do I see quite how Germany can actually invade us. The months — and perhaps the years — to come, though, must bring dreadful sorrows and sufferings, at best.

If I were strong enough to do even a bit, I should not feel so despondent. Edith is full of work and spirit. . . .

*To F. J. Stimson*

BOSTON, 8 *April*, 1917

Whatever one's hopes or doubts, there can be no hesitation in deeply, earnestly approving the President's course during the past week. His address to Congress is admirable. So far as one may tell, from public prints, what has occurred since indicates a higher degree of preparation, or at least of foresight, than had seemed the case before. What shakes me, as I have written you too much in the past, is that his course for a full term has failed to win my confidence — particularly in his appointments; and at the same time has seemed singularly and distrustfully confident in himself. In a word, perhaps, he seems to me now impatient of anything but acknowledged inferiors to himself; and this at a time when the country needs its best men everywhere.

My mood is doubtless odd — it would not otherwise be mine. And my obstinate illness, as you see, has broken what nerve I ever had. I am tremulously older than my years, in a world always too much for such infirm powers as mine.

Meanwhile, there is something deeply impressive in the general feeling hereabouts. It is not careless, but wholly grave; it seems nearer appreciation of a great crisis than anything I remember before. At the same time, it is outwardly calm. Except for flags everywhere — there is one at my library window, as I write — you would hardly know the difference from the times just past and stretching back in memory. No one is hysterical, no one overwrought, no one changed — unless it be in implicit revelation of gravity. The meeting at the Club, just before which I wrote you last, was remarkable: some two hundred men, as quiet as if nothing serious were in the air; some short, firm resolutions; no discussion; a unanimous vote; and a dispersing as quiet as if from a religious ceremony.

The more folks know, the graver they are: Howard Elliot, for example, whom I chanced to meet yesterday. He said nothing but quiet commonplace, agreeing with me that there is chance of long and hard trial to come. No one can foresee. For my part I should be glad if the doctors found my case anxious as distinguished from troublesome. I can't do anything at all; I hate uselessly to survive; and I fear that I dread the realities seeming so close at hand. After all, one would n't be human if there were n't in him some touch of cowardice to conquer. Here, I think, I am at one with many — perhaps with most; and as we don't mean not to conquer ourselves, the country will end the braver for our self-conquests. . . .

*To Sir Robert White-Thomson*

PORTSMOUTH, 21 *May*, 1917

. . . Edith is busier than ever, having just been made the head of a committee organized to stir up the women's clubs, etc., of Massachusetts to help in the sale of the "Liberty Loan," the huge national issue of bonds about to be made for war purposes. The government has proceeded, to my mind, demagogically in this matter, refusing to employ experienced banks, or to pay any commission whatever, even expenses of advertisement and postage. Yet they hope to get some three hundred millions, at $3\frac{1}{2}$ per cent, over-subscribed. The bankers, to be sure, are doing all they can to help. Dear B[1] has been working himself sleepless, for one; and has devised an advertisement, now in every shop window, intended to appeal to the patriotism of the common people:

U MEANS YOU
S MEANS SUBSCRIBE
A MEANS AT ONCE

Of course, U.S.A. is the regular abbreviation for United States of America.

Half the college are already in officers' training corps. Six French officers have been sent to give military instruction at Harvard, and thoroughly good men they are. Last week, at a special convocation, the degree of LL.D. was given to Joffre, who arrived so tired that he could hardly walk. I was chosen to escort him in the academic procession. A fine, bluff, honest

[1] Barrett Wendell, Jr., had entered the Boston office of Lee, Higginson & Co. in 1905, and is now a member of the firm.

old fellow he seemed; but too exhausted by long, fast, sleepless travel for any talk. Viviani turned up next day, too late for his degree. Immensely clever and eloquent I thought him; but not of deeply trustworthy quality — thoroughly a politician in type. Mr. Balfour has declined to come to Boston, I fear by reason of the intense Irish feeling among most of the city government. I wish I might have met him. . . .

*To the same*

PORTSMOUTH, 27 *June*, 1917

. . . My illness has lately been troublesome again. Though they assure me that it is not dangerous, it is dreadfully depressing. Two weeks ago, however, I had a wonderful and tonic surprise. My portrait has been painted[1] as a gift to the college from certain friends. I did not know who, or how many, they were until suddenly asked to dine with them in Boston — the matter having been quietly arranged with Edith. There were some fifty or sixty in the company, and as many more names who could not be there. The speeches were simple and really affectionate, touching me beyond words. And my Harvard colleagues gave me a beautiful piece of old Sheffield plate — a singularly graceful tureen, which had once belonged to my great-grandfather's kinsman and dear friend, Judge Morris, of New York. They were almost of an age, one born in 1730, the other in 1731, and they corresponded intimately for some fifty years, occasionally visiting each other. So it is almost a piece of family plate. I wish you could see it in this pleasant old house.

Of public matters I will say nothing. The spirit of America is admirable now; but we are not yet awake. . . .

*To M. A. DeW. Howe*
[*After the death of Wendell's brother Evert*]

PORTSMOUTH, 30 *August*, 1917

. . . And as for me, far more than half of those nearest me have long been somewhere else than here. I have now a queer

---

[1] By Charles Hopkinson.

feeling that whether we fall asleep or wake blinking, it will be in nearer and dearer fellowship than one can find much longer in the sunlight.

Be sure of my gratitude for your words of sympathy, and that I shall always stay

Sincerely, affectionately yours,<br>BARRETT WENDELL

*To Sir Robert White-Thomson*

PORTSMOUTH, 31 *August*, 1917

It will grieve you to know that my last surviving brother, Evert, has died, in Paris. He went there, a few weeks ago, to make arrangements for some relief work for our troops. He arrived ill, the trouble proving to be diabetes. It must have been of long standing, though I think he did not know it. At the American hospital he was cared for by Dr. Lambert, an old friend. William was at hand, and Jac's wife and her two boys — now both in the ambulance service — were there too. He died on Monday, the 27th.

Whether you knew him, I am not sure. He was one of those rarely happy human beings who never quite outgrew the innocent buoyancy of boyhood. He never had any regular occupation; but devoted himself incessantly to uniquely personal charitable work, largely among boys who without his care might have become criminal. His exuberant enthusiasm, the while, made him hosts of friends everywhere. No one was more popular, more beloved, or will be more widely and deeply missed.

My consolation is that until the last he enjoyed his full strength, and that the nature of his disease was such that even if he had recovered he must henceforth have been invalid, or at least confined to a regimen which, beyond almost any one else, he would have found intolerable.

There was never happier life, nor gentler death.

As for me, I grow slowly better, until I begin to hope that before long I shall be able to work a little. I have more than one literary project in view. . . .

*To the same*

BOSTON, *Christmas*, 1917

. . . The gravest Christmas within my memory, I find this, though not yet saddened by the private sorrows so soon to come. The spirit of America deeply impresses me; we hesitated long, — I think too long, — but one can see now that we approach the test we have accepted in a mood of wonderful earnestness. Everywhere one feels a calm courage, strangely different from the over-excitement and blatant confidence with which our Civil War began, and with which our brief Spanish War was suffused throughout. These tremendous years develop a moral dignity which shames one's moments of misgiving for what may come. . . .

## PROFESSOR EMERITUS IN ACTIVE RETIREMENT

### 1918–1921

THE attentive reader will have noted in the preceding chapter one highly characteristic sentence in a letter of Wendell's: "I have a genius — if I have any gleam of such thing — for being honestly but profoundly in the wrong." The accuracy of the word "profoundly" in this statement will be estimated as variously as individual opinions are wont to differ. Not so with "honestly." Wendell's own opinions concerning affairs and men underwent extensive changes between his early "mugwump" days and his later years of extreme conservatism. Towards the end of his life he wrote, of an eminent figure of the generation before his own: "I greatly disliked him, and he me: but I can see now the big qualities of him." It is easily imaginable that, with a further extension of his years, he would have expressed himself concerning later figures with something less of finality. But his contemporaneous opinions are preserved in these pages not only for their revelations of Wendell's honest immediate views but for their permanent value in the history of opinion. What most of his friends were saying he made no scruple of writing. Thus there are passages in his letters, especially in the last two chapters of this book, which must be counted an essential part of the recorded beliefs of his time.

There are two formal expressions of his own political beliefs to which special attention should be drawn. These are found in an address, "The Ideals of Empire," which he gave before the American Academy of Arts and Letters in New York, April 18, 1917, and in his Phi Beta Kappa address, "The Conflict of Idolatries," given at Harvard, June 17, 1918.[1] In the first of these deliverances he traced the succession of ideals of world-empire from the earliest times to the present, and — writing before the question of a League of Nations was flung into the pit of political controversy — brought his address to the following conclusion: —

What will come of this war on which we are now entered, no man can tell. What may come of it is an attempt to establish by common consent a world-empire in which each state, large or small, monarchic, aristocratic, or popular, shall have an acknowledged right to independent existence. In such an empire the common authority of all would protect the independence of each part, enforcing the law of peace, sparing those who submit to it, checking oppression, suppressing rebellion. All this such common authority must do, not in a name foreign to any, but in a name common to every part — for such common authority must be based on the humble and devoted consent of all. That name has not yet been proposed, except in vaguely general terms, like a League to Enforce Peace. But we of the United States may surely be forgiven if we think of it as a name in which, as in the name of our own country, all separate names may merge — the United States of the World.

In "The Conflict of Idolatries," his conclusion, if somewhat less concrete, was equally idealistic. "The old order," he declared, "must ceaselessly change, yielding place to new. Broadly speaking, the conduct of human affairs must take one of three forms — each sometimes beneficent. Government must be either monarchical — concentrated in a single ruler; or aristocratic — concentrated in a ruling class; or popular — diffused among the

[1] The addresses were published in the *Harvard Graduates' Magazine*, respectively, for June 1917, and September 1918.

people. So long as any of these forms works for the welfare of society, it is healthy. When any of them plans only, or chiefly, for its own good, it is ailing and soon falls into deadly sickness."

The gist of the matter, as he saw it, appeared in the final paragraphs: —

Until our conflicting idolatries, forgetting the clashes of their logic, can thus perceive their errors, there is little chance that idols will so much as begin to crumble; for until then, whatever the fluctuating fortunes of arms, no cult will ever quite admit the right of another even to existence. Then, however, each and all may gradually and wonderingly come to understand how their common and ideally noble end of justice can be approached only by those who will renounce all pretence to absolute authority, and will humbly seek inevitable law, consoling themselves under its bondage by unfettered freedom of the spirit. Nothing less than that unseen freedom of the spirit can surely lead us towards the spiritual communion needful if we are ever to approach with mutual confidence our final end of peace.

To-day, this seems far away. What we most need now is practical counsel. No one can yet give it surely. Only two things are certain. The first is that we must never shrink from the day's work, as God gives us to see it. The second is more subtle, but more enduring: we must keep our spirits loyal to righteousness.

Another "occasional" address of these later years was that which Wendell delivered in New York, February 22, 1919, at the commemoration of the centenary of the birth of James Russell Lowell, under the auspices of the American Academy of Arts and Letters. Written in response to a hasty summons, at a time when his physical energies were narrowly limited, it was yet a performance revealing Wendell at his best. In comparison with the essay, "James Russell Lowell as a Teacher," in his early volume, *Stelligeri*, it embodies, through its interpretations of the biographi-

have doubtless overrated it as a production of scholarship. An English reviewer, in the "Musings without Method" of *Blackwood's Magazine*, held it up as a revelation of "the sad results of abolishing the humanities," and scornfully referred to the short cuts of translation — which Wendell commended to his readers with but a faint apparent hope that they would spend much time on it — as "Greek without tears." In the American *Classical Weekly*, a Johns Hopkins scholar, Professor David M. Robinson, showed a clearer apprehension of Wendell's purpose and the value of its achievement, for, besides pointing out, as such a reviewer must, what the litany would call some of the "negligences and ignorances" of the book, he hailed it as "fascinating and inspiring" — a book which will make laymen and scholars alike "read with a livelier interest the best classical authors." Furthermore, he declared: "Professor Wendell was no theorist or propagandist or pseudoscientist. Scholars who are prejudiced against such books may well learn a lesson from this work, which is full of the soundest generalizations that hit the nail on the head almost every time." Such an appraisal of his work, by an American classicist, knowing both the subject and the audience for which its treatment was intended, would have seemed to Wendell himself a substantial reward for this last labor of his mind and spirit.

This labor was performed partly at Portsmouth, partly in a little room at the Boston Athenæum, of which Wendell was a devoted trustee and frequenter from 1890 till his death. Here too he wrote, in the autumn of 1918, an historical account — unpublished — of the Boston firm of Lee, Higginson and Company, of which his son Barrett had recently become a member. At Portsmouth, in the summer of 1919, he wrote "A Gentlewoman of Boston, 1742–1805,"[1] a biographical sketch of Catherine (Wendell)

[1] Published in the Proceedings of the American Antiquarian Society, October 1919

Davis, one of the daughters of his Boston ancestors, John and Elizabeth (Quincy) Wendell. Made up largely of bits of correspondence found among the family papers in the Jacob Wendell House, this was a production in which he took a lively interest and pleasure.

In spite of all the limitations of his strength, the brief period of his retirement from his profession of teaching was thus a period of substantial increase in his written work. It was also a time in which there was a corresponding increase in the honors bestowed in recognition of this work. In 1913 Columbia University had conferred upon him the honorary degree of Doctor of Letters. Harvard awarded him the same degree in 1918, and in 1920 he received, in recognition of his interpretation of France to the English-speaking world, the honorary degree of Doctor of Laws from the University of Strassburg, restored to its French control. Nearer home, he was elected, in the spring of 1919, to the presidency of the Tavern Club of Boston, in succession to Henry Lee Higginson, and in June 1920, to the Board of Overseers of Harvard College. In all these recognitions it is not over-fanciful to perceive a blending of the local and the universal proper to one so deeply a Bostonian and at the same time so much a citizen of the larger world.

Through these final years neither failing health nor absorption in the tasks to which he had set himself impaired his activities as a correspondent. The letters to his friends, on the contrary, show him outgiving as ever in his friendships, and perhaps more than ever serious in his moods and his expressions in regard to men, affairs, and life itself.

*To his daughter Mary*

17 *February*, 1918. — ... My habit now is to get up a bit before ten; to get before eleven to the Athenæum, where I can manage to write from one to four pages in two hours; to lunch

THE JACOB WENDELL HOUSE, PORTSMOUTH, NEW HAMPSHIRE

at the Somerset or the Tavern; to get home by three or so; and thereafter to read, or doze, with breaks for tea or dinner, till eleven. To do anything active of an afternoon or evening generally means restless nights; these mean painful "giant-baby" days — a vicious circle. . . .

11 *April*, 1918. — . . . To-day, while I was working at the Athenæum, I heard a band in Tremont Street; and looking from my window across the new green burying-ground, I saw through the trees, just over our old Wendell tomb of the 1730's, a British tank waddling down the street. After it came the band, followed by two or three hundred recruits, who carried our flag and the British and a third. This was white, with two blue stripes, and a blue device in the middle which at first I could not make out. All of a sudden I recognized the "Seal of Solomon." It was the flag of Zionists, enlisting for their own independent Palestine: a mere dream, I suppose, but a dream that revives the hopes of the Maccabees. Anyhow, it thrilled me. . . .

## To A. Lawrence Lowell

[*At the Harvard Commencement exercises of this day, President Lowell had conferred the honorary degree of Doctor of Letters on Barrett Wendell in these terms: "Barrett Wendell: devoted as a teacher; ever steadfast as a friend; a writer on many themes; a seer who beheld the soul of France before it shone forth brighter than ever through the darkness of this war."*]

BOSTON, 20 *June*, 1918

DEAR LAWRENCE: — The degree conferred on me to-day comes at the very time when, as a matter of family sentiment, it means more to me than it could have meant either sooner or later.

Among my earliest memories are a stiff old portrait, always called "Uncle Eyre," which has been in my Portsmouth house for more than a hundred years, together with the manuscript of his Salutatory oration, delivered at Harvard in 1718. He was John, son of John and Catherine (Brattle) Eyre, of Boston; his mother's second husband was Wait Still Winthrop, Chief

Justice of Massachusetts. She was the "Madam Winthrop" of Sewall's Diary. "Uncle Eyre" married Ann, daughter of Henry Sherburne, of Portsmouth, where he subsequently lived, and died without surviving issue. His wife was aunt of my great-grandmother Wendell, born Dorothy Sherburne. Through her the portrait and the oration descended to my grandfather and my father, and finally to me. Together they began, when I was a child, my feeling of intimate personal relation with Harvard.

Five years ago, when my aunt Sarah Barrett died, I found among the things she left me a stained little silhouette profile of my grandfather's elder brother, John Barrett, of the class of 1818, and the manuscript of the Commencement part he delivered in that year, just a century after "Uncle Eyre's." He died about two years later. He was the eldest son of John and Elizabeth (Brown) Barrett, of Boston, Milton, and Braintree. His most eminent ancestor was Roger Williams, from whom his mother descended through the families of Sayles, Almy, and Greene.

So the Phi Beta Kappa oration I gave on the 17th combines with the degree given me to-day truly to begin in 1918 a third century of family Harvard tradition, blending the two others.

In sentimental mood, I write on an old sheet of paper found at Portsmouth in a portfolio which belonged to my grandfather Wendell; and I shall bring you to-night in an old portfolio which came to me from the Barretts, photographs of Uncle Eyre's portrait and of Uncle John Barrett's, together with the original manuscripts of their Commencement parts, and a photograph of me taken during my last year of Harvard teaching — some eighteen months ago. To these, as soon as I can have it properly copied for myself, I will add the manuscript of my Phi Beta Kappa oration, given last Monday. Together, you see, they record the beginning of this third century of Harvard tradition in my family.

If you think them interesting enough to give to the college I should be glad to have them kept together in case this be not inconvenient. For I like to fancy that in 2018 there may chance to be at Harvard some one of my line who might add to them records to begin another such century.

How much your formal words touched me to-day I will not try to tell you. Only be sure that I am always

Affectionately yours,
BARRETT WENDELL

*To Nancy Schenck, aged three days*

PORTSMOUTH, 23 *August*, 1918

My DEAR ANNE: — Your message of birthday congratulations is welcome not only as testifying to a friendship which has lasted all your life, until we may both assume it consecrated by the full strength of beloved tradition. It is welcome also because it implicitly assures me that you may always be trusted to make good use of your time. In the two days since I last heard of you, it seems, you have acquired two beautiful names which will always be precious to you, and in due time to somebody else.

So far as nativity goes — which I take to concern the cycle of the year — you are a little my senior. . . . In the matter of longevity, accident has arranged matters otherwise. You will not, I hope, feel that I presume too much on this secondary advantage when I venture to suggest that you will do well to keep on as you have begun, and make it a rule to acquire something beautiful every day. Among objects which I may consequently call to your attention are virtues, plate, prayers, works of art, beaux, wisdom, and modestly increasing affluence. Other desirable things will doubtless occur to you. Whatever the treasures you thus acquire, I dare hope that they will never quite hide from you the glowing and constant — though deeply respectful — affection of

Your very devoted
BARRETT WENDELL

*To H. M. Kallen*

PORTSMOUTH, 23 *August*, 1918

Your message of birthday greeting brings me deep pleasure. I was half afraid that you might resent the perhaps extreme candor with which I set forth when I last wrote you my devotion to principles of the past. Somehow, therefore, a telegraphic accident which befell your despatch seems to me delightfully apt. You probably addressed me by the dignified title of *Professor*, but by the time it got to me it had subsided into *Private*. This, incidentally, is the only military dignity to which I am entitled, after having served my time in the Cadets, *c.* 1875. It seems to me, as well, the most fitting handle imaginable for all names in the Utopia to be.

Forgive this trifling. Though better of late, I still feel wobbly — not sure of myself. And be sure that I am constantly

Gratefully and affectionately yours,

BARRETT WENDELL

*To the same*

PORTSMOUTH, 8 *September*, 1918

. . . Before long now, my Phi Beta Kappa address will appear in the *Graduates' Magazine;* and in due time I shall have some pamphlet copies. Concerning the war, and all, it says what I have to say at present as clearly as I can make it. To get it printed at all was troublesome. I cannot feel, with you, that in such a Lucretian chaos as is working about us any utterance is much worthwhile. To speak with assurance, in any case, one must see clearer light than is yet mine.

Your own view, you will surely understand, impresses me much as a passionately sincere anti-Semitic propaganda might impress you. There is somewhere a Greek chorus, not quite decorously frowned on by Macaulay in an off-hand comment on Wordsworth's sonnets: "Τὸ μεν μῆ θυσεῖν," and so forth, if I have my Alexandrian accents straight: "The best fate is not to be, and next to that, is sinking back to that whence we merged into being." The only earthly approach to social justice must be made not by individuals but by generations; social penalties take at least a century to mature; and, in brief, the trouble I find with this passing moment is mostly that those who incur them violently resent their instant inconvenience, instead of trying to discern the secret of social law. There is no health to be sought through destruction. Our world, I think, is on the verge of unwitting suicide. Over it, by and by, another will come, but not a different; for there is a cosmic social law as inexorable as the laws which keep the planets in their course. . . .

## To Francis Rawle

PORTSMOUTH, 27 *September*, 1918

MY DEAR MR. RAWLE: — The pleasure brought me by your kind word about my Phi Beta Kappa address is the greater because it comes at a moment of invalid discouragement. To write the address took me six months; I made five full copies in my own hand, not to speak of a half-finished version which was evidently going all wrong. My effort throughout was to reduce what began in mental chaos to real, as distinguished from merely apparent, order; and carefully to command the excesses of a temper naturally unsympathetic and I fear repellent. Certainly, I never did more serious, persistent, honest work, trying hard to say something which might really help others to think. My long illness, too — I have been invalid since March, 1914 — made me feel throughout that this might well prove my last literary work.

It was kindly received enough; and old friends said pleasant things at the time. No one but the *Graduates' Magazine*, though, would publish it; and even my always kind publishers — my old friends, the Scribners — gently pointed out that in times like these they could not again bring out for me a volume of essays for which the prospects, based on former such books of mine, were disastrously unpromising. So, except that my conscience was clear, those months of work seemed wasted.

Forgive me for troubling you with so long and so intimate a letter. It implies, I fear, the general weakness of health which must keep me mostly inert. It is impelled, though, by real gratitude. Your kindness in taking the trouble to write me has brought me the only word of sympathetic approval which has come from any but the intimate friends who heard the speech; and what you say shows that, at least for you, I have accomplished something of what I tried to do.

Gratefully and sincerely yours,

BARRETT WENDELL

*To F. J. Stimson*

PORTSMOUTH, 7 *October*, 1918

Until your letter came, some two weeks ago, I still hoped for another glimpse of you. After all, though, that visit of yours here was so flawless that it will always stay among the perfect memories. Of all my friendships, yours has been the nearest and the dearest since we were boys at Harvard. To find it, after these accidental months of silence, boundlessly itself was happy beyond any words I can find. I feel old — and indeed I have considerably survived all but one of my generation — the men I mean. . . .

This morning's papers have the new German Chancellor's peace speech. Though nobody could distrust Germans more suspiciously than I, one phase of the present situation seems to me perhaps misapprehended. We generally assume that, left to themselves, they would do it over again. Unless I am all wrong, there is more than even chance that their own measureless sufferings and miscalculations might well prevent them from doing so. The future danger from them I suspect to be less in their military power — on the whole proved in every sense unduly expensive — than in their economic, which is based on a more profoundly honest willingness to work without excessive reward than is to be found in other European nations. Dishonest as men, they are honest as craftsmen; even though counterfeiting, they will do their best, content with low wages, beer, and a sense that in this respect Germany really is on top of all the rest.

What will happen between now and when — if ever — you get this scrawl, I don't venture to guess. Just conceivably they will withdraw from invaded territories to their own boundaries. If so, but I should think hardly sooner, the fighting may stop. The one thing not to be surprised at is surprise. Old and crabbed, I can't trust things as I should like to; but it is amazing to find how much lately said and done by our government seems to me right. . . .

*To the same*

PORTSMOUTH, 17 *October*, 1918

. . . As I grow older, by the way, I find a new meaning in the sea. Whatever happens on shore, nothing can scar the everlasting waters. They are the still unmastered substance of our planet, unconquerably elemental; and when the sky gets pure of earth above them it stays limitlessly so, too. All of which were better in a sonnet if I could make one. Old Ocean makes even Nile and Ganges seem as modern as Cæsar, or Alexander, or Hindenburg.

To-day's newspapers are misty with rumors of abdicating Kaisers, and a child-emperor whose picture looks queerly as one fancies the King of Rome might have looked a century ago. Poor little "Aiglon"; I have never felt sure that civilization would have been the worse for him. As John Ropes used to say, the fatal trouble with the Bonapartes was that they were not gentlemen. Whatever the faults of the Hapsburgs, they had their breeding. Here, and wasted, was the one chance to see what might have come from the force of the one strain and the quality of the other. The Prussian princeling is too purely royal; just as republican magistrates, God help us all, lack the heritage of sovereignty.

To-day I am all alone here — Edith gone to Boston, whither she proposes, I understand, to take me next week. I have seen nobody; and heard only polite acknowledgment of my still-born "Conflict of Idolatries." The most painfully true comment thereon came from one of our colleagues, generally held precise in use of critical terms; he had heard me give the address with much pleasure, he said, and he found it on reading to be "entertaining as ever." Such is the fruit of six months' effort on my part seriously to think. . . .

> "God made the only world he could,
> And when the work was done
> He said that it was very good —
> I disagree, for one."

When I repeated that quotation to a Washington woman a little while ago, she pronounced it "the essence of Beacon

Street." She may have known what she meant; I failed to grasp more than the expression of her thought. . . .

## To R. W. Curtis

BOSTON, 17 *October*, 1918

. . . Dr. Munthe's[1] view of Wilson seems to me penetrating. I have known Wilson for more than thirty years, though I have not seen him, I think, since 1909, when he stayed with me at the time of Lawrence Lowell's inauguration. He was then President of Princeton. He is to my mind a man of what we used to call ministerial habit of mind; that is, he has the qualities of a Presbyterian parson, convinced that he cannot make a mistake. Uncontradicted, he is pleasant, widely informed, intelligent to a certain point. Contradicted, he is fanatically malignant; for he believes himself absolutely right and he is not imaginative enough to be generous in feeling even though he might accidentally be so disposed. Personally I have never happened to come in conflict with him; those who have done so are unanimous, so far as I have known, in feeling that when it comes to business you cannot trust him, any more than you can generally trust a parson in matters of affairs. The smug inconsistencies of his conduct as President I fear to be characteristic. Certainly there is hardly a man in this country in whom I could feel much less personal confidence. You will therefore see how glad I am that the recent elections have made Congress on the whole Republican — particularly as the domestic policy of Wilson tends toward doctrinarian socialism. . . .

## To his daughter Mary

BOSTON, 11 *November*, 1918

. . . To-day what seems to be true news of German surrender makes Boston pandemonic. The crowd is good-natured, happy, orderly; but frightens me. It is like a gamboling wild beast. What I think of is Russia, and the red flag in Germany. Contagious revolution will be worse, if it come, for what I think civilization, than another turn of the fortunes of arms

[1] Axel Munthe, Swedish doctor at Rome and Capri.

might have been. Yet I so detest Germany that I can't help gladness for its shame. What I most dread is sentimental democratic sympathy with the German people. If in time they can manage popular government as it has been managed — for all its errors — in France, they will work a miracle.

I write from the Athenæum. Even here, the din is such that I can't pretend to work this morning. It began at four, with uninterrupted sounding of steam whistles for four whole hours. Think of the fuel!

Mamma is joyous as ever. . . .

*To F. J. Stimson*

BOSTON, 26 *January*, 1919

. . . I promise to be so long in dying as probably to outlive our generation; meanwhile, I can manage a little work, an hour or two a day at most, and seldom get through twenty-four hours without exhausting pain. I am therefore a bit appalled by an invitation which came only two or three days ago, and seemed in essence mandatory, to replace Cabot Lodge as eulogist of J. R. Lowell at the Centenary Celebration arranged by the American Academy of Arts and Letters, in New York, a little more than three weeks hence. I must do my best. After all, I think, Lowell's course in Dante has meant more to me than any other of my college studies; and few are left now to whom he is more than a more or less classic fact in literature. I shall try to treat him as human, and as American in that deepest sense which means that a man has no vestige of personal tradition not wholly native; thereby his fresh linking of our sympathy with England becomes the more wonderfully significant.

In the February *Scribner's*, which I will send you as soon as I receive a copy, is an article[1] which really springs from your first, off-hand comment at Portsmouth on my Phi Beta Kappa speech. The end, you said, is there too abrupt, and should have been developed. I wrote this supplement in September or October; to my surprise, Bridges accepted it. Two or three unexpected people have already said kind things of it. . . .

[1] "Law and Legislation"

*To the same*

BOSTON, 9 *March*, 1919

. . . Beveridge's *Marshall* is not yet finished — much less out. He has Paul Thorndike's house this year, where he purports to be working at the biography for twelve or fifteen hours a day. I never met him till this year. He interests me; a very live wire I find him, but perhaps imperfectly strung. He seems to me intellectually honest and remarkably alert; but neither deeply wise nor cautiously prudent. He presided last night at a mass-meeting, addressed by Borah, to denounce Wilson's League of Nations plan. Well-considered or not, this can hardly be accepted by the Senate without amendment. On the whole, I should think, public sentiment is tending against it. Lawrence Lowell, who has been starring in the West and South with Taft, thinks that Wilson's disregard of Congress has dished the party for 1920, unless the Republicans are stupider than ever — as indeed they may be.

My dearest younger friend, Frederic Schenck, suddenly died last week, just when he was thought completely convalescent from pneumonia. It stuns me; it is like losing one of my sons. . . .

*To E. S. Martin*

BOSTON, 17 *February*, 1919

DEAR DAN: — Now it is all over, I can tell you that a day or two after your little book[1] came it mysteriously disappeared. I hunted for it high and low. Just when I was in utter despair it turned up, on Thursday, in full light on a parlor table, just as if it had flown back of itself.

So I really read it only yesterday — my first undisturbed two hours. And instead of the merely formal word I was afraid I should have to send, I can tell you how tenderly admirable it seems to me. There is an implicitly prophetic quality in it, too. Long before the grievous need for any such word came, the word was written, mostly unawares and therefore the more deeply true. I hardly know, either, a portrait more such as one would most love than that which by chance you

[1] *Abroad with Jane*

had, for frontispiece. The costume might have looked fantastic; instead it helps merge the memory in the life, brave, absorbing, consoling, just. The past is the only sure thing this side the shadows or the light — whichever may come. As we get towards evening, there is nothing more wondrous, more beautiful, more nearly explanatory than the memories when we would have nothing changed.

Always sincerely and affectionately yours,

BARRETT W.

*To the same*

BOSTON, 23 *February*, 1919

DEAR DAN: — It was a real disappointment not to have time for talk on Friday; but, as you know, Mrs. Robinson and my wife had me in their clutches; and really could n't wait. Even the glimpse of you is pleasant to remember.

So neither then, nor when I hastily wrote the other day, was there any moment for a word about your tract. You never did anything better; of its kind, it seems to me a little masterpiece; and I should think it might make much appeal — not in our own circle, yet in another almost limitless; for the individual man to whom it may chance to speak directly may be found almost anywhere.

The comment I should personally make on it implies my own limitations. So far as I grasp your meaning, the Christ you touch on is the Christ of the New Testament. Somehow, in this aspect, I have never felt the full force of the Christian ideal and message. Historically considered, the Gospels tell the story of a remarkable man who lived under extremely fixed earthly circumstances, remote from any we know, and died before he was old enough to have much experience. Here are distinct terrestrial limitations, both of time and space, which for my part I find that I must consider, if I would grasp the meaning of this or that passage, for all the spiritual genius undoubtedly there.

On the other hand, there is an actually divine Christ — best known to me through Dante — in whose limitless existence the highly localized incarnation is only a physically conditioned episode. We get, you see, straight to the Church — humanly erratic throughout its history, yet so divinely inspired that even at its worst it can bring spiritual consolation. I put all this clumsily; and I am not orthodox in subscription to any known creed. But the limitless, eternal deity somehow touches me personally much closer than the same spirit momentarily incarnate in a remote province of the Roman Empire. The true question, I suppose, is how one may not forget the letter in perception of the spirit. For one, the New Testament may be the better guide; for another the Church.

Yet both have their human limitations. Truth can't be imprisoned in any words or formulas. It is only when we forget these from beginning to end that we can begin to merge our selves in eternity — the sole thing which can ever reconcile human consciousness to the fatal evanescence of its earthly lot.

I write clumsily, pretty tired by that New York excursion, and the unmemorable utterances I got off yesterday in memory of Lowell. But I think you will see something of what I mean.

Always sincerely and affectionately yours,

BARRETT WENDELL

*To the same*

BOSTON, 23 *March*, 1919

Your letter and that excellent Easter meditation mean so much that it is hard to write even a bit of what thoughts and words they stir in me. Both of them I find wonderful in simplicity, sincerity, beauty. So both make instant and strong imaginative appeal. Yet nothing can comprise all truth. The surest truth of all is that before very long the wisest man must come to where knowledge ends and belief must begin. The evidence of things unseen can be found only in faith.

And here, if I am not all astray, comes the most incredible of paradoxes. Faith itself is in essence not a creed but an art, fundamentally at once submissive and hopeful. The submission is to what we may call divine will — the power which makes things as they are on earth incessantly other than we would like them to be. The hope is that somewhere beyond earth there may be that which shall eternally console.

Now, just at this point, I have all my life been at odds with most of those I care for most. It began when I was a little boy; and when my dear old happily evangelical grandfather Barrett discoursed to me about the blessedness of immortality; the occasion was the death — from acute indigestion, I believe — of a farm horse, thereby extinguished from existence. To my grandfather, the horse's lot was therefore deplorable; even at six or seven, already delighting in sleep, I found it enviable; and saying so, was rebuked and prayed over for total depravity, though neither punished nor unkindly treated. Before long, I somehow reasoned out that immortality was welcome to most men because they want it; in other words, faith in it brings them consolation. As I did n't want it, — nobody could tell why, — and as we all agreed that God is good, I saw no reason why I should not privately console myself by a precisely opposite act of faith: if I don't trouble God too much while I am these passing years awake, why should n't he be good enough to let me sleep *in requiem æternam?* Few, I know, agree with this impulse. Yet that simple act of childish faith has helped me through more than fifty years. I should be the last to urge it dogmatically. The miracle it manifests is the manifold efficacy of faith. Each of us may most wisely believe that which to him brings most comfort, shunning the man of intolerance, charitably admitting the limitations of all humanity, and bearing as bravely as may be the burden of the flesh.

Meanwhile, I suppose, I stay "invincibly ignorant" to the doctrine of both Church and Gospel. Yet no one more deeply recognizes the measureless consolation to be found by others in the one, the other, or both.

Always affectionately yours,<br>BARRETT WENDELL

*To the same*

BOSTON, 26 *March*, 1919

By chance I have just come across a book, not itself remarkable, which brings together very simply many instances of how Christianity has irradiated London slums. Harold Begbie: *The Little That Is Good.* (Cassell. 1917)

It is not worth ordering, but if you come across it in a library I think you will like to glance through it. Nothing could more harmonize, I should think, with your own view of Christian teaching.

And I should be the last to combat this, except when it is presented to me as a universal truth. To my mind, you see, what is food for most may be at best innutritious for some. The aspects of God, of eternity, of Nature — whatever you will — are too infinite for comprisal within even the noblest formula.

Just who Begbie is I do not know; nor have I turned to *Who's Who*, which would probably tell. Years ago, about the time when William James was concerned with *Varieties of Religious Experience*, he called my attention to the first book of Begbie's which he had come across — perhaps the first of all. I forget the name. The genuineness of the cases of conversion there set forth had greatly impressed James; though of course James was as far from orthodox dogma as any human being could be. At the time I did not find Begbie so noteworthy as James thought him. As I remember, that book — like the one I mention to-day — was carelessly flung together, evidently the work of a busy man, mostly occupied with other and better things than pen and ink. Coming back to Begbie now, I am much impressed by his sincerity and earnestness, though in more ways than one it does not appeal to my instinctive sympathy.

Affectionately yours,<br>BARRETT WENDELL

*To the same*

BOSTON, 27 *March*, 1919

Our letters have crossed, as such things often do. Here is Tarkington's good, brave, honest paper. I don't care for his novels; when I once met him, I was surprised to find him — so far as I could see — sound to the core, humanly real, only superficially if at all Bohemian; and this article makes me pretty sure of the personal impression. What is more, I cannot doubt that what he says will bring comfort to measureless grief and spiritual agony all about us.

Only, asking no more than something as near compensation for what I must bear as I can find, I would rather stick to my blind old faith — Topeka or Boston, as you choose. Knowledge must forever stop somewhere; grant that, and so long as you let others alone you may wisely let your own, I believe, stop where it will.

As for Boston and me, you are at once right and a bit short of data. Everybody has his own nature to reckon with. Mine, forty years ago, demanded more or less unconsciously two environing conditions: a settled relation to my surroundings somewhere — a sense that I belonged where I was, and was part of it; and separation from domestic authority deeply affectionate and yet incessantly irritating on both sides. By inheritance I belonged in New England; we have lived and married here ever since 1714; and my family lived in New York, where their very self-centred and happily self-sufficing existence was contentedly going round and round in a quiet little 38th Street eddy. Also I fell in love, most fortunately, with a girl who belonged here, and preferred to stay where she belonged. Also, the chance which called me to work at Harvard was the only opportunity I ever had to do anything so useful as to present a demand.

The limits of it all I see as plainly as you can; but there are limits even to the penetrable stellar universe. It is only a question of size. Life, even for one so comfortably fortunate in a small way as I have been, often seems mostly toil and trouble. At sixty-three, it seems to me that I have toiled here to more effect and have had trouble in less poignant form than could have been the case anywhere else. The Lord called and I answered; and if peace comes at last, I shall know Him instead of only believing Him good. Peace I have always yearned for. Four or five of my earlier books purposely ended with the word.

Affectionately yours,

BARRETT WENDELL

*To the same*

BOSTON, 30 *March*, 1919

This letter from Tarkington I am glad to see. It strengthens my impression of his quality; my first prejudice, of years ago, was mistaken. Incidentally, his generation in Indiana seems to me the most nearly important literary fact of just that period in America. It never got far, but it was genuine, faced things squarely, tried to be true rather than imitative, and was native. The laureate of it, though, was Whitcomb Riley, who does n't loom large beside Whittier — on the whole our most deeply Yankee poet; the statesman of it is my interesting friend, Beveridge, whose public views and utterances don't come quite up to Webster's. I give the period about fifty years — 1865 to 1915, let us say. I respect Indiana; but I don't expect it to survive Athenianly.

As to his subject, I dabbled in it thirty years ago — being able to write "automatically." The paper on the Salem Witches in my *Stelligeri* (1893) tells why I dropped it. I also made a story on the subject ("How He Went to the Devil") which Arthur Ware printed in *Two Tales;* but I can find no copy of this work. In general, I have thought occult experiment dangerous to critical intelligence and to strict sense of truth; both William James and Richard Hodgson — pretty intimate friends — unwittingly went, as I saw them, a bit to pieces. So far as I remember, only one friend whom I have known well bore the full moral test of this exploration without harm and on the whole with benefit. This was old Mrs. Dorr, George's mother, a woman of such remarkable quality that I have no better name for it than genius. With her the magic seemed white; elsewhere I have found it at best greyish. . . .

*To the same*

BOSTON, 30 *March,* 1919

In my scrawl of this morning I forgot to put a word about the Ingersoll Lectures.

George Goldthwaite Ingersoll, of the Class of 1815, was my grandmother Barrett's cousin. He was an old-fashioned Unitarian parson, full of the dignity of the cloth, abhorring radicalism, and devoutly believing in personal immortality. His only surviving child, "Cousin Carry Ingersoll," who finally had no nearer relatives in my generation than I am, was a woman of considerable character, much eccentricity, fundamental loyalty to traditions, and vigorous tendency to think for herself. This made her, in her father's opinion, dangerously radical — particularly when they got to dispute about immortality of the soul. He died, as I have it, in 1863; I can just remember him, occasionally turning up at my grandmother's. Cousin Carry survived until 1892 or thereabouts. Her will, an extremely detailed document, disposed of a small estate so elaborately that most of it got nowhere. Her largest bequest was for the foundation for the Ingersoll lectures, in honor of her father's memory; but whether her secret intention was to demonstrate the truth of his faith or that of her vigorously opposite opinions nobody could ever decide.

She sent me not long before she died a fine old family chair and the Harvard memoranda — now given to the College Library — on which I touched in *Stelligeri*. I gave my grandmother's photograph of "Cousin George" to Lawrence Lowell, who has hung it in the President's office at Cambridge. Thus, between Cousin Carry and me, the stately old fellow's memory is fairly secure at Harvard. And God was once so good as to bring me into contact with President Eliot just in time to prevent him from introducing the first or second Ingersoll lecturer as one who came to set forth truth on a foundation lately made by the piously affectionate daughter of a "worthy country apothecary." I almost wish I had let him say so; for if the dead can rise, the furious forms of Cousin George and Cousin Carry would most likely then and there have materialized; both were aristocrats to the core, though of no deathlessly eminent origin. And what they might have done to C. W. E. I hate to think, for he is a great big good man as ever was.

*To the same*

1 *April*, 1919

. . . As to vodka, I am inclined to think intoxicants the social sedative which has kept Western society from exploding. They anæsthetize discontent. National prohibition I rather expect to blow things up at almost any time.

It's all too much for me. I like to go to sleep, and dread waking up.

*To F. J. Stimson*

BOSTON, 2 *May*, 1919

. . . If I were you, I would keep clear of England. From here, or from Argentina, one can still fancy it Victorian. That age was great, after all; stupid, if you will, but not foolish. And decent folks had their rights as well as the rôle. It's dead and gone, like her plump Majesty, and poor King Edward, done to death by the regicidal fooling of the Ministry whose follies and recklessness made Germany and methinks England dead and gone altogether. She has not proved so; only her new phase is to me as displeasing as the Commonwealth would have been to Walter Ralegh. I would rather dream of the Queen, and pray, like him,

> May God so guide me when my time shall come
> That I may pass to where she lives undying.

This age of ours grows literally obscene — thrusting into sight everywhere the foulnesses which are better ignored. . . .

*To Nancy Schenck, one year old*

PORTSMOUTH, 23 *August*, 1919

MY DEAR NANCY: — The picture you sent me for my birthday is a great pleasure. As I look at it, you seem so much like your papa that I feel almost as if he, and not only you, were comfortably gazing at me — too content quite to smile, but with all the smiles of loving kindness ready to break out at any instant when they might be needed. It will be what we now fancy a good while before you grow up, as he and I have grown, to an age when nobody remembers for a while whether folks are old or gray. When that time comes, I can wish you nothing better than that you shall give as much happiness to those who know you as he has given to those who have known him. The best thing anybody can come to be is one of whom the thought makes others happy.

You are three days older than I am, you may remember after all. So perhaps the little things I sent you for your own birthday did not get to you quite in time. I was not so prudent as you were, in remembering how slowly — like all great things

— the processes of our government are apt to move. Sooner or later, though, the parcel post should bring you the trifles. And I am sure that, whether you happen to care much for them in themselves or not, you will like to think that they bear assurance of how much I like to think of you; so, you see, you are beginning life in just the way I have hoped you would live it always.

Give my love to Mamma, and to Grandma, and be sure that I am always

Your very affectionate<br>BARRETT WENDELL

## To Mrs. Frederic Schenck

PORTSMOUTH, 26 *August*, 1919

. . . I love that picture of Frederic more and more. Somehow, as I look at it on my table here, it brings — just as his presence always brought — a sense of helpful, buoyant strength. I shall take it to my little room at the Athenæum when we go back to Boston; that is where I shall totter along with the work I could never have begun without his help. . . .

## To H. M. Kallen

PORTSMOUTH, 30 *August*, 1919

Our leisurely post-office brought me your birthday greeting only yesterday; so this word of the pleasure that came with it, and with your loving word, is not so much delayed as it might seem.

They tell me I look better; so I suppose I do, and may be. Various things quite beyond my control, though, keep me from feeling so — not only the utter confusion which befogs world-air, but matters more personal. I am glad for your gladness that I was born; I am not sure that I share it, at least with the Puritan thankfulness for the mercies vouchsafed me. In most ways my sixty-four years have been remarkably free from care, no doubt; the weight of them, perhaps, begins to perplex me beyond words. Cares of the imagination are probably penalties one must pay for want of actual cares. More and more, I like falling asleep, and dread the relentlessness of sunrise.

All the same, your friendship, constant through so many years, helps. It would be happier for us both if we saw things alike, perhaps. I am not sure, though, that our very differences are not better, or at least more deeply meaning, than agreement would be. For whatever turn the course of affairs may take, neither you nor I, knowing each other, can ever doubt that things which look desperate to him look right to men as honest, and as honestly devoted to human welfare, as he.

A little while ago, I mentioned "Sunrise." That is the title of the only thing I have written this summer. It will appear in *Scribner's Magazine* when the present volume gets to page 470. I will send it to you in due time. You will find it to have one great merit — comparative brevity. And it sums up, as well as I can, the mood in which one who feels too old for change sees change surging everywhere. . . .

Sincerely and affectionately yours,<br>BARRETT WENDELL

*To Mrs. Frederic Schenck*

PORTSMOUTH, 11 *September*, 1919

DEAR CIVILISE: — It is not, I think, any treachery of memory which has deprived me of any such recollections as you hoped I might have. It is rather that, close and dear and confident as my friendship with Freddy had long been, there was always on his part a fine, beautifully instinctive reticence about the matters most deeply, tenderly his own. He never hesitated to speak his mind, or his moods. But what meant to him most of all never came to the surface of his speech. One felt it, one knew it, one was immeasurably glad that it was his; one never touched on it at all.

What I am sure of is the beautifully deep purity of happiness you brought him. Until you were more than part of his life his life was incomplete — as all lives must be to begin with, and most must be always. Then, when he came to know what you were to him, there seemed nothing wanting. He was always, increasingly, his own happy best; sure, without telling his certainty perhaps even to himself in formal words, that he was among the few who need in this world only what they have.

Those months, now your flawless memory and mine, had for him, as they had really, a beauty which cannot even be shadowed in words.

And to me, if you will let me say so, this is more than a consolation now; it is a constant happiness which nothing can ever cloud or change. As one grows old and feeble, there is no reality comparable with that of what has been. If this be troublous, it will stay so as long as consciousness keeps one alive. If it be gently joyous, it will help beyond compare to gladden what without it would be sorrowful shadows. And what was true of him will stay true always. He lived to know, through you, the best that life can give to any human being. He was worthy to know it. And by and by—for no future in this world stays very long —we may all come to feel, in loving him, a solemn gladness that, having known to the full what life can bring, he has been spared the weight which the years begin to make heavy for such as live so long as I have lived already.

Always affectionately yours,<br>BARRETT WENDELL

*To Senator Lodge*

PORTSMOUTH, 25 *September*, 1919

MY DEAR LODGE: — Will you forgive a word of comment on the Report[1] of the Committee on Foreign Relations, read in my invalid bed this morning. The comment is not substantial but formal. As you have known for years, I trust you implicitly; and when I do not everywhere agree, I am sure both of your sincerity and of an experience on your part so measurelessly beyond mine that the expression of dissent would be beyond my power or my right.

But when it comes to style, — to the savor of any piece of writing, — I feel in my own field again.

Just here, unless I am all wrong, the tremendous strain of these past months has told on your nerves a little more than you perhaps realize. In consequence, I find throughout the report implicit evidence of a feeling which might easily be mistaken for something rather partisan than completely na-

---

[1] On the Treaty of Versailles.

tional. This is not quite easy to define or to specify. So far as I can decide, it shows in a frequent tendency to irony, which results in an effect of opposition to opponents rather than of serenely asserted principle. The older I get, the more I believe that any such tendency is particularly mischievous. When one's purpose is positive, it can be achieved only by winning support of the doubtful. And this, I believe, is rather repelled than allured by any negative or ironic mood. Of one thing, I am certain; you are always at your own best when most simply assertive.

On general principles, too, I think that one is always wisest to assume an adversary honest in purpose, however mistaken in conduct or method. Does not Franklin somewhere in the *Autobiography* touch on some such practice, as most efficacious in his own expression of practical dispatch?

Forgive this perhaps impertinent word. I have had a miserably invalid summer. The worst of it is that the doctors pronounce my discomfort nowise dangerous. They are good, though, neither for wits nor for temper. But they do not prevent me from staying always

Sincerely and affectionately forever,

BARRETT WENDELL

*Senator Lodge to Barrett Wendell*

[*In making the foregoing letter of criticism available for publication, Senator Lodge asked that it should be followed in print by his reply.*]

27 *September*, 1919

DEAR WENDELL: — Thank you very much for your letter of the 25th of September. Let me say first how sorry I am to think that you have been suffering from anything this summer and have been forced to lead in any way an invalid life. Anything that happens to you is of deep interest to me and I only hope you will be able to throw it off. It is a comfort to know that the doctor says there is nothing alarming about it.

Of course, I am only too glad to have you criticize anything I do and to know your opinions about it. I am aware that there are one or two touches of irony in the report, but my object was to make it as brief as possible and state in the most concise form the reasons for the committee amendments. I do not think that I attacked anybody except in defending the committee against the wholly unjust charge of delay. I simply gave the facts in that regard and it seemed to me only just to tell the country how much we were hampered by the fact that the President would give us literally no information, and that we had to get such information as we could from the press, from some witnesses we called, and from private sources. That is not the way that a Committee of Foreign Relations of the Senate should be forced to proceed. All I said about the President's statements to us when we met him at the White House was that they were before the country and that the people could judge how much information we received from them. I suppose that may be considered as irony. I then discussed our trade with Germany, that being one of the arguments which has now died out, that we were preventing commerce with that country, which simply was not true. It seemed to me that I had to meet those two criticisms upon the treaty. I have looked over what I said in describing the amendments and they seem to me to deal wholly with the principles involved. It may be my stupidity, but I cannot detect in those anything but declarations as concisely as possible of the reasons which influenced the committee in making amendments and proposing reservations. The last paragraphs are a general statement of the attitude which I think the United States should take. I have just reread them. If there is anything personal or sarcastic in them, I failed to see it. I may be wrong in the position I take, but it seems to me at least a general position. The only places that I can find where it is open to the charge of showing personal feeling is in the defense of the committee in regard to delays, and something I said about Mr. Lloyd George, whom I used as an illustration, to the effect that other people did not think the ratification of the covenant was going to lower the high cost of living. I may have put it in an ironical way, but it seems to me a fair answer.

Greatly to my surprise, the report had a large success, and is being called for by the thousands in all parts of the country, owing, I imagine, to its simplicity as much as to the statement about reservations and amendments.

Perhaps you are right about the irony. It seems to have struck some people, and I am ready to admit that irony is a dangerous weapon. But I am afraid I still believe that the irony I used about the President's conversation with the Foreign Relations Committee was perfectly reasonable. It was better than a blunt statement that he gave us no information, and it erred on the safe side and certainly followed Emerson's rule as to the strength of understatement.

With best thanks for your note, believe me,

Ever yours,

H. C. Lodge

*To H. M. Kallen*

Portsmouth, 11 *October*, 1919

There was delay in sending me the October *Scribner's;* so the copy I promised you goes only to-day. "Sunrise" is the only thing I have really managed to do in four months. The months have been invalid. I hope for better conditions when we go back to Boston in a fortnight or so.

As to America, you know my long opinion — that no one can be of any nation who feels bound to any other. Historically ours is English, in law, language, and general tradition. It absorbed my Dutch and French strains before 1750. It has rather lingered behind England than hastened ahead; it has rather reverted than progressed. It cannot be its full self till the continent has repeated the history of the now decadent Atlantic colonies. This culture I take to have been analogous to the forced culture of a germ. That I seem of the past and feel so, is true; yet I believe myself and my kind the nearest thing now extant to what Americans, if they persist, shall be a century hence.

Fundamentally we believe in fair play, which is a different thing from privilege, whether those who seek privilege seek it in the name of Truth or of Labor. We believe, too, that at least a century is needful to work out the course of social justice in any line of descent; and furthermore that in our country each century has thus far done so as nearly as may be this side Paradise, Utopia, or Chaos. Something of this I meant to write after "Sunrise," under the title of "Genealogy and Social Justice"; but for the moment I am unable to write at all. In Boston I shall recur to my book of "C.-L. I" lectures: "The Traditions of European Literature." My wits are happiest when not helplessly concerned with matters of the grieving, uncontrollable moment. . . .

*To the same*

PORTSMOUTH, 18 *October*, 1919

Good for far less even than usual nowadays, for the past two months, I have only just finished reading Salter's *Nietzsche;* and I can hardly exaggerate the pleasure it has given me. I am not skilled enough to comment on his views of a subject to be read only in a language I do not understand. His setting forth of his views, though, is masterly. I shall be at pains to remember anything about so difficult a matter when the writer has so simply and gently taken the pains to do his own task adequately. To understand, one has only to attend. The book thus becomes as interesting as it is stimulating. To me the matter is new. I take it to be a systematic statement of something in itself never reduced to system — the kind of thing that might be done with Emerson. I am surprised to find how much of it appeals to me as approximately true. If I can express my point of disagreement, it is that in discarding God, and so on, Nietzsche appears to neglect the general fact of cosmic law on which much of the idea of God is more or less based. His superman is after all an idol. If we must have idolatries, I come to believe, the safest are those sanctioned by the ages. Slavery to something beyond ourselves is inevitable. And so on. You will see what I mistily mean. If all the old formulas prove mistaken, there is little reason to expect the new to be much more valid.

But, on other grounds than this I find his views of democracy very like mine; and his views of elastic aristocracy as well. Where I most dissent is where he condemns the state of society which has been ours. It is as imperfect, no doubt, as man or as the Church. But like them, it has possibilities of good as well as of evil, of growth as well as of decay. Our wisest course, I think, is to observe and to obey its laws.

In one way, Salter's work almost vexes me. When a man can think so clearly and can write so well, he ought — one feels — directly to express himself, as James did, rather than to subordinate his expression to the interpretation of another thinker. To be a dignified disciple, one must have a very big god indeed. . . .

*To F. J. Stimson*

BOSTON, 30 *November*, 1919

. . . When the police strike occurred we were still at Portsmouth. So it seemed remote. The election of Coolidge, under all the circumstances, was reassuring. As to the treaty, I am confused; feeling sure only that both sides are patriotically honest, and that in my opinion the confusion of peace with the League of Nations made the submitted document politically short-sighted. Peace should have been made at once; the League certainly deserved as long and as careful discussion as finally led by compromise to the Constitution of the United States. To mix them together could hardly help either delaying peace or hurrying us into engagements which, if not scraps of paper, might have led to dangerous entanglements. . . .

You will have heard of Henry Higginson's death, two weeks ago — a clot resulting from what was thought not dangerous surgery. The morning of the day he died he dictated eight pages of reminiscences to be sent me as a kind of appendix for an account of Lee, Higginson and Company which I had made for B, and which fortunately happened to please H. L. H. This last letter of his is full of character and spirit. The Tavern had a meeting in his memory on the 24th, when I had to take the chair. Henry Rogers spoke, and Wister, and Philip Hale. "*Integer vitæ*" was sung, and "*Meum est propositum.*" It lasted almost an hour; but the whole company was so deeply at one that it seemed neither gloomy nor long. Facing them all the while, I felt the quiet solemnity of their willing immobility. It had an almost ritual dignity, utterly sincere.

As for life, it is of course a tragedy, in the sense that for every human being, and for the planet itself by and by, there must come earthly extinction. To see the comedy beyond, one must have such faith as Dante's, whom I take to have held comedy a thing so enduring as to imply happy life forever after. This, large or small, must always be a matter not of material reality but of spiritual belief. "Doubtless," as Increase Mather put it, "there will be no settled good until the second coming of our Lord." *Dies iræ* occurs to me. Anyhow, "*Solvet sæclum in favilla*," if we can believe the daily prints. . . .

## To R. W. Curtis

BOSTON, 18 *January*, 1920

. . . As to Lodge, my notions are not quite clear. I not only like him personally, to the point of affection, but I confidently believe him a man of simple and genuine public spirit. His experience is very great; he knows a good deal more than most men have forgotten; and he thinks not with a politician's adroitness but with our nearest approach to the foresight of a statesman. Furthermore, in his insistence on the constitutional responsibility of the Senate he is profoundly and admirably right. At the same time, though I personally care for him and admire him, he has always impressed me as weakened by one or two limitations disadvantageous to himself and sometimes mischievous in their effects. For one thing, he is not sympathetic either in temper or in address. He does not quite understand the mood of honest opponents; and he has a trick, even among his friends, of so putting things as to excite, when you do not agree with him, instinctive resentment. At the same time, this very same trick appeals to petty prejudice among people who for the while think with him. A regrettable consequence has always followed: when really large and constructive in his purposes, he has managed to impress people as a rather cynical opportunist at best. When he asserts principle, when he is positive, he is often admirable; but he is not judicious in his inflexibilities. When he resists others, when he is negative, he tends unintentionally to emphasize dissensions. He never consciously plays with the weaknesses and the vices of others to win his game; but he does unfortunately strengthen weak hands without meaning to.

What has troubled me of late has been, first, his exacerbating influence at a time when the world needs, I think, conciliation of dissentient impulses. He gives stimulants when wiser practice would prefer sedatives. And in one respect, with full recognition of his immensely greater knowledge than mine, I have never been able to agree with two opinions of his which now seem to me unusually dangerous and thus cause my second and deeper trouble. In private as well as in public, intimately as well as politically, he honestly distrusts both England and Japan. That both have aspects dangerous to us anybody would agree; it does not follow that these comprehend the whole story. That there is plenty of dangerous American prejudice against both England and Japan is clearly true. The more this is excited, the less promising world-future looks to me. And Lodge, I think, excites and heats it injudiciously. For my own part, I believe that one most important factor in world-order must be control of the sea. Agreement with England can manage the Atlantic; agreement with Japan can manage the Pacific. Disagreement with either must confuse the control of an ocean. So, even for the best of constitutional purposes, I should hesitate, if responsible, to do anything toward avoidable dispute with either.

I wallow beyond my depth, you will doubtless have remarked already. It has pleased the Lord to keep me from where my splashings can do any harm. Of all incapacities to run things, my own appears to me the most limitless I have ever come across. . . .

*To the same*

Boston, 26 *January*, 1920

Calvin Coolidge's statement,[1] which I enclose, may interest you. It was published this morning, to the complete surprise of even the politicians, I believe. The political situation I don't pretend to understand. Clearly, though, the regular Republi-

[1] The announcement in which the Governor of Massachusetts declared: "I have not been and I am not a candidate for President."

cans here were trying to boom Coolidge, and the Roosevelt-radical group were trying to split the party again by booming Leonard Wood.

Coolidge's statement seems to me in any case clever. It should hold the party together, and prevent his candidacy unless he looms larger in Chicago next June than now looks likely. If he does, it does not commit him; but gives him a chance to come forward with far more strength than would otherwise be probable.

Whether it is sincere is of course another question. To me it seems so. I know him a little — a small, hatchet-faced, colorless man, with a tight-shut, thin-lipped mouth; very chary of words, but with a gleam of understanding in his pretty keen eye. He writes everything, they say, with his own hand. A friend of his told me that when he decided to act against the striking police last autumn, he was frantically warned that it might prevent his reëlection as governor. All he said was, "The country won't go to hell if I'm not elected." His majority, a few weeks later, was the largest ever known in Massachusetts.

The chances are, no doubt, that he will not be dreamt of in Chicago. If he is, I incline to think that he may turn out to be a Yankee Lincoln — a local lawyer large enough to handle things memorably. . . .

*To Mrs. John L. Gardner*

[*In answer to a note of congratulation on the selection of Wendell as President of the Tavern Club.*]

BOSTON, 1 *February*, 1920

DEAR MRS. GARDNER: — No one but you would ever have taken the pains, in illness, to send just such a message as comes from you. Only that word "pains" — unless it be true of the illness — is all wrong; for through all the years I have known you there has never been a time when you have not gladly and helpfully spoken just the word one needs to persevere. You can hardly help helping.

And even in itself this new word means more than I can quite find words to tell you. Howells was our first man of letters

324 BARRETT WENDELL AND HIS LETTERS

here when they made him president; Mr. Lee was a first citizen — perhaps incontestably our first. Norton was in his own way the first man of his time among Americans; Henry Higginson, as a private citizen always devoted to public interests, had lived to be *facile princeps* hereabouts. There was no successor for men like these. The choice fell on me in a way which I could hardly refuse without causing perplexity. But no one knows better than I what a change the nomination makes; it is not yet an election. So it is good to know that this inevitable sinking of a prime tradition into something secondary has the other aspect which your words make uppermost — of a challenge to do one's best.

Just why I add the very different thing which was uppermost in my viscous wits yesterday I can hardly tell. You probably know the five lines attributed to Hadrian — his farewell to life: —

*Animula vagula, blandula,*
*Hospes comesque corporis,*
*Quae nunc abibis in loca,*
*Pallida, rigida, nudula,*
*Nec ut soles dabis jocos.*

I needed them in something I am writing, and could find no English version which seemed a bit right.

Vital spark of heavenly flame

is lovely, but far too free. So in the course of the morning I hammered out this: —

Gentle breathlet, ever fresh,
Guest and comrade of the flesh,
Whither goest thou now away,
Pale and stiff, unclothed of clay,
Laughing no more, no more at play?

I don't pretend it good; but it may perhaps interest you as the latest result so far of more than forty years' effort to make our English language say what I want it to.

Forgive this excursion; and be sure that I am always

Gratefully and affectionately yours,

BARRETT WENDELL

*To R. W. Curtis*

BOSTON, 29 *February*, 1920

Your kindness in sending me Keynes's book has made me famous. Everybody hereabouts wants to read it; and what copies were allotted to these parts were sold out on the spot. So I am politely accosted at every turn by folks who want me to lend it. The list grows long enough to last till another leap year. At this moment, Jack W. is deep in the book, which I let him have yesterday.

It is the most interesting discussion I have seen of the questions before — and beyond — us all. It seems to me as honest as it is clever. Of course, one therefore accepts it as gospel, till one stops to think. Then one remembers a single word, "inequitable," of which I have forgotten to note the exact place. It is a mere current adjective, applied to the state of economic things and social in the past. These it assumes us to agree wrong. I don't agree. Taken for all in all, to my mind, no family for centuries has been able to behave in a socially constructive way through three generations without emerging; nor not to, without something very like submergence, or disquieting symptoms thereof. This I believe true of high and low alike. I take it to be, for the larger purposes of social welfare, an impressively equitable condition of affairs. If so, those who resent it because more than one generation is needful for firm social structure are bound not for the heights but for the depths.

When one gets to economic detail, it is to me only less bewildering than technical mathematics, because the terms, instead of being $x^\pi$ and $y^\eta$, are apparently intelligible and have the power of exciting visual and other material imagination. In fact, they thus get for such as me the more mischievous; for I have to stop and realize that I can't understand things which I feel as if I could. Experience of economists as colleagues has tended to a belief that they really are almost equally deceived by themselves. I admit, though, that my sympathies are blindly Tory, and that I never knew an economist whose reasoning did not end in more or less pestilent radical propaganda. They are also more sentimental than I — spelling MERCY in capitals and pronouncing it, *Justice*.

So, though I can't tell you why I can't accept Keynes throughout, — who throughout interests and persuades, — I don't think I can. If he is inspired, I am not. Or, to put it better, he is so reasonable that I can't help regarding him with suspicion. At least he has over me the advantage that he can write seriously without preaching — whereof I spare you more. . . .

*To F. J. Stimson*

BOSTON, 7 *March*, 1920

. . . They have made me president of the Tavern Club, to replace H. L. H.; and I am nominated for candidacy for the Honorable and Reverend the Board of Overseers, of which the president is an eminent jurist named Robert Grant. Also, as I think I wrote you, the University of Strassburg, on the occasion of its resumption by the French, distinguished itself by conferring the degree of doctor on Lawrence Lowell, Haskins, and me. So I begin to feel grandly great. The secret of my success I take to be that I have published no book since 1909. . . .

*To Professor E. K. Rand*

BOSTON, 19 *April*, 1920

DEAR RAND: — . . . I am reminded of a comic experience of my own. In '94 I published an unimportant book about Shakespere — remembered, though, by two readers I am rather proud of, particularly as I sent it to neither: Quiller-Couch and Mrs. Wharton. After due consultation of current authority, I arranged the plays and poems in conjectural chronologic order, and then discussed Shakespere's development as thus indicated. At the beginning of each play or poem, I put in brackets a few lines indicating why it was placed where it was. Then I wrote as fast as the pen would run — the whole book was written, with writer's cramp to bother me, between Commencement and September 15th, 1894. Concerning the dispute as to whether "All's Well," etc., is or is not the lost "Love's Labour's Boon," I thus wrote (p. 246): "The question can never be definitely settled." Some years later, I received — I forget from whom — a now long-lost thesis in some 150 printed pages, exhaustively examining all available evidence on the matter; and concluding, in all gravity, "The final word has been spoken by Wendell," it proceeded to quote, with full textual accuracy, my priceless gem of Nineteenth Century English.

Now nobody knows better than I that I am no scholar — and therefore of no consequence to learning. Yet one thing I did in my teaching seems to me right. I tried to make pupils read things, and not weight their unsteady heads with things that had been written about things — historic, linguistic, whatever else. My task as a Harvard teacher was to give glimpses of literature to men who would generally not be concerned with it in practical life. That I never forgot. Any scholar can help make scholars; but lots fail in the process to humanize. My real duty, as I saw it, was not scholarly but humane.

Always yours,<br>BARRETT W.

## To R. W. Curtis

PORTSMOUTH, 15 May, 1920

. . . Cabot Lodge turned seventy the other day. When I last saw him — six or eight weeks ago, at dinner — he seemed remarkably well; but inclined to talk of anything else rather than of the public matters which have occupied him so tremendously: Shakespere, for choice. I never felt his power more, even though implicitly. What is more, as I have told you before, I believe him really a statesman, and not, as so many think, an opportunist politician. His work I argue to have been admirable and constitutionally faultless. I wish it might have been done with less emphasis on American loyalism or provincialism. The conceit of this country pales John Bull. The real question is not whether a thing is American, but whether it is good. In the old days, — alas, no more, — Ohio champagne, doubtless American, was not quite French; as to California claret, it had one uncompromising virtue — it would n't mix with water. But then, neither would it make man drunk. . . .

*To Lindsay Swift*

PORTSMOUTH, 27 *June*, 1920

DEAR LINDSAY: — Your good word is welcome. Its news of how the class dinner was irrigated deepens my gloom that I could not be there; only I prefer the slow, enduring, copious exhilaration of good wine to the swift throbs of even the best liquor. God help us all. The Second Chapter of the Gospel according to Saint John still keeps faintly alive my hope for innocent conviviality in Paradise — except that when there is neither marriage nor giving in marriage the custom of wedding feasts may perhaps fall into regrettable desuetude.

As to the Overseers, I propose that '77 start a petition to the General Court that the present system of election be replaced by some such provision as this: —

"From the passage of this Act and forever thereafter, all vacancies in the Corporation or in the Board of Overseers of Harvard College shall be regularly filled first by members of the Class of 1877, who shall succeed to office in order of seniority of birth, and secondly, when, in the Providence of God, there shall no longer be enough members of the said class to fill all vacancies, or the said class shall have become altogether extinct, by the oldest living graduates of Harvard College, who shall succeed to office in order of seniority of graduation, seniority of birth, and — in case of twins or triplets — alphabetic precedence."

It must be clear to us all that the greatest evil in the modern world is suffrage. By this very slight constitutional amendment, it might be cured altogether.

*To H. M. Kallen*

PORTSMOUTH, 18 *July*, 1920

As you slowly grow to know, I fear, the years have made me little better than one of the wicked. So, though not yet immune from remorse, I can't feel so penitent as if I still cherished hope of salvation, when I remember how long I have left you without a word of thanks for "Pluriverse"[1] — which I take to

---

[1] A posthumous book by Benjamin Paul Blood, edited, with introduction, by H. M. Kallen. Blood was the subject of an essay, "A Pluralistic Mystic," in *Memories and Studies*, by William James.

be a present in anticipation of the birthday soon to make me a full sixty-five.

In spite of your preface, I can't pretend to understand it; but I can really feel in it a sincere and original effort, on the part of one wise enough to rest content with thinking, to understand the incomprehensible. Just now, partly by reason of age, partly of infirmities, and mostly of despair, I give up effort to understand. It has been an anodyne relief from the unanswerables besetting me everywhere to give what lazy working brains I have managed to rescue from nothing for the past year or more to the writing out of my earlier lectures in "C.-L. I". Beginning with Greece, and proceeding no further than Dante, I have kept my wits away from all the modernities; and dealing only with traditions, — as distinguished from any manner of interpretation, — I have found pleasant the task of perhaps giving other folks, who want to think, old material to think with in a little better order than I found it in. The volume is now being printed and, if the world lasts, will appear in the autumn. But the world now seems to me perilously close to the climax of Virgil's infernal vision: —

*Terribiles visu formæ Lethumque, Laborque.*

Secularly prophetic, he makes Labor — with a capital L, and in 'Ell — the acme of evil.

Forgive this levity. I am better than I was a year ago; but far from steady on my shrinking legs, thus typifying pretty much everything, as now revealed by the public prints. If you stray hereabouts this summer, be sure to let me know. For the next month or so, the house will probably be full with the family; but there is always room at the arid table which the so-called Freedom of our country forbids me longer to bedew with anything wherein the germs of cheerfulness and good-will can be analytically detected. All the same, you know how glad I always am to see you.

*To the same*

PORTSMOUTH, 23 *August*, 1920

The Chinese poems not only bring the pleasure of new assurance that your friendship is of the realities, but also have a strange and happy implication of their own. This is easier to feel than to put in words. We live in times beyond us all; and, as we are whirled this way and that, no two of us can see from quite the same angle the light of the passing days and the shadow of the passing nights. All the more, it is vastly helpful to turn to other centuries and to other regions than our own; and, thinking together in the candlelight of what has been, to find ourselves as truly at one as when, looking forward, we long for what we should most wish to see about us. After all, the difference between a reactionary and a radical, at heart, is only that the one longs to retain whatever is good and the other to destroy whatever is evil. Neither can ever be quite right or all wrong.

My summer has passed busily, with proof of the book about European literature which in two years I have made out of the notes of the first half of "C.-L. I"; the rest of the notes (1300–1900) will fill two more years. Then I shall be sixty-seven; but still, as always,

Sincerely and affectionately yours,

BARRETT WENDELL

Through these final letters the traces of Wendell's indefatigable industry and unwavering friendship are seen to run like threads of steel and gold. There were many moments when his old whimsical humor expressed itself, as in these words from a letter (25 January, 1919) to Judge Grant: "You and I may not quite have got to the evening of life; but we may think of ourselves as in its tea-time. Wherefore, we shall play our parts best now if we make-believe, so far as may be, that it is always afternoon — the day's work done." For Wendell himself, as it happened, the day's work was by no means yet done.

What the completion of his *Traditions of European Literature* meant to him is suggested in a memorandum made by Mr. Bolton, Librarian of the Boston Athenæum, in which so much of the work on this book — a triumph, on merely physical grounds, of energy of spirit over bodily weariness — was done: "May 24, 1920. B. W., overcome with emotion, squeezed my hand, and could not talk. Finally he managed to say: 'I've finished it! The book!'"[1] Even then there were months of arduous self-imposed industry still to come. On June 29, in Portsmouth, with all the proof-reading of his last book still before him, he began an English version of Egenhard's *History of the Translation of the Blessed Martyrs of Christ, Marcellinus and Peter*, a narrative in Latin, which attracted him by reason of its animated accounts of European life in the ninth century. "The attempt to translate it, with the constant aid of Teulet's French version," he wrote, "will give semblance of systematic occupation to what might otherwise be drearily invalid hours this summer." The last of the ninety-seven large pages of manuscript was inscribed, at the Athenæum, "Finished 8 Nov. 1920, 1 P.M." Here also, on the very next day, he began the sequel to his *Traditions of European Literature*. Three months later he died. On the day of his death Mr. Bolton made this memorandum: — "I went down and sat in his chair where he had been for so many months, writing his last book. Very sad. At the left were two stout vellum volumes, the 1581 Petrarch; in front, Browning's *History of the Modern World*, Grant's *History of Europe*, with Dante and more Petrarch; at the right Oliphant's *Episodes in a Life of Adventure*. His notes on manila cards were neatly stacked and his blank book lay open. He had been writing of Petrarch, and, referring to Griselda, said: 'I am not quite well enough to verify this memory. 21 Dec. 1920.' He had begun this second volume with the sub-title, *Six Centuries of Modernity*, 7 November, 1920, and was, he records, 'very languid.' Part I was: 'Finished 7

---

[1] It is a curious coincidence that this biography is completed in the same place, precisely four years later.

Dec. 1920, with more effort under illness than anything I ever remember writing before. B. W.'"

The last occasion of his leaving his own house was on Friday, December 3, when he occupied the president's chair at the Tavern Club, at a luncheon in honor of General Nivelle of the French Army. Though physically unfit for any effort, Wendell met the needs of the occasion with an impromptu speech glowing with his love for France. When the company had dispersed, I found myself standing beside him. "Will you give me your arm to the head of the stairs?" he said; "I don't feel quite sure of getting there." So I accompanied him to his motor; and, once over his own threshold, he did not step across it again. For some months he had been suffering from pernicious anæmia. On Saturday, February 5, 1921, pneumonia set in. On the following Tuesday, February 8, he died. Two days later the funeral services in Trinity Church, Boston, filled with a multitude of friends, former pupils, men and women representing the widest variety of interests, were rather like the last tribute of respect to a great public figure than to one who was primarily a teacher and writer, and in private life merely the truest of friends, the most devoted of husbands and fathers.

The immediate testimony in written words, printed and unprinted, to the affection and respect inspired by Barrett Wendell's life was overwhelming in its very bulk. A passage from a single letter, written by a German colleague of Wendell's at Harvard, Professor Kuno Francke, contains such implications of a pervading generosity of spirit, even in relations involving sharp differences of view, that it may well stand in evidence of qualities universally endearing: "Let me only say that your husband was one of the few who during these last years of despair helped me to bear what had to be borne, without losing all hope in humanity. His generous words of friendship and his chivalrous high-mindedness have been a light for me in many a dark hour. And as long as I live, I shall feel united to him through a spiritual kinship which knows no racial divergences or national contrasts."

This book, in its endeavor to represent Wendell "on his own terms," preponderantly through his letters, is essentially Wendell's book. Yet it should be said that by no means all of him is to be found in the preceding pages. In particular, and through what after all may be an exaggerated respect for his own strong instinct of privacy, the great and abiding happiness of his domestic life is rather suggested than recorded. In scores of unprinted letters his solicitous concern for everything that touched the lives most closely bound to his own, his remembrances of family birthdays and other anniversaries, his whole-souled sharing of joys and sorrows found the warmest expression. His children and grandchildren, the constant procession of friends through his house in town and in country, filled his days with happiness. Though his own reports of it all have seemed rather for private than for general reading, the intensity of his feeling as the affectionate head of his own household must be recorded with a final emphasis. This may best be expressed through some words from the "Recollections" of his younger daughter, Mrs. Osborne, writing thus about both her parents: —
"It is impossible to think of my father without my mother. To her much of his success was unquestionably due. They were so constantly together, that even in her rare absences from home she was the more associated with him because he was so obviously lost without her. He depended on her for everything; her resource in meeting his varying moods, her calmness, saneness, patience, and unalterable devotion, were unequaled. For forty years together she shielded him from the petty irritations of

daily existence; she bore the brunt of domesticities of which he was ever utterly impatient, and, although no children could have had a more loving and conscientious mother, she was always able to meet his swiftly changing needs. His very dependence on her shows, more clearly than any words, how deeply he loved her. No man could have had a better mate; I know no couple who loved each other more completely."

The man that Barrett Wendell was, not the man he thought himself or that some others thought him, is the man these pages have sought to show forth. Honest, pure, and original of mind; chivalrous and generous often to the verge of the quixotic; given to decking serious thoughts in the motley of jest and caprice; but, to the core of his being, faithful, and wise, and kind.

# BIBLIOGRAPHY

## Books

1885
*The Duchess Emilia: A Romance*
Boston: James R. Osgood and Company; New York: Charles Scribner's Sons, 1896.

1887
*Rankell's Remains: An American Novel*
Boston: Ticknor and Company; New York: Charles Scribner's Sons, 1896.

1891
*Cotton Mather, the Puritan Priest*
In "Makers of America" series. New York: Dodd, Mead and Company.

*English Composition*
New York: Charles Scribner's Sons.

1893
*Stelligeri, and Other Essays Concerning America*
New York: Charles Scribner's Sons.

1894
*William Shakespere: A Study in Elizabethan Literature*
New York: Charles Scribner's Sons.

1900
*A Literary History of America*
In "The Library of Literary History." New York: Charles Scribner's Sons.

1902
*Ralegh in Guiana, Rosamond and A Christmas Masque*
New York: Charles Scribner's Sons.

1904
*A History of Literature in America.* In collaboration with Chester Noyes Greenough
New York: Charles Scribner's Sons.

*The Temper of the Seventeenth Century in English Literature*
New York: Charles Scribner's Sons.

1905

*Selections from the Writings of Joseph Addison*, edited, with introduction and notes, in collaboration with Chester Noyes Greenough. In "The Athenæum Press Series." Boston, New York: Ginn and Company.

1906

*Liberty, Union, and Democracy, the National Ideals of America*
New York: Charles Scribner's Sons.

1907

*The France of To-day*
New York: Charles Scribner's Sons.

1908

*The Privileged Classes*
New York: Charles Scribner's Sons.

1909

*The Mystery of Education, and Other Academic Performances*
New York: Charles Scribner's Sons.

1910

*La France d'aujourd'hui*, translated by Georges Grappe.
Paris: H. Floury; London: Nelson, 1912.

1920

*The Traditions of European Literature*
New York: Charles Scribner's Sons.

### Miscellaneous Writings

1876–1879

Contributions to the *Harvard Lampoon* listed in *Lampoon* indices, Volumes I–VII.

1884

Letters on the Democratic Convention in Chicago, signed, "From a Looker-on in Chicago": *Boston Daily Advertiser*, July 10 and 11.

1888

"The Last of the Ghosts": *Scribner's Magazine*, February.

1891

"Some Neglected Characteristics of the New England Puritans": *Annual Report of the American Historical Association for 1891*. Washington, 1892.

1892
"The Dean of Bourges" (Poem): *Scribner's Magazine*, January.
"Were the Salem Witches Guiltless?" *Historical Collections of the Essex Institute*, February.
"How He Went to the Devil": *Two Tales*, April 30.

1893
"John Greenleaf Whittier": *Proceedings*, American Academy of Arts and Sciences, May 10.
"Impressions at Chicago": *Harvard Monthly*, October.

1894
"Francis Parkman": *Proceedings*, American Academy of Arts and Sciences, May 9.

1896
Introduction to Shakespere's *As You Like It*, in "Longmans' English Classics": New York: Longmans, Green and Company.

1898
"Composition in the Elementary Schools": *New York Teachers' Monographs*, November.

1899
"Samuel Eliot": *Proceedings*, American Academy of Arts and Sciences, May 10.
"The Relations of Radcliffe College with Harvard": *Harvard Monthly*, October.

1901
"William Whitwell Greenough": *Proceedings*, Massachusetts Historical Society, February.
Review of *The Clergy in American Life and Letters*, by Daniel Dulany Addison: *American Historical Review*, April.
Review of *The Transit of Civilization from England to America in the Seventeenth Century*, by Edward Eggleston: *American Historical Review*, July.
"A Review of American Literary Phases" in *Studies in American Literary Life:* Philadelphia: The Booklovers' Library Press

1902
Review of *The Literary Diary of Ezra Stiles, D.D., LL.D., President of Yale College: American Historical Review*, July.

1903

"The American Intellect" in the *Cambridge Modern History*, Volume VII. Cambridge: University Press.

1904

"Our National Superstition": *North American Review*, September.

1905

"Le Président Roosevelt": *Revue Politique et Parlementaire*, February 10.

1907

"Impressions of Contemporary France: The Universities": *Scribner's Magazine*, March.

"Impressions of Contemporary France: The Structure of Society": *Scribner's Magazine*, April.

"Impressions of Contemporary France: The French Temperament": *Scribner's Magazine*, June.

"Impressions of Contemporary France: The Republic and Democracy": *Scribner's Magazine*, July.

"The Influence of the Athenæum on Literature in America" in *The Influence and History of the Boston Athenæum:* Boston: The Boston Athenæum.

1908

"The Privileged Classes": *Journal of Education*, February 27.

"The United States and France": *International Conciliation*, August.

1909

"Charles Eliot Norton": *Atlantic Monthly*, January.

"Abbott Lawrence Lowell, Twenty-Fourth President of Harvard College": *Harvard Graduates' Magazine*, March, "De Præsede Magnifico": *Harvard Graduates' Magazine*, September.

1910

"Henry Cabot Lodge, Statesman": *Boston Herald*, May 1. Introduction to *Cowboy Songs and Other Frontier Ballads*, collected by John Avery Lomax. New York: Sturgis and Walton Company.

1912

"Edmund March Wheelwright": *Harvard Graduates' Magazine*, December.

1913

"A New England Puritan: Cotton Mather": *Quarterly Review*, January.

"A Fantasy Concerning the Epitaph of Shakespere" in *Anniversary Papers by Colleagues and Pupils of George Lyman Kittredge*. Boston and London: Ginn and Company.

1915

"William Roscoe Thayer, as Editor of the Harvard Graduates' Magazine": *Harvard Graduates' Magazine*, September.

1916

"Henry James, An Appreciation": *Boston Evening Transcript*, March 1.

1917

"Ideals of Empire": *Harvard Graduates' Magazine*, June.

1918

"Japan and Righteousness": *Scribner's Magazine*, July.

"The Conflict of Idolatries": *Harvard Graduates' Magazine*, September.

1919

"Law and Legislation": *Scribner's Magazine*, February.

"A Gentlewoman of Boston, 1742–1805": *Proceedings*, American Antiquarian Society, October.

"Sunrise": *Scribner's Magazine*, October.

"James Russell Lowell": *Commemoration of the Centenary of the Birth of James Russell Lowell*. New York: Charles Scribner's Sons.

# INDEX

# INDEX

References to Wendell himself are indicated by **W.** It has not been attempted to list all the persons and places seen at home and abroad and mentioned casually in his letters.

## 346    INDEX

Printed by McGrath-Sherrill Press, Boston
Bound by Boston Bookbinding Co., Cambridge